MW01049894

THE FALL LINE

Following page. Untracked, untouched snow on undeveloped ski terrain in Colorado, a state boasting a thousand mountains over two miles high that will be able to absorb much of the future growth of the sport.

Roach Photos

The Fall Line

A SKIER'S JOURNAL

by John C. Tobin

MEREDITH PRESS / NEW YORK

FIRST EDITION

SBN: 696-59607-5
Library of Congress Catalog Card Number: 78-93839
Manufactured in the United States of America for Meredith Press

To my devoted wife, whose understanding attitude
toward my bachelor ski weekends
can only be compared to the attitude of a Frenchwoman
toward her husband's mistress.

Preface

At Sun Valley high on the ridge of Mt. Baldy, a snow cornice has formed at the top of Easter Bowl. This cornice resembles a giant wave, and like a wave it stands poised, ready to break. The formation has been created by eddying currents of air depositing snowflake upon snowflake in the lee of the mountain. Its massive flowing lines, endlessly curling under, make the cornice a work of sculpture.

Suddenly wind hits the cornice, which has outgrown its strength, causing a barrel-shaped section to break off from the rest. The impact from such a section of cornice hitting a slope can simultaneously trigger an avalanche. But this time the rounded section rolls easily down the Easter Bowl slope, leaving an almost perfectly straight line etched on a light cover of new snow. This line defines the steepest route down the hill, and marks what skiers call the fall line.

When a skier is on a steep slope he feels a thrill as he swings into the fall line. An easy maneuver, this should be the most relaxed moment in skiing. Yet it is often a moment of fear, because the fall line means speed, and speed may mean loss of control and possible danger.

Foreword

In the past thirty-five years few sports have grown as fast and changed as much as skiing. From a handful of rugged individualists using primitive equipment and equally primitive style on logging trails and hilly pastures, skiing has evolved to the fashionable, sophisticated sport of today. Every aspect of the sport has undergone a radical transformation: from the equipment, the apparel, the skiing and learning techniques, to the multimillion-dollar new-town resorts.

Not the least of the changes is the skier himself. He used to be of the same stamp as the mountaineer. I think, a nice kind of natural snob, relishing the tightness of his group, enjoying a sport that few had ever tried, and even fewer had mastered. Those early skiers, who had mostly been first exposed to skiing in the Alps, imported the *Gemütlichkeit* and *Kamaderie* of skiing, so that even now these expressions seem to connote skiing. But that has really changed now. The spirit is there, but it is different, and few of the older skiers who shared the early heady growth of skiing are particularly pleased with the popularization of *their* sport.

Jack Tobin is an anomaly. He fell in love with the sport at a tender age and never fell out of love. It hasn't mattered to him that the sport matured. He has accepted every change with the understanding of a parent, and he has changed too. In this book he records the personal feelings and observations of a skier swept along by the changing tides of the sport. In one chapter we catch the original spirit of early skiing on Suicide Six in Woodstock, Vermont. The names and faces are all there, but most important is Jack's recapture of the mood. In another chapter Jack examines Stowe ten or fifteen years later. Other names, other faces, and another sort of skiing spirit. His recollection of anecdotes and people is remarkable. And there are way-stops in between. Just about every major resort and every major figure in skiing gets a mention somewhere. The reference is not always flattering, but is always firsthand, direct, and stated in the context of a larger love affair.

Ski racing is the recurrent theme that runs through the book. Jack was a reasonably hot racer prior to World War II, an improved racer trying to compete with the kids in the late forties and fifties, and finally, in the sixties, one of the best veteran racers in the United States. As a racer of long standing he has traveled widely with greater opportunity to meet the personalities of the sport: the racers, the pros and the ski-area operators.

In some ways I was a part of the horde of racers that followed Jack and those colorful racers of the late thirties (I don't think any of them *weren't* colorful!). I was raised on the tales of their legendary prowess, of who schussed what and when. I never considered going to any college other than Dartmouth, and in retrospect, I think it was because of the towering impression of the Dartmouth racers of the thirties and late forties. I knew them all by name and feat, much as another kid might know the batting averages of his favorite ball players. Some of these Bunyanesque heroes were still racing when I began to climb through the ranks, but there weren't many, and Jack Tobin was one of the few who stuck with it.

Now, as time goes on, I am racing less and working more, but I still run into Jack several times a year in the veterans' races. He is a class or two ahead of me; but I suspect he trains harder than I do, and I think he takes it more seriously. I know his memory is better than mine for specific races.

The last time I saw him he happened to mention that his best showing in a veterans' race was in the Hochgebirge Cup of 1966, one of the foremost annual veterans' races in the east. He recalled that I had won, Egil Stigum, another ex-Dartmouth racer, was second; George Macomber (ex-MIT and the 1950 United States FIS team) was third, and he was fourth. At the prize giving, I commented that I owed my success to a practice session the day before with Jack Tobin, which had earned a chuckle because everyone knew that Jack had not skied well in practice. Did I remember?

As he recounted it, I did. And then I thought: How did he remember such a trifling incident, including the finish order, the year of the race, and the small joke. If I had asked he probably could have told me the times we turned in, how many gates the course had had, and what kind of snow it had been held on.

When I heard he was writing this book, it occurred to me that he was a natural to do it, with his knowledge of the people and places, his abiding love of the sport, his perceptive eye and ear, and his great memory for anecdote and detail. I was not disappointed with the final product. I think it tells the story of American skiing in its formative years as well as it can be told.

Waterville Valley, New Hampshire July, 1969 — Tom Cochran

Contents

THE FALL LINE

1

Birth of a Skier

Salvador Dali tells us that his memories go back to the womb. This may be so; certainly the richness and hallucinatory character of his paintings would indicate that he had an earlier start than the rest of us.

But I too can remember being held upside down, slapped rudely on the back, and emitting a loud cantankerous cry.

Admittedly the circumstances were somewhat different. I was then in the fifth grade, ten years old, lying on my back in the snow. I had trudged through a snowstorm with a friend. We were both on skis for the first time, on a slope called Flood's Hill in a public park in South Orange, New Jersey. My first run down this hill began with a few entranced moments. I was breaking track in new snow and moving with quiet swiftness, enjoying a completely new experience. However, my sense of balance was soon confounded and at the steepest part of the slope, very much on schedule, I hurtled forward into the snow, my toe-strap skis releasing and flying off in opposite directions. There I was, lying on my back, almost upside down, and with a thick layer of powder snow caught under my shirt in frigid contact with my skin.

So like a baby, I cried resonantly when slapped on the back, having no profound thoughts about what lay ahead. Actually a new life was beginning for me, but I was far too miserable, damp, and cold to sense in any way how important skiing was to become to me.

In fact, I prevailed upon my friend to return home immediately. I was so thoroughly disenchanted with the sport that I did not ski again that winter or the following year.

When I was in the seventh grade, we had an unusually severe winter for New Jersey, with a continuous cover of snow for about two months. Inevitably I went back to Flood's Hill for the mass sledding and skiing activity. Skiers were then in the minority, but I had enough of the pioneering spirit to be more interested in that sport than in sledding.

The year was 1932, but it could just as well have been 1877, because we were engaged in simple toe-strap skiing, a form of skiing several thousand years old. We were using long light ash skis with flat stained tops and etched decorative lines. These carried the name of the famous old New York sporting goods store, Alex Taylor. They had natural wood bottoms with a single groove for stability when running straight, and straight running was about all that could be accomplished on those skis. The front end had the classic elongated telemark tip, which, unknown to us, served a function in the turn of the same name. The most notable part of the skis was the toe-strap binding, a weak link between skier and ski. A broad heavy leather strap fed through an opening in the ski itself, and there was a corrugated rubber foot pad. When the foot was firmly forced into the toe strap, and the skier's weight slightly back, he had some feeling that his skis were under him. The turns and maneuvers associated with modern downhill skiing had not been perfected, and would have been quite impossible with this binding.

So those of us who skied on Flood's Hill that winter had to be content with straight running. We would point our skis down the hill and ride it out, squatting slightly and leaning back, coming to a gradual stop on the flats—not very graceful, not very imaginative, no more than a boyhood diversion. We did build simple jumps, but it was chance rather than skill which determined if our skis would stay with us when we were airborne. Despite the limitations of the toe-strap binding with the free heel, it is still the most perfect safety binding ever conceived, and none of us received more than minor cuts and bruises.

My skiing life had begun, but it might have ended right here on Flood's Hill. However, the year 1932 marked the approximate time when a number of developments took place that have been largely responsible for the growth of modern skiing. Through a combination of fortunate circumstances, I became intimately involved in these developments and was carried along on the incoming tide of this exciting sport.

2

Genesis of the Modern Sport

Skiing as a method of winter travel goes back three or four thousand years, and is deeply ingrained in the history of northern countries. Since it involves a principle simpler than the wheel and more advantageous during the snow months, it may go back even further. The home of this ancient sport is Scandinavia, particularly Norway. Today we think of the Scandinavian countries primarily in terms of cross-country skiing and jumping. The classic Holmenkollen competition in these two events started in 1892. However, early downhill running was a true Norwegian development, with the telemark and christiania * turns named for the towns where they originated.

In Europe, ski vacationing in the Alps began before the turn of the century. The famous Kandahar Ski Club was founded in 1879, and the Ski Club of Great Britain in 1902. One of the earliest English skiers was the famed author of the Sherlock Holmes series, Sir Arthur Conan Doyle. And the 1920's saw the British, who are enthusiastic pioneers, making frequent ski and winter mountaineering trips to the famous resort towns of Switzerland, Austria, and Germany.

* Christiania is now known as Oslo.

The winter mountains have a clean beauty, an almost spiritual quality. Men who have a true love for the mountains are more drawn to them at this time of the year than at any other season.

In winter mountaineering, the ski is a means to an end, and the hazards are more often avalanches, than hazards such as the skier's speed and loss of control. In the 1920's as today, there were a number of people tragically killed each year while skiing on steep, snow-laden slopes which gave way under critical conditions of time, temperature, and physical consistency. However, downhill skiing on patrolled slopes has seldom resulted in fatal accidents.

As skiing proficiency increased, interest turned from ski touring to down-mountain running. Downhill races became quite popular in the years from 1925 to 1930. There was probably broader participation in racing around 1930 than at any period in the history of the sport, and racing played an important role both in publicizing the sport and in improving equipment and technique. The British Ski Year Book for 1929 lists the results of ninety-three downhill and slalom meets held during the previous winter season.

Interestingly enough, some of the early forms of downhill racing were novelty events. One such contest was a bag-snatching race. The competitors descended a course studded with ski poles on which were hung paper bags. The object was to finish the race in the shortest time with the greatest number of bags.

A second novelty event, and one of the important early downhill races, was a throwback to the days when skiing was mostly a form of winter mountaineering. This was a roped race, where two skiers would go down the course roped together, very much like alpinists skiing a glacier over hidden crevasses. One reason this race survived for a number of years was that certain race officials were concerned about safety, the idea being that one roped racer would restrain the other, and that, hopefully, two madmen would not be paired together.

The first British ski championship meet took place at Scheidegg in 1922, and was a combination of downhill race and style competition for telemarks, stems, christianias, and jump turns. Points were to be awarded in the style competition very much in the same manner as figure skating. Since this meet brought skiers together from different Alpine resorts who were seeing each other ski for the first time, each frantically practiced his turns up to the final moment, desperately trying to perfect maneuvers at which others appeared superior.

The primitive downhill race of 1925 was perhaps the purest ever run. There was simply a mountain to be skied. There were no rules, no prescribed route, and few officials. The racers climbed the course together, examining the terrain. Occasionally a skier would leave the group to tramp out a segment of his course or to make a mark in the snow above a particularly steep spot. At the top of the mountain the racers gathered in line for a simultaneous start. This was known as the *geschmozzel* start, a German word almost as amusing as *Obergurgl*, which is also in the skier's vocabulary. This mass start made the race literally a free-for-all. Although the slopes were wide open, the danger of a pileup was always present, particularly when several skiers would spot a common objective like a set of tracks where they had climbed up. Sometimes three or four leading racers would arrive there together and go down in a tumble, giving those following an advantage. Occasionally a racer would notice a shortcut, and peel off, only to find slow going in heavy snow, or with victory in his grasp, look back to measure his lead; and down he would go. This race with its *geschmozzel* start is still remembered nostalgically by veteran skiers. In all forms of modern downhill racing, interval timing is now used, with one minute between runners being considered a normal and necessary margin of safety for the competitors.

The early downhill courses were sometimes fairly long runs with drops of over 2,000 vertical feet, comparable to present-day race courses. Shorter, more serpentine runs, around sets of flags, were soon devised, and these became known as slaloms—from the Norwegian word meaning "sloping track." Sir Arnold Lunn, one of the great pioneers of skiing, is generally given credit for inventing the modern slalom.

Such were the primitive days of downhill skiing. A race two miles in length would perhaps be won in 9 minutes' time, with the winner 3 minutes ahead of the second man. The same race today might be over in less than 2 minutes.

The father of modern skiing is generally conceded to be Hannes Schneider, of St. Anton in the Arlberg. His first ski school was set up to train Austrian ski troops who fought in World War I against the Italians. For three years Austrian and Italian ski troops fought to a stalemate in the Ortler-Cevedale region of Italy. The Ortler Plateau is at an elevation of 12,500 feet, and on it was located the highest artillery emplacement in World War I. Since this area was snow-covered the year round, skillful mobility on skis was militarily essential. Knowledge of the mountains was important too, as in December of 1916, 10,000 soldiers were killed by snow slides in a 24-hour period. On the Austro-Italian front there were more casualties from avalanches than from military action. Twenty years later, at the summit of the Königspitze one could still see cannon embedded in the ice.

After World War I Hannes Schneider and his instructors continued to develop the system of ski turns which had proved so effective on the windswept snow and ice of the Ortler Plateau. All of the turns in this early Arlberg School, crude though they were, had a similarity to modern turns, and like the modern ones, could be divided into two types—steered and swing-weighted.

Progress was also being made in equipment. As the skier progressed, the free-heel toe-strap binding was replaced by steel toe-irons into which the boot could be wedged. Various restraining leather straps, with and without a heel spring, were attached to these or to the ski itself. Through a diagonal pull, working like the spring on a screen door, these straps tended to keep the heel on the ski, giving the skier some backward and forward stability. Interestingly enough, the binding known as the long-thong (*lanière* in Europe) had been in use for a score of years. In this harness arrangement, the strap is attached to the ski and then wrapped around the ankle and heel of the boot in several crosshatching moves, making the foot very much a part of the ski. This is the binding which, with a safety-release toe-iron, is used by all experts and racers today. And inevitably it gave the early skier a new degree of security and control.

The skis were fairly stiff planks, with ridgetops, and they were made from tough resilient American hickory. The wood ski still survives, and up until about four years ago was standard for slalom, never having been replaced for this purpose by the metal ski and only recently by the fiber-glass ski. The wood ski now consists of a number of laminations, technically engineered for the required combination of flexibility, curvature, and torque. American hickory is still the only accepted wood used by the best ski manufacturers everywhere.

Most early skiing took place in deep unbroken snow. As skiing activity increased, skiers found themselves more and more on packed-out, skied-over slopes and trails, which in Europe came to be called *pistes.* These packed-out slopes had a hard surface which at once wore down the skis' wooden edges, yet required a sharp biting action to avoid excessive skidding. Accordingly, various forms of metal, fiber, and plastic edges were affixed either to the sides or the bottoms of the skis. Incredibly enough, the single groove on the bottom, a part of the classic ski design, still survives and performs the function of giving the ski stability, so that it tends to run straight without slithering.

In the mountain resort towns of Europe, cable cars were made available for skiers' use. These lifts had been built originally for the summer tourist trade, but the worldwide trend toward skiing would never have taken place without such facilities for skiers to ride up. Although many new types of lifts have since been developed, in Europe the cable car is still standard on important mountain runs. Apart from the personal advantages to the skier, availability of uphill facilities has inevitably led to improved performance, for a skier can now easily accomplish five to ten times more downhill running than he could when he had to climb.

So the Arlberg technique, better equipment, and use of cable cars resulted in sweeping changes in the style and speed of skiing. In downhill racing, it was as if an explosion had taken place. Prior to 1930, the ski turn was unreliable as a means of changing direction and speed. Even the most experienced skier struggled from one turn to the next. Consequently, other methods had to be employed, particularly on steep slopes and in variable snow. The most reliable of these was known as stick riding. In this maneuver, the skier placed both ski poles between his legs and rode down the hill like a witch on a broomstick, with a rooster tail of snow streaming behind him. His speed was controlled by the amount of pressure applied to the dragging poles.

There was at this time fairly widespread use of and considerable debate on a maneuver known as the planned sitzmark, which took two forms. In one, a skier would take a pitch, such as Devil's Gully on the Murren run, absolutely straight, striking terror into the hearts of observers. However, just when it appeared that he was on the brink of disaster, he would fall in such a manner as to bring himself to a stop. He would then rise to his feet and proceed on his way, having picked up time on more conservative skiers who zigzagged down the pitch. The other form of planned sitzmark was much less dramatic. Here the skier simply spread his legs at the top of a pitch, sat down, and bounced along on his rear end until he reached flatter terrain.

Skiing officials have frequently tampered with the rules of downhill racing. Shortly after 1930, stick riding was forbidden. The planned sitzmark was legislated against in certain races either by putting a no-control disqualification on the steep pitches where it might be used, or by eliminating a runner who fell on any part of the course. The modern racer has such precise control over his destiny that he need not resort to such primitive maneuvers. However, the planned sitzmark endures as an important part of the beginning skier's repertoire, since at times it is his only means of survival.

But the battle over the open downhill course versus a controlled race still goes on. The early 1930's saw a number of controlled downhill races. In these races, ski officials, perhaps overly concerned with the risks of high-speed skiing, prevailed over the majority of racers who were confident they would exercise judgment in the interest of safety. And gates were set through the entire length of the course to force the skier to take a prudent line as well as to slow up his progress on the steep sections. One of our three Alpine events today, the giant slalom, has evolved from the controlled race. This is a medium-speed, smooth-turning test over a course nearly as long as the downhill, and since the turns come one right after the other, it requires a powerful carving action with the skis and is an excellent test of physical conditioning. The downhill, however, remains a largely uncontrolled race. There is great interest in designing better and safer courses. If gates are used, they are there to define the course in open sections and to keep skiers away from dangerous rocks, ravines, and tricky reverse curves that tend to throw them into the woods. Racing officials have an abiding sense of vigilance, and do not permit a downhill race to be held when the track is extremely icy or the visibility limited. The result is there are remarkably few fatal accidents in the downhill, a race which is one of the most exciting events in the world of sports.

One of the great downhill races in Europe is the Parsenn Derby at Davos. The course is seven miles long, with a vertical drop of 4,500 feet. In 1926 this race was won by Peter Gruber, from Davos, in the time of 22 minutes 30 seconds. In 1929 there were 138 entrants, including skiers from Vienna, Zurich, the Arlberg, and many English from Klosters, a popular Swiss resort the English still frequent today. The race that year was won by David Zogg, a first-rate Swiss skier of the day, in the remarkably improved time of 17 minutes 59 seconds.

Probably the first true international championship in Alpine events was a Fédération Internationale du Ski race which took place at Murren, Switzerland, in 1931. The F.I.S. is still the governing board of worldwide racing. The men's slalom event was won by David Zogg, and the men's downhill by another Swiss named Walter Prager, who was later to become the Dartmouth ski coach. Walter Prager made quite a name for himself in another race, at Sestrières, by coming off the last steep pitch in the air, performing a perfect forward somersault, landing on his feet, and crossing the finish line without a trace of snow on himself.

At the 1932 Winter Olympics in Lake Placid, New York, downhill skiing was not yet important enough on an international level to be included in the program. The two Nordic events, cross country and jumping, did take place. But in the 1936 games at Garmisch-Partenkirchen, and in all winter Olympics thereafter, the downhill and slalom events have figured prominently.

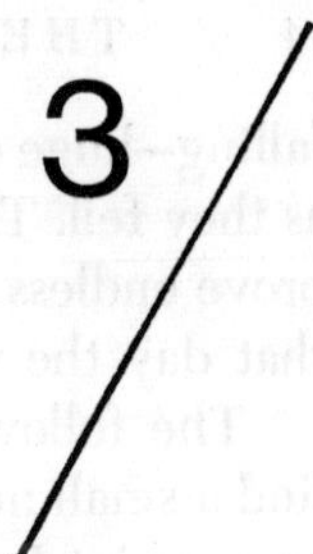

Early Skiing at Choate

The year 1933 found me at the Choate School in Wallingford, Connecticut, where I did very little skiing my first two winters as hockey was then my number-one sport.

However, I remember a snowstorm during my first year. The school was given a holiday, and I went out on my Alex Taylor toe-strap skis for over six hours. I was alone most of the day, since there were only a few other skiers in school. Touring the Wallingford countryside, I experienced for what was really the first time the thrill of powder skiing and soft snow underfoot.

Deep powder skiing on steep slopes in an unbroken track is considered the epitome of enjoyment and accomplishment. The skier makes smooth swings, with snow sometimes up to his hips, and a clear unbroken slope ahead. There is constant uncertainty about whether he will be able to retain his equilibrium. But when he reaches the bottom of a hill, his etched tracks stand out as incontrovertible proof that he has mastered a piece of unexplored territory. Sadly, I was never to be a deep powder skier. Instead my thrills were to come from mastering hard-packed snow.

My principal pleasure as I trudged around that day came from feeling a part of the storm. There was little or no wind, and the temperature was near the freezing point, with heavy snowflakes falling—huge clusters of crystals which you could almost hear land as they fell. The storm seemed to have a special quality. Would it prove endless and completely engulf the world? Probably not. But that day the wonders of winter were opened to me.

The following year I skied off and on, and was surprised to find a small nucleus of friends who enjoyed it as much as I did. At some point I decided to give up hockey, the only sport at which I had ever been good, in favor of skiing, at which I hoped to excel. Hockey and skiing combine certain elements, for there is plenty of action in each, and both require a good sense of balance and speed.

Skiing gave me a feeling of importance. I felt at home as a skier at once. I had an edge over others in balance, and derived a tremendous satisfaction from coming to grips with the challenge of this new sport. As a thin, somewhat awkward youngster whose father had been an all-American football player at Dartmouth, I was discovering through skiing a new role which would enable me to become an entity at school and to develop a personality of my own.

At Choate we skied on elongated hills which, as we learned in geography class, were glacial moraines known as drumlins. These hills were steep enough for learning basic balance and early turns. Our ski sessions were certainly informal; we had little idea of what we were doing, and even less knowledge of what we were supposed to do. There was a Norwegian carpenter by the name of Fred Whiting who worked for the school, and he often joined our group and took it upon himself to be our ski coach.

Downhill skiing burst on the scene with a tremendous fanfare in the mid-thirties. These were the winters of snow trains, magnificent new trails built by the Civilian Conservation Corps, and sweeping victories for the Dartmouth ski team.

Snow trains out of Boston and New York were very popular. Usually these trains took skiers on one-day jaunts to the snow country and back. A Boston & Maine advertisement in the winter of 1934 announced a round-trip excursion rate between Boston and Greenfield, New Hampshire, for $1.75, urging readers to "Put new joy and zest into living, and leave an afterglow that lasts from week to week." Still pretty good copy.

Conservatives who fear government spending will be relieved to know that the trails built by the youths of the C.C.C. camps in the thirties were an important and highly successful investment in a sport which has proved to be an economic mainstay for both Vermont and New Hampshire. These trails were given such terrifying names as Nose Dive at Mt. Mansfield, Thunderbolt on Mt. Greylock, Wildcat at Pinkham Notch, and Hell's Highway on Moosilauke. There is also the Taft Trail at Cannon Mountain, which although it was not named for the prominent conservative leader, may have given Republican watchdogs a feeling that some good would come out of the C.C.C. Actually these trails were built with an incredible amount of foresight, well ahead of their time, both in location and design. The areas where they were laid out are by and large the centers of Eastern skiing today. Also the steepness of the terrain and the design of the courses were engineered for a grade of skiing that was yet to come. The early races on these sensationally named trails sometimes attracted as many as four or five thousand spectators who lined a course to witness the new daredevils of skiing.

Among these daredevils were a sprinkling of old-timers whose names are now legendary—Alec Bright, Bob Livermore, Sel Hannah, Al Sise. All still ski actively, even participating in veterans' races. A whiz-kid generation of Dartmouth skiers was also very much in the limelight. Foremost was Dick Durrance, who was born in Florida, learned to ski at Garmisch-Partenkirchen as a schoolboy, and returned to this country to become America's number one skier. In a race on the Taft Trail in 1934, he covered the mile and a quarter course in 2 minutes, 44 seconds, averaging thirty miles an hour, and beating his nearest competitor by more than half a minute. He brought back from Germany the tempo turn, a high-speed, highly stylized christie. There were other Dartmouth skiers in the headlines—Ted Hunter, the most graceful of them all; the Bradley and the Chivers brothers, skilled in jumping and cross-country as well as the Alpine events; Eddie Wells, who skied in a deep crouch, well forward, almost falling out of his loosely laced boots; and Harold Hillman, who was an erect, confident-looking skier. These boys, who received tremendous press notices, dramatized the sport. And overnight, skiing became headline material.

Not only was interest and participation in skiing on the increase, but such important developments as the advent of the first rope tow at Woodstock in 1934 were taking place as well. The evolution in technique and equipment had begun.

Skiers now outfitted themselves with steel-edged skis, and a magnificent new binding called the Kandahar, with a cable and spring arrangement to keep the boot in the toe-irons and down-pressure on the heel. This binding, which made the foot seem part of the ski, became the standard ski binding for the next ten years.

Skiing technique changed less rapidly. The few ski books available were often contradictory, and I developed an early prejudice against book learning when it came to skiing anyway. We had some idea of stem turns of the steered variety, where the skier puts his skis in the closed V position of a snowplow. These turns are made simply by weighting one ski more than the other. The weighted ski then becomes the steering one, turning the skier in the general direction it is pointed.

But stem turns are dull and belong to the early days of skiing—early both in terms of the sport's history, and each skier's development. Our Norwegian coach taught us the telemark. This turn is a great show-off maneuver, since when properly executed it is truly graceful. The skier advances one ski, trailing the tip of the other alongside the advanced boot. He is then in the position of a fencer who lunges at an opponent. The weight is on the forward ski, an inward-turning twist is applied, and the trailing ski is brought around very much as if it were a coupled railroad car. The result is a classic pose, with outstretched hands, like a ballerina poised on one leg.

No sooner had we learned this turn than we realized how impractical it was. One had to have perfect balance to advance the first ski to such an extent, and in order to change direction, it took considerable scrambling to advance the other foot. Linked turns required both great proficiency and a wide trail. Also, we were proud of our new down-pull bindings, and to accomplish this turn, we had to have a free heel, since the heel of the trailing foot was supposed to come completely off the ski.

We did learn the open christie, better described as the scissors turn. Here the skier must separate his ski tips so they are pulling apart. He then puts most of his weight on the ski pointing in the desired direction, leans back, and skids around on that ski, with the outside, unweighted ski hopefully being brought along. We found this to be a most useful high-speed turn and learned it with surprising ease. This old-fashioned turn differs in body movement from modern turns because the skier must lean back rather than forward. Actually this may be more natural if he is inexperienced. All these efforts were aimed at avoiding the situation made infamous by the Charles Addams skier whose tracks have straddled a tree. The open christie returned when the Austrians came to this country for the 1950 F.I.S. meet at Aspen, and in close slalom work they utilized the maneuver as a way of both finishing one turn and skating to a high line for the next.

Naturally we worked on the pure christie, a turn where the skis remain parallel throughout. However, our version was similar to the side thrust a ski jumper makes on the flats near the end of the outrun. The jumper must make an emergency stop, and he does this by unweighting his skis in a quick, almost hopping movement, twisting the unweighted skis at right angles to his former direction, and skidding to a stop. The result, as intended, is more a skid than a turn. In downhill skiing, the result is also more a skid, only here the intention is to turn rather than to brake. The classic terminology in skiing contains a name for this old-fashioned turn which is most appropriate—the jerk christie. Used by most nonexpert parallel skiers today, this turn results solely from an anxiety to get around as quickly as possible, and consequently is not a thing of great beauty.

Our little skiing group at Choate was extremely pleased to have learned the basic stem, telemark, open christie, and our own form of pure christie. As we progressed from one step to another, we thought we were keeping abreast of new techniques. However, all these developments had been covered in a book published in

1913 titled *How to Ski,* and written by Vivian Caulfield, one of the early stalwarts of the sport.

At some point we decided to form the Choate Ski Club. Our organization was more fraternal than athletic, as those of us who were drawn to skiing at this early stage were a pretty mixed group. We all found in this sport, however, an important and exciting new outlet and the ski club achieved status as we organized trips, and even entered a few meets.

Our first ski meet was held in the winter of 1936 at the Eaglebrook School in Deerfield, Massachusetts. This was a four-event meet—downhill, slalom, cross-country, and jumping. The downhill was a short, steep course through the woods, ending up on a practice slope. Most of us had never skied a trail that challenging, and it is a wonder no one was hurt. I remember "Spiff" Little of Mount Hermon, who was later to become a fellow member of the Dartmouth ski team, going off the course deep into the woods, and emitting schoolboy curses as he worked his way back to the trail, still on his skis, to place fairly well in the race. "Spiff" must have received an impressive scare, for after that he always tended to race in a well-thought-out, carefully controlled manner. In the slalom I put to work my open christie, which I had learned only a few days earlier, and placed fifth or sixth, best of the Choate runners. The slalom course utilized the old style slalom gates, with knee-high flags enabling much easier entry and egress than the tall flags which soon replaced them. The cross-country course, though relatively short, was a terrible chore for most of us, since we ran it on full-weight downhill skis. I recall envying Reese Harris, a tall, slender boy from Hotchkiss, well equipped with narrow cross-country skis, proper bindings with locked-in toe and free heel, light boots, and long poles. Whether Reese was the winner, I do not remember, but he certainly looked the part.

There was a neat little steep-walled U-shaped gully on the course, where we dropped straight down and then suddenly found ourselves shooting up the other side. The trick here was to keep the weight over the skis. I think I made it, and since I seldom forget bad or embarrassing falls, I probably did. In the jump, we Choate boys used our heads, for none of us entered the event. The jump was built on a steep hill which overlooked the Eaglebrook School buildings. There was no real outrun. The landing hill went suddenly into an uphill slope, ending abruptly at the sharp edge of a driveway beside the school. If the jumper made a good jump and a solid landing, he reached the end of the uphill slope with considerable speed, and became airborne again as he hit the edge of the driveway, landing in a pile of hay which was supposed to prevent him from crashing into the school building. Jumping is a great spectator sport, and none of us was disappointed in the show that day at Eaglebrook. The jump, needless to say, was poorly designed, and abandoned immediately after the first meet.

During vacations of my last three years at Choate, I went skiing with some of my schoolmates. Christmas we went to Gore Mountain at North Creek, New York, an area that has always had good early season cover. The main attraction there was a bus which went up a plowed road to a point near the summit. This bus enabled us to "ride up and slide down." The trails were poorly designed and narrow, with sudden sharp curves, and although we enjoyed ourselves, North Creek does not stand out in my mind as an outstanding ski area.

Spring vacation we headed for Mt. Washington in the White Mountains of New Hampshire for superior skiing under breathtaking condition. Mt. Washington is widely known for almost always being "socked in." The highest natural wind velocity ever recorded was clocked by the summit observatory at 231 miles per hour. The mountain storms are so severe that every few years fatalities occur when people are lost on the mountain. Midwinter skiing on the upper sections of the mountain is almost nonexistent. Skiing above the timberline does not begin until early March, and even then it is limited by caprices of the weather.

We always had superb weather at Mt. Washington. And during those long cloudless days, skiing under a hot sun on fast spring snow, we were carried away by the dramatic beauty of true Alpine skiing. Mountains, like most things in life, are judged on a relative basis. Mt. Washington, however, is imposing in all of its proportions. The mountain is 6,280 feet high, rising from the floor over 5,000 feet, to dominate with its sister peaks in the Presidential Range, that part of the north country. The timberline ends at the 4,000-foot level, providing vast and steep snowfields.

The only way to take the measure of a mountain is to climb it yourself. And Mt. Washington should be climbed in the winter. The mountain is in a national forest, and it is ordained that any man who would ski there must conquer it on foot. If the National Forest Service should ever entertain the idea of putting a lift on the mountain, old-time skiers would rise up in arms.

Climbing, a skier senses the full proportions of the mountain, breathes in air touched by hemlock fragrance, and is treated to incredible vistas of snow-covered rocky slopes. It takes a lot of energy to struggle up to the open slopes, but it is an exhilarating experience, and the climb goes fast.

The ice sheet which at one time covered New England has left its marks on the mighty mountain. On the southeast side is a huge bowl known as Tuckerman Ravine. This is a glacial cirque, carved out as the ice sheet receded. And the bowl formed is an almost perfect parabolic curve, looking like one half a giant radar reflector. All winter long the prevailing wind from the northwest blows snow from the cone on the summit into the lee formed by the steep boulder-gutted rock walls of the ravine. The snow builds up in this bowl, filling it to a depth of one hundred feet. Slopes rise from the center of the ravine in all directions, at gradually steepening angles right up to more than fifty degrees, the steepest angle at which snow can hang without constantly avalanching. The ravine has two big craggy shoulders, one on the left known as Boott Spur, and one on the right known as Lion Head. Here and there are massive outcroppings of rock which are never quite covered with snow.

Tuckerman Ravine never looks the same. Winter after winter the snow drifts in differently. Sometimes the cover is lean, and the bowl has exceptionally steep snow walls with narrow slopes between the rock outcroppings. Other times it is plush, with longer, less steep and broader slopes, making it appear as though the snow would like to cover the rocky walls in their entirety. The snow surface is also ever-changing, its texture going from wind-blown fine powder to coarse-grained corn snow, sometimes wearing wind-wave marks or even striations from falling ice particles. Sometimes the surface gradually recedes, with snow line and snow level diminishing under the increasing warmth of the spring sun. There are some aspects of the ravine, however, that do not change. A right gully and a left gully provide exciting entrances from the snowfields on top, while the main entry is by the famous Head Wall itself, slightly on the right side of the bowl, between two large rock fields. Another appealing feature of the ravine is a large outcropping, a third of the way up the bowl. This always pokes its head from the snow, and is known as Lunch Rock.

We had great times skiing there. The weather alone can provide an element of enjoyment. Anyone skiing in the ravine on a sunny day has the impression that the walls of the bowl are serving as reflectors, concentrating the heat of the sun on the exact place where he is standing. The full, salubrious effect of the sun combined with the Alpine beauty of the scene had a lasting effect on our young and impressionable minds.

Remembering our lack of ski technique, I marvel at the apparent ease with which we skied the steep slopes and even the Head Wall of the ravine. Perhaps by skiing at Tuckerman we were learning to relax in the fall line. Since the slopes rise ever so gradually to their full steepness, the skier adjusts to steep-slope skiing in small steps, each time starting from a higher point up the bowl. Still there is a point where there is no halfway measure. And here a skier must prepare himself for going over the wall. As he walks up, generally on the right side of the wall, he puts his feet into firm footholds made by others. When he nears the steepest part of the wall, mountaineering takes over, and a giddy feeling in the stomach makes surefootedness difficult. So steep in fact is the slope at this point, that the climber, who is carrying his skis over one shoulder, has to swing the hand holding them to the side, to keep from hitting the snow ahead. Once past the steepest part, he finds his view back down the ravine obscured and has the feeling of looking over a precipice, not knowing where the bottom may be. But the skier remains aware of the exact positions of the rock faces below him, and can now plan the precise course he is going to take over the wall. Up here at last, he is on more normal ground. Though when this easier section has been reached, there is a desire to go even higher, in order to have more of the easier skiing for warm-up turns before reaching the critical point, where a fall could be dangerous.

From the slope on the cone above the ravine, the skier sees a concave snow horizon, and since he cannot see the rocks or any part of the slope below, he must use this snow line very much like a pilot on instruments would use his artificial horizon. The arc of this snow horizon, combined with his earlier careful noting of rock positions, enables the skier to swing down in a traverse to the left and make a right turn above the steep section, knowing full well that this is no place for a fall. Then he goes from another traverse to the right, into the unbelievable steepness of the center wall, where he either runs so much in the fall line that he picks up fantastic speed and goes below the rocks on his right, or he takes a slower line which forces him to make a turn in order to avoid these rocks. The turn must be executed on the steepest part of the slope, where the angle is fifty degrees. The skier, as he goes over the wall, is very much aware that he is not merely accomplishing a feat, he is making a performance. Activity in the ravine has stopped, and all eyes are on him. Gradually his confidence picks up with his speed, because the full expanse of the bowl is before him and he can see the broad, gently sloping runout at the bottom. He is flushed with a sense of achievement and skis with ease and exhilaration, at record speed.

In many years of skiing at Tuckerman Ravine, I only fell once going over the Head Wall. The snow was somewhat heavy and rotten, and I vaulted forward, spraining my ankle. But the damage to my ego was considerably greater than that to my ankle, for when you fall high up the ravine, you slide or somersault for one hundred yards or so, until the slope eases off and you can stop yourself.

I remember meeting a girl above the Head Wall, a girl named Cynthia Taft. I watched her ski the wall with skill and grace, and I am sure I never talked to her anywhere except on the snowfield above the ravine. Still we became quite friendly, and exchanged letters after spring vacation was over. I was impressed by a girl who could master this kind of skiing, and would certainly like to have known her better.

A Choate master named "Finky" Gurll was part of our spring vacation group. A stocky, nice-looking man with extreme bowlegs, he was a delight to watch on the slopes of Tuckerman Ravine, skiing with feet close together and knees a foot apart.

We stayed at a boarding house, called Abbott's, in Jackson, New Hampshire. After a full day's skiing, we would return there late in the afternoon. With the temperature in the sixties or seventies, and not a sign of snow for several hundred yards, we would sit out on the porch drinking beer and basking our well-baked faces in the last hours of sun. There was a true feeling of fellowship at such moments as Dick Dickinson, Milton Tootle, Mr. Gurll, and I looked out at Mt. Washington, which had provided us with yet another day of thrilling skiing.

4

The Starting Gate

Man's fondness for sliding takes many well-known forms, particularly among youngsters. However, few of us at any age can resist a long glide down an icy sidewalk. Skating is a popular form of sliding, and the first few steps on ice at the beginning of a season make a skater especially aware of this. Sledding, tobogganing, and bobsledding will always be part of the winter's fun. In the Hawaiian Islands, a traditional sport is tea-leaf sliding. Here one sits on a giant tea leaf, holding the stem in his hands, and slides down steep slopes over heavy, matted vegetation. The limitation to this pastime is there can be only one run per tea leaf. Dancing, too, is a form of sliding. And there are other links between dancing and skiing as well.

Skiing is sliding in the grand manner, though many people ski today because it has become "the thing to do." The sport is so much in the spotlight that Madison Avenue uses skiing to promote automobiles, cigarettes, and soft drinks, in an attempt to associate the product with a chic, energetic, sports-minded leisure class.

Ski clothes tend to flatter male and female alike, and in recent years the influence of ski attire has been felt throughout the fashion world. Après-ski outfits of ten years ago have become the "at home" dress of today.

The sports world is undergoing a lesiure time boom, as the shorter work week combined with rising incomes is making possible broader participation in all forms of outdoor activity. Vast numbers of people have taken up skiing, and many travel on their vacations to the Alps, the true home of downhill skiing, and even to such far-off places as Chile and Japan. For the less wealthy and adventurous, there is the weekend jaunt, which can be almost as much fun as a trip to Zermatt. And so the vacation home has become very much a part of the modern ski scene.

The enthusiasm of those who ski attracts others to the sport. Often this interest develops in the family, and all members rush off to the slopes together. Occasionally a parent has harbored a lifelong yearning to ski, and in promoting it as a family sport, satisfies his own desires. But the fact remains there are few other sports a family can do as a unit with equal involvement and enjoyment for all.

Skiing is one of the best ways to come to grips with winter. There are many ways of turning your back on winter. Some people run south, while not a few others, ostrich-like, resort to heavy drinking indoors. But skiers look forward to their season with intense excitement.

Skiing is thought to be a dangerous sport, especially by the nonskier. However, skiing at the intermediate level or above is seldom hazardous to one's life. Ski injuries are almost exclusively of a nonpermanent nature. Ironically, it may be the safest sport of all for many of us. In this fast-moving world the social pressures in the community and the necessity for success in business keep the individual motivated to the point of agitation. Many people who turn to skiing are intense and introspective. They need an outlet for their energy and ambition. Skiing then may have an important and as yet unrecognized role in mental health.

A desire to exercise, and to do so outdoors, brings a large number of people to skiing. A person must be in fair physical condition to have any real interest in becoming a skier. Those who are overweight usually and wisely stay away. Also, individuals who do not exercise regularly and who lack stamina and muscle tone are aware that skiing offers special hazards for them. Before going out on a slope, either as a beginner, or at the start of a new season, each skier should do conditioning exercises. The skier who is well into his winter season has attained an added spring in his step, strength in his backbone, and a keenness of mind, all of which help him face the hurdles of the day.

But for each skier, the sport also has a special inner meaning: The winter countryside and the mountains may be the important thing, or it may be the companionship of enjoying with others a pleasant way of life. One bond which all skiers share, however, is the battle between control and noncontrol. A skier who is only a few days into the sport realizes how this tug-of-war is linked to his very survival. As he progresses, he takes great pleasure in knowing how fast he can go without taking undue risks. Even the "hotshot" racer faces this challenge on a steep bumpy schuss like Exhibition Run at Sun Valley, which no one takes straight. So every skier must find his own level of control.

While I have now mentioned a few of the more obvious reasons why people begin skiing, some are more deeply buried.

A friend of mine, Dick Sarkisian, went to school at Williams College under the shoulder of Mt. Greylock, where he had many opportunities to ski during his four winters there. He resisted skiing's temptations, but there must have been a buildup in the deep recesses of his mind. For after he graduated he took a trip around the world, and one day when he was in India he had the rare treat of seeing from Darjeeling the full grandeur of the Himalayas. His subconscious ambitions were spurred. Right then and there he took up the sport. And he has remained a dedicated skier to this day.

Paul Gensior, an artist, says that snowstorms provoked his interest in skiing. He enjoyed walking in them, particularly at night, and loved the way the snow mantled the countryside, almost seeming to stifle all life beneath it. But no matter what the duration or magnitude of the storm, nature's strength was there. For Paul the aesthetic experience of wanting to be part of a snowstorm is what lured him to the greatest snow sport of all—skiing.

Jim Robison, president of Indian Head Mills, made an unusual start in the sport. Beautiful Bridget Schwarzenbach talked him into buying a large A-frame chalet which belonged to a friend of hers and was located on the Spruce Peak mountain road at Stowe. Some nonskiers are leery about investing in ski equipment, uncertain whether or not they will take to the sport. Jim was so sure he wanted to ski that he bought a house without seeing it, before he even ventured out onto the slopes. The second winter after his purchase, I skied with him, along with Bridget and her husband Bobbie, leading them down the difficult Chamois Trail on Mt. Mansfield. Although this was a tough test for Jim, he did exceptionally well for someone who had taken up skiing only one year earlier at the age of forty-five. As is so often the case with resolute people, Jim has become a very good skier.

Jane Burbank, the attractive wife of a Westchester architect, was for a long time interested in skiing, but the fear of getting hurt had restrained her from taking up the sport. However, she saw two people in successive winters break their ankles getting in and out of cars on her icy driveway. This experience convinced her that she should no longer deny herself the pleasure of skiing. Jane has picked up the sport with some ease and is apparently much less inhibited by fear than others who have started earlier or more impetuously.

Why some people make better skiers than others, is difficult to define. Sometimes someone starts the sport because he knows he will do well at it; for instance, an active person looking for a way to stay fit during the winter season will turn to skiing.

The sport requires a special form of coordination. The skier uses his entire body, but depends more on his legs and sense of balance than on anything else. It does not follow that because a golfer has a low handicap he will be one bit more adept at skiing than his high-handicap friend. Consequently, many good skiers are unsuccessful in other sports. However, there are two particular activities in which ability seems to carry over into skiing—sailing and dancing.

It seems extraordinary at first glance that skiing and sailing should go together, or that skill in one should imply skill in the other. These two sports complement each other on a seasonal basis —that is obvious. Not so apparent are the other aspects which link them. However, both sports require man to master the elements. In sailing, nature's rhythms in the sea and the wind are controlled by man's rhythms with the tiller and the sails; in skiing, the mountains and the snow are controlled by the skier's entire body as he carves out his turns. Neither sport receives a mechanical assist to forward motion. Instead there is more the illusion of speed or the challenge of a specific situation than speed itself. Each sport requires concentration, with tremendous attention to detail regarding such matters as equipment, preparations, and mental attitude. And though both require time and money, perhaps the greatest link between them is that the mountains and the sea appeal to the senses in the same way.

The other activity where proficiency carries over into skiing is dancing. The movements of dancing require the same balance and coordination as the turns of skiing, and a sense of rhythm and a lightness of foot are essential to both. But it is not the highly trained dancer with a large repertoire who necessarily makes the best skier. It is more frequently the relaxed, uninhibited exhibitionist, enjoying himself in spite of not knowing the precise steps, who will be at home on skis.

5

Skiing for Dartmouth

One afternoon in 1938, late in November of my freshman year at Dartmouth, word passed around that Dick Durrance was going to conduct a class for freshman ski squad prospects. We were to assemble at the Vale of Tempe, a steep-walled ravine that runs through the Hanover golf course. The campus had not even seen its first good frost, yet we were told to bring our skis. This practice session was to take place on wet grass!

For most of us this was our first chance to see Dick Durrance ski. For me, it was more than that, since I had never seen any top-caliber racer on skis. And for all of us I am quite sure it was our first and only experience skiing on wet grass.

That afternoon the unusual conditions could not be compared to a good-to-excellent rating on natural snow. There had been a short heavy rain during the middle of the day, and the steep slope, which had a slick heavy grass surface, provided fairly fast running. Good edge control was a necessity, since the skis tended to slide away from the turn. Dick Durrance, as mild in appearance as he was formidable on skis, was stocky, short, partly bald, with a friendly face and soft speaking voice. He conducted a tightly structured lesson, and we were so busy absorbing what he had to say, and trying to put it to work, that we hardly noticed we were skiing on grass.

Dick's lesson led up to a high-speed christie with a slight stem throughout. He emphasized the tremendous control, flexibility, and quick reactions that were possible from this position. Also he did this simple turn with such facility that there was none of the usual braking action associated with the stem. As he performed the turn, the stemming action was more body movement and thrust than snowplow, because the skis were so nearly parallel. We learned that we could take advantage of the stem, shifting our weight with ease from one ski to the other, without the disadvantages of its awkwardness and braking action.

Dick Durrance was a great one for ski safety. In downhill races he would almost invariably be faster than any man on the course, but his margin of control was always well planned. Having skied most of his life, including nearly a dozen years of competitive skiing on the international race circuit, he has never had a broken leg or other serious ski injury. Although Dick taught us a basic ski technique for safety and speed in both tight slalom work and high-speed downhill running, he was actually retarding our technique, because on a long-term basis, the stem, no matter how slight, had to go. Any form of the stem is a difficult habit to break, and some of us have spent the better part of twenty-five years trying to get rid of it. On the other hand, in fairness to Dick, anything that he tried to teach us in 1938 would have been far removed from contemporary, angulated, heel-thrust parallel skiing.

When the snow appeared that winter, regular afternoon practice sessions were the order of the day at spruce-studded Balch Hill, overlooking the Hanover plain. Both freshman and varsity squads trained together under the sharp eye of coach Walter Prager, and the group was overweighted with freshman hopefuls. What I lacked in background and skill was offset by an intense desire to become a Dartmouth skier. In the early time trials I placed high enough to be certain of a berth on the freshman team.

I remember well my first day of real skiing with members of the Dartmouth ski squad. About a dozen of us had gone up to Franconia Notch to stay at a Dartmouth Outing Club hut at the foot of Mt. Lafayette, overlooking Cannon Mountain across Echo Lake. The skiing was exceptionally good for mid-December. After riding the new aerial tramway which had just opened a few days earlier, we schussed the Taft slalom slope, where I skied at about the same speed as upperclassmen Charlie McLane and Bob Skinner. Of course, little did they know how unsure I was at that speed!

Most of the races I entered my freshman year were on short, narrow, and relatively slow Class C trails, courses that always unnerved me more than the steeper, longer, Class A trails. On the short courses, the race was over in about one minute, and there were possibly one or two critical points on the trail where speed had to be maintained for any kind of a showing. On the Class A trails a run was more cohesive. Here a skier had an opportunity to find and hold his stride through any number of schusses and difficult turns. My log of results on Class C trails features such entries as, "Fell near finish, couldn't get up," or "Wax race–eighth place out of twenty," or "Had hell of a time–fortieth place out of fifty-seven." I did place third in the Fisk Trophy Race at Woodstock, but was 12 seconds behind the winner, Harold Hillman.

In March I entered the White Mountain Ski Runners' Race on the Wildcat Trail. This was my first race on a Class A trail, and I desperately wanted my A rating. Today to get into Class A a skier must earn F.I.S. points by skiing faster than those in the class above him. Before World War II one good run on a good day would qualify a skier for the top racing class. In that race on the Wildcat, my time was 2:41.2, which gave me twelfth place. More important, it gave me my A rating, since a time of under 3 minutes was the requirement.

In late March, 1939, I went back to Mt. Washington for spring vacation. But the weather was generally bad, and I was sick with influenza. Just when I was scheduled to head home for a few days with my family, the weather broke, my health returned, and the mountain took on the look of grandeur I remembered from my Choate spring vacations. It was frustrating enough to have to leave under such circumstances, but worst of all, the third American Inferno Race was to be held from the summit of Mt. Washington to the Appalachian Mountain Club hut at Pinkham Notch. A telephone call asking my nonskiing family for permission to stay was notably unsuccessful, and April 8 and 9 found me in the snowless Oranges of New Jersey, heartbroken not to be racing down a mountain I knew and loved so well.

However, back in Hanover I was elated to learn that even though the sun had been shining in New Jersey, the race on Mt. Washington had been postponed to April 15 and 16 because of bad weather. My class A rating qualified me for the Inferno, and I sent in an application blank.

In the spring the Dartmouth skiers always stayed in Gorham, New Hampshire, which was north of the mountain and inconvenient for Boston skiers. We were aware of our near monopoly of the town. Our two favorite places to stay were either with "Ma" Rollins or "Ma" Wilson. Only about a dozen of us could be put up at Ma Rollins', where we were treated practically like members of the family. The price was low even in terms of the noninflated dollar—$1.25 per day for bed, two meals, pack lunch, and after-dinner song entertainment by the Rollinses. For those who wanted to come and go at their own choosing, Ma Wilson had around fifty beds on the second floor above a restaurant. The beds were scattered in corridors and over doorsills in a manner which appeared haphazard, but which was calculated to provide the maximum number of lodgings. The price was 25 cents per night, and only 12½ cents if a double bed was shared.

From Ma Wilson's window on Saturday morning, April 15, the weather seemed very questionable. We could not even see the mountain, and the overcast looked like snow. Nevertheless the entire Inferno crew—patrol, officials, racers, chief-of-course Walter Prager—started up the mountain. We bulldozed ahead into the teeth of a snowstorm, right up into the ravine itself, before calling it quits, leaving a batch of guide flags just below the Head Wall. But on the wooded Sherburne Trail down below, several inches of new snow gave us perfect conditions for some skiing. Still there was little excitement in the air, since it appeared that the Inferno might have to be canceled Sunday for the fourth and final time that year because of weather.

A thrill awaited the early risers at the Ma Wilson establishment next morning. From our second floor windows we had a truly magnificent panorama of the Presidential Range. The sky was deep blue and cloudless and the mountain was dazzingly white, with a touch of hoarfrost over new snow. But at Pinkham Notch the summit weather report on the Appalachian Mountain Club hut bulletin board indicated that the race was not by any means a certainty. Gusts at the summit were up to eighty miles an hour and the temperature ranged between ten and twenty degrees.

Down in the notch there was little hint of such windy, cold conditions. Dressed lightly for the climb, we stripped to the waist just a short way up the trail. Usually skiers climbing to the ravine proceed up the narrow fire trail which holds an even climbing grade throughout. However, we went up the lower wooded part of the Inferno racecourse, the Sherburne Trail, to study carefully the line we would take. The higher we climbed the warmer we seemed to get, and we became quite sure the race was on.

The first American Inferno Race, which took place in 1938, was won in 14 minutes, 41 seconds. Dick Durrance won the second Inferno the following year, in 12 minutes, 35 seconds. Although rigorous tests of mountain skiing, these races were not true downhills, since skiers had to stem down the narrow fire trail. Everyone knew that the record would be broken by a big margin this year, because the new Sherburne Trail, a broad, fast, intermediate-grade course, would enable much greater speeds. Also, a powerful-looking skier, Toni Matt, known as the demon from St. Anton, had spent all week meticulously studying the upper slopes on the cone of the mountain, the Head Wall, the ravine floor, the Little Head Wall, and the entire Sherburne Trail. All winter Matt and Durrance had had a running duel, with Matt usually leading. In addition, there was a sense of drama in the air because this was the Inferno, a race from the summit of Mt. Washington to Pinkham Notch at the bottom, with a vertical drop of 4,300 feet over a course just under four miles long, which included one of the steepest skiable slopes in the world.

As we reached the Little Head Wall the air temperature dropped nearly to freezing, and the wind howled above the rock walls of the ravine. Each year, as I have mentioned, the ravine looks a little different. This year the scrub spruce and boulders were covered from the floor of the ravine down to the Little Head Wall. Some years the skier had to make slow swings through mammoth boulders, and in other years a path had to be clipped through the tops of underbrush.

At the Head Wall we could feel a great wintry blast of arctic air. We studied with keen interest that part of the course which would give us a line from the top of the ravine, down across the floor to the Little Head Wall. Once over the top of the wall and without its protection, we became fully aware of the accuracy of the summit weather report. We could now see the entire cone section of the racecourse. Walter Prager had put in a series of flags to guide the runner from the top across the snowfield up to the critical left turn, and then to the right turn above the wall. The left turn was a turn away from the traverse of the cone and toward the Head Wall. The right was a check turn above the rocks, leading into the actual traverse over the wall. The guide flags were single flags, not gates, and it was not mandatory for the racer to pass near them, but they did lead to the correct ravine.

The closer we got to the summit, the fiercer the wind became. The last two hundred yards of the course consisted of a rock field which should have been studied very carefully. But most of us, nearly frozen at this point, walked hurriedly on to the shelter at the top. At the summit itself thick ice coated the ground, the hotel, the meterological tower, and Camden Cottage, the climbers' cabin. Before entering the cabin, we had to secure our skis to keep them from blowing away. Inside, forty-two runners and a half-dozen officials crowded together, teary-eyed and coughing. Someone had started a fire, and wind coming down the chimney caused a heavy layer of smoke to fill the cabin. Walter Prager called the Dartmouth skiers into a corner for a message more philosophical than competitive. He wanted us to enjoy ourselves, and stressed the drama of the event. To Durrance he pointed out that Matt would be nearly impossible to beat because of his week's practice on the mountain. Dick, then, along with the rest of us, was to ski his own race and enjoy the run.

The starting arrangements for this race were unique. It was so cold that having a starter outside, or even rotating starters, was impossible. An electric bell had been rigged to give a 5-second warning and then ring for "go." Then, as each racer left the start, which consisted of two lonely ski poles jammed into the ice, the next racer would go outside to get into his bindings. Joe Dodge, hut master and pioneer of radio-telephone communications for racing, was the starter, safely behind the window of the hut at the summit.

Matt was one of the early runners. What happened when he went down is a matter of history. Walter Prager, who was standing at the top of the Head Wall waiting for his Dartmouth boys to appear, noticed Matt's speed on the snowfield of the cone. As Toni approached the wall he made his S turn to the left and then right, and seemed to be checking in a conventional manner. But instead of completing his final turn, he pointed his skis straight down the Head Wall. The several thousand people in the ravine who had come up to watch Matt and Durrance ski this famous course were spellbound as Matt did the unbelievable and schussed the Head Wall. Attaining a speed of perhaps seventy miles per hour, he shot across the floor of the ravine, his ski tips reverberating with a noise of gunfire as he hurtled over a snow surface that was frozen into wind-wave ripples. At the bottom of Little Head Wall his speed was so great that he was the only runner to coast up a slight incline at the beginning of the Sherburne Trail. He skied the entire course with strength, skill, and speed.

When Dick Durrance approached Water Prager in his S turn at the top of the ravine he slowed down enough for Walter to shout to him, "Take it straight! Matt did!" Dick responded with a smile and proceeded to comply with Walt's earlier instructions, running the wall conservatively, about the same as the top dozen runners. Over all, Dick ran a magnificent race, but he was still one full minute behind Toni Matt, who halved the old record and skied the course in 6 minutes, 29.2 seconds.

My run in the Inferno was the most exciting thing that ever happened to me on skis. In the starting gate I had a lonely moment with the mountain. It was quite a thrill to be standing at the summit, on the knife ridge of the Presidential Range, taking a look behind me down toward Bretton Woods, then ahead at the rocky slope and the snowfields beyond, with Wildcat Mountain standing out against the blue sky and the distant Atlantic coastline in the haze below. When the starting bell rang, it did not take much of a push to get going, since there was a forty mile an hour wind at my back. After not more than fifty yards I realized that I had no path through the rocks. I resorted to an unplanned sitzmark, got up, and before I really got going again, the rocks closed in once more and forced another sitzmark. This time I saw my way through, and swung into the long half-mile traverse toward Tuckerman Ravine. Way ahead I could see the figure of Roger Peabody, who had started one minute before me. The snow on this part of the course was a windblown, mirror-smooth surface. Going before the wind almost at the speed of the wind itself, I heard no noise save the sound of my skis in a slight sideslip. For most of the runners this was the fastest part of the course, the kind of easy speed that skiers revel in. At the top of the ravine I made my S turn with great care and swung into my Head Wall traverse. Soon I was going faster than I had ever gone on the wall. Gradually straightening out, I headed for the ravine, where the snow surface was a bit softer than at the top because it was less windblown. I was amazed at the number of spectators lining the bowl. As I went across the ice waves on the floor I realized that some people were standing on my line. I held my ground, figuring they would give way. My style was far from effortless at this point. With feet wide apart, I hung on for dear life, and the group at the top of the Little Head Wall suddenly ran clear of this approaching apparition. Over the Little Head Wall on my intended line, I picked up even more speed, but cursed as I came to a full stop before the incline that led into the Sherburne Trail. Shouts of encouragement told me that everyone but Matt had stopped here, and I was on my way again, poling madly. The upper stretches of the Sherburne consist mostly of easy, straight corridors. My skis ran swiftly over a corn-snow surface that had dried out and was starting to freeze. In the middle section of the course a wetter and slower surface alternating with shaded, faster patches of snow caused me to rock back and forth as I went from one consistency to the other. Riding the bumps presented a constant challenge, and when I hit the S turns on the last half mile of the Sherburne the snow got even heavier. My legs began to feel like putty after the toughness of the course, two weeks off skis, plus two falls near the start, and I took three more falls. Coming down the last pitch before the finish, I had one more hurdle—the bridge across the brook which was covered with giant snowdrifts. Three times I went from standing erect before I hit a drift to a full crouch as I went over it. Then I collapsed to a skidding stop as I crossed the finish line. While I was still lying in the snow, Charlie McLane thrust a can of beer into my hand and congratulated me on my run. My time was about 3 minutes longer than Matt's, but I placed thirteenth, and all the skiers who beat me were big names in Eastern racing.

There were only three racers who skied the course without a fall—Toni, Dick, and Ed Wells, who was third. Harold Hillman, who was fourth, would have had a no-fall run, had he not tangled up with a runner he was trying to pass. All forty-two runners finished, and without injuries. Charlie McLane took one of the few falls in the ravine area. He had stayed on his Head Wall traverse as if in a trance and found himself in a head-on collision with the top of a scrub spruce. One skier, Bob Egelhoff, overshot the Head Wall and skied toward Boott Spur. He ended up going down the left gully with a time of 16 minutes, which under the circumstances was quite remarkable. Alec Bright, already well known as a skier, at forty-one was the senior racer by about ten years, and placed fourteenth.

Matt's feat surely stands as one of the great downhill victories of all time. Many legends have been built up around his run; some say that he caught an edge at the top of the Head Wall and was forced to take it straight. I personally place little faith in this story. Others say that on one of the turns near the finish Matt bounced from a bump to a tree, then from the tree onto the trail without falling or losing any speed. Two weekends after the race three of us climbed up the Sherburne Trail. We never found any edge marks on the trees near the finish, and in any event this part of the Matt myth seems highly unlikely.

The college boys thought of Toni as the strong silent type. After Pearl Harbor he enlisted in the Army, where despite the language barrier he became an officer in the ski troops. After the war Toni tried professional boxing in the heavyweight class. Today he directs the ski school at Catamount in Hillsdale, New York, and remains as always a well-liked, much-respected person.

The American Inferno has not been held since then. In 1953, a shortened race, dubbed the "castrated Inferno" by Pinkham Notch's Joe Dodge, was held just below the center of the Head Wall. In at least a half-dozen other years, efforts to hold the race were frustrated by Mt. Washington weather.

In 1940, the year following the Inferno, it was Dick Durrance's turn in the duel with Matt. Dick had been skiing hard all winter while doing public relations and photography work for Sun Valley. In the downhill of the Harriman Race, which took place on the Warm Springs Trail, Dick was the man to beat. On an exceptionally steep part of that course known appropriately as the Steilhang, Dick skied straight down with tremendous speed. At the end there is a sharp turn to the left into a gully, and Dick, unable to hold his turn, skidded into the up-bank of the gully, straddled a small pine tree, almost hit a big tree, and took a momentary fall. Then at the bottom he came toward the finish with such tremendous speed that he could not stay on his feet, and he fell again, sliding under a rope into some bushes. He lost several seconds, but scrambled across the finish line to win in 2 minutes, 56 seconds, beating Walter Prager, who had made a no-fall run, by 4 seconds, and beating Matt very handily by about 19 seconds. That evening at the banquet Averell Harriman said as he handed the cup to Dick, "Don't you ever do that again."

By my second winter at Dartmouth I had at least established myself as the best downhill skier in the sophomore class. The last of the big names, including Durrance, Wells, Howie Chivers, and Dave Bradley had graduated the year before. However, I was not by any means assured of a berth on the varsity. The weekend before Dartmouth Winter Carnival I went with the B team to the Williams Carnival, where we all were skiing as four-event men. The downhill race was held on Mt. Greylock's Thunderbolt, a trail

I had skied the three previous weekends, once in practice and twice in races. Because the course was icy that day, a half-dozen control gates made of heavy saplings had been strategically placed to slow us down and keep us out of the woods. The gates, however, had the effect of tripping up many of the best runners, including hotshot Bob Meservey, who as a freshman was skiing on our Dartmouth B squad. More than a few racers had bruises on their bodies as well as their egos. As for myself, my ego was sky-high since I was at home on the icy course, and I won my first victory on skis, 20 seconds ahead of the others.

In the slalom, I was told that I skied with a complete lack of style, but my confidence must have pulled me through, because I won this too. I was a passable cross-country skier, placing eleventh on a course that was beautifully laid out in the rolling countryside of Williamstown. As a jumper my aptitude was about zero, and in addition I had had very little practice. Since I had won the downhill and the slalom, I was given quite a buildup by the announcer at the Sheep Hill jump. Coming down, I was characteristically off in my timing, jumped too soon, and landed at the top of the knoll. I then proceeded to run the rest of the jumping hill in an ungraceful downhill crouch. The crowd, thinking the announcer had made a mistake, laughed good-naturedly. My second jump was not much better, and I was last among those who stood up. Still I had done well enough in the other three events to win the Skimeister Award. My teammates often jokingly referred to me as "Skimeister," since I was obviously not by any means a true four-event skier. However, as a result of the Williamstown races, I became a member of the Dartmouth varsity.

The single most compelling factor in my ambition in the sport was my desire to attain as much of a name in Dartmouth skiing as my All-American father had in football. I suppose I failed, for fame on skis eludes all but a small handful of skiers. In our group Charlie McLane, 1940, and Bob Meservey, 1943, were the most consistent winners, but we were all part of a forgotten generation of Dartmouth skiers. The Big Green stars who had preceded us were associated with the beginning of the modern sport as well as with a period of almost absolute Dartmouth dominance.

Our coach, Walter Prager, stressed individual safety rather than personal glory, and honor for the college rather than fame for the team. Walt's greatest role was giving last-minute instructions at the top of a course. While reviewing the critical points on a trail, he would emphasize the importance of turning way ahead of a turn on the course, in order to cut the curve close to the woods on the inside or uphill side. This was a faster and above all safer line than the one near the trees on the outside, downhill side of the curve. Walt taught us that anticipation is a key to all kinds of skiing—from slalom racing to open slope skiing where there are moguls on the course. Also, Walt was a great one for getting us psychologically primed for a race. He had more success with others than he did with me, however, because I became too "psyched up" for a race. Skiing was my only sport, and I had probably set sights that were too high for someone who was not raised in the snow country. Typically, in my first Dartmouth Carnival, I fell in the slalom right at the feet of Dean Neidlinger and my father, who had never seen me ski before.

Walt's safety record among members of the varsity during his twenty-year tenure as coach was perfect. The records of Otto Schniebs, his predecessor, as well as of those who followed him, right through Allison Merrill, the present-day coach, have likewise been unblemished. That is, in modern times no member of the Dartmouth A team has ever had a serious accident while training or racing for the college. This once again proves that the danger in the sport can be eliminated even from racing by a well-planned approach.

Although Walt was not so impressive in teaching us ski technique, he was very effective in the fine points of racing. In practice sessions he would teach us to ski with minimum edging to eliminate chattering on hard snow and to maintain smoothness through a slalom run. Above all we were to keep our weight over our skis and our bodies well poised so as not to get caught in the folly of having our weight back. If he did not put us into a ski technique mold, it may have been because he did not accept the current version of the Arlberg method.

Without asking Walt's permission, we all tried to emulate Toni

Matt, then the idol of the slopes. This vogue involved certain motions above the waist which we now know had no bearing on the dynamics of the turn. To describe the movement as simply as I know how, there was first a great counterswing, with the inside shoulder and hand going well forward. The outside shoulder and hand then followed through, rotating in the direction of the turn. The result was a posed look, with the outside hand well over the outside ski. In skiing today, the upper part of the body is kept out of the turn, facing downhill throughout. The hands touch the pole to the slope in a light, quick, uninhibiting manner, to trigger off a turn and set up the weighting and unweighting of the skis.

As young-looking as his Dartmouth skiers, Walt was a much-respected, well-loved coach. He was of simple Swiss ancestry, and his fame as a skier as well as a coach never in any way changed his unassuming manner. Whenever he raced against us in open competition, he would win more often than not. At all times conscious of good sportsmanship, he insisted that we conduct ourselves in an exemplary manner. Dartmouth's honor would not be lost through someone's fall in a set of slalom gates, but it could easily be compromised through thoughtless egotistical behavior.

Walt's skiers were a spirited, unpredictable group, who often showed a positive genius for breaking the rules of the college and of society, without getting either Dartmouth or themselves in trouble. Walt in his wisdom seemed to be able to take our brinkmanship in stride. In his final year, Dick Durrance stood up on the speakers' table at the carnival banquet in the presence of Dean Neidlinger and other dignitaries as well as members of the press, to give one of the most humorous inebriated performances in the history of the college (that Eleazar Wheelock had founded with "five hundred gallons of New England rum"). And Dick's favor with Dartmouth and the skiing community was never higher than it was that night.

A typical practical joke occurred outside the restaurant below Ma Wilson's rooming house in Gorham. A car loaded with skiers was all set to head for Mt. Washington when a latecomer came out of the restaurant. He started for the car, but stopped and yelled, "I've forgotten something." Then as the straggler wheeled around to reenter Ma Wilson's, John Litchfield, Dartmouth ski jumper and baseball team pitcher, fired a fast snowball at him. But Litchfield's aim was high, and he shattered the overhanging neon restaurant sign. Hearing the noise, a policeman came out of Ma Wilson's and spotted the intended victim running away from the scene of trouble. Meanwhile, Litchfield and his gang calmly took off unnoticed for the mountain. Late arrivals at the Pinkham Notch hut gave Litchfield the word that the cop had successfully locked up the innocent victim for the day in the county jail. Litchfield and company proceeded to enjoy the day's skiing, devoid of any pangs of conscience.

Charles McLane was in many ways our most colorful skier. Like most members of the varsity, he was a Phi Beta Kappa in addition to being a senior fellow. But he was still something of a screwball on the slopes. He raced with tremendous competitive spirit, featuring fantastic recoveries and a complete absence of style. However, there was plenty of style in the way he would let loose with a spontaneous volley of cursing at the end of a bad run. Spectators and officials at the finish line came to anticipate his characteristic outbursts. Walter made it clear that it was Charlie's unique prerogative to let off steam in this fashion. I remember that in the 1941 Eastern Championship at Franconia I had a tense, chattering, somewhat slow no-fall run. When after the race I indulged in some swearing of my own, Walter stopped me by raising one menacing finger as if to remind me that my name was not McLane.

Bob Meservey was our greatest stylist, skiing in a way not too unlike the French method of the early 1950's. With humorous intent he ordered some reinforced leather polo helmets for his teammates and appropriately labeled them "crash-pots." Today racers wear scientifically designed crash helmets for the downhill as well as for the giant slalom. Our generation actually had little need for such protection since our lacquer-bottomed broad-edged skis as well as our unrefined technique slowed us down. In addition, although we were whittling away at speed records, we were not psychologically ready to push speed to its full limit. Walter consequently looked with some disdain at our white crash-pots.

One of our standard jokes on a race day was to pick a most unlikely shortcut through the woods, pack it out, and ostentatiously discuss it in great detail as other competitors came up the trail. The good skiers knew that it was a joke, but the inexperienced competitor, who would never think of taking a shortcut, would seriously believe us to be quite mad, with the crash helmets adding the finishing touch.

On the Sunday of carnival weekend during my sophomore year I was entered in the Fisk Trophy Race on Suicide Six at Woodstock. The top part of the slalom consisted of a series of linked turns through open gates. Skiing with a hangover, I missed a set of flags to the left as my attention was on a set directly below me. Since I realized much too late that I had gone by the gate, I simply skied straight down the hill, bypassing the rest of the course and disqualifying myself. When I came to a stop, Walter came up and gave me the only real tongue-lashing of my Dartmouth racing career. He told how Friedl Pfeiffer had been criticized for bad sportsmanship and exhibitionism when he schussed a slalom slope in an important race with thousands of people watching.

The Dartmouth skiers also had a talent for après-ski group singing. There always seemed to be special lyrics to suit an occasion, and sometimes we even had a song ready for something that hadn't yet occurred. At the Hochebirge Race on the Taft Trail in 1940, the host club's legendary veteran skier Alec Bright went off into the woods for one of his many leg breaks. That night at the Hochebirge banquet we were ready with a song, but we were not alone, since most of the other teams had songs available for such a foreseeable Bright accident. So out of great respect for someone we all loved, we held what amounted to a wake for the skier who was resting in the Littleton Hospital.

My good friend, Jake Nunnemacher, was captain of the ski team my senior year. In every way Jake lived and acted the part of the ideal Dartmouth skier. One day the two of us had quite a scrap. Walking out of the hut at Pinkham Notch, we simultaneously spotted a knitted Norwegian cap hanging above the swinging tavern-type Appalachian Mountain Club sign. We immediately turned toward each other to see if the other had noticed, and then raced toward the prize. A 10-minute struggle ensued as we tried to shinny up the pole that held the sign. One of us would get part way up only to be pulled down by the other. Finally Jake flattened me so that my breath was knocked out for about two seconds, which was all he needed. The big throng of skiers watching the struggle gave Jake quite a hand. I must say that afterward I was somewhat mollified because the hat looked so well on him. Jake was a blond, pink-cheeked lad with perfect Germanic features. And the hat, brown-and-white with a high peak and earflaps, became his trademark. In World War II Jake was the only Dartmouth ski team member to be killed. He was shot in the back of the neck during a mopping-up operation a few days before VE Day. I have often thought that if the German soldier who shot him could have seen Jake's face he never would have pulled the trigger.

Almost every year Dartmouth skiers race in the West where they have often distinguished themselves. For Christmas of 1941 I was scheduled to go to a national intercollegiate meet at Sun Valley. Because this was a few weeks after Pearl Harbor, my family had decided that I should go as it might be my last real vacation before entering the service. Sun Valley was even then a magnificently designed ski community. A small group of well-spaced buildings complementing one another were set among several open rolling hills, one of which was Dollar Mountain. Semi-wooded Mt. Baldy, with its 3,000-foot vertical drop, loomed big. To the north the well-named Sawtooth Mountain range etched its jagged outline against the sky. Years ahead of its time in every way, Sun Valley was tremendously impressive to me as a young Dartmouth skier. My first night there, I found myself, true to Sun Valley tradition, having a drink at a table with Veronica Lake, filmdom's star of the year. And on Christmas Day a new snowfall made the winter scene in every way appropriate for the holiday.

A few days later the downhill was held on the Canyon Run, which featured the fastest American racecourse of that time. This long schuss is a broad, bumpy open slope feeding into a steep-walled fairly narrow ravine. About two thirds of the way down the slope the racer hits terminal velocity, where he relaxes, knowing that wind pressure will keep him from going one bit faster. I placed third in the downhill, having taken a quick nervous fall just after the start. After the first run of the slalom I was 9 seconds ahead of Bill Redlin from the University of Washington, the national amateur champion of 1941, who had had a spill. In the second run it was my turn to fall and Redlin ended up the winner, beating me by two tenths of a second. I was still very pleased, however, since it was my best performance in a major race.

During the last semester of my senior year I skied harder and did less academic work than ever before, yet I had a Phi Beta Kappa average for the first time. Most of my teammates planned to join the mountain troops, but I decided that I was too emotionally involved in the sport of skiing, and that the time had come to make a break. So I turned my back on the ski troops and entered the Navy. For about a year I was a PT boat officer, after which I spent the rest of the war in the submarine service.

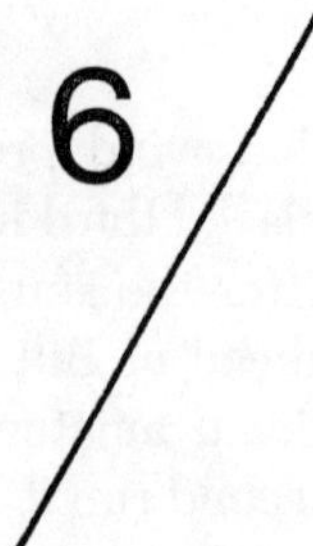

The Four Seasons

There are really only two ways to end the ski season. Although they are quite different, either can be a satisfactory means of leaving winter behind. Sometimes the season ends with a late April weekend, blessed with the unexpected bonanza of seventeen inches of moist spring powder to provide nearly perfect snow conditions. After such a weekend the skier says to himself, "This is the way to end a season, to remember it at its height." Or the season may end in the classic way, under a hot sun, with the brooks running strong and bare spots showing most of the way down the mountain. On the last few hundred yards of the trail the skier feels that the wet corn snow, already rotten right through to the ground and mixed with mud, will disappear before his eyes.

Whichever way, the ending is complete and the skier is anxious to get on with the rest of his life. So deep has been his involvement with the sport that he has perhaps subordinated studies, job, and family. However, no matter how much of a "nut" a skier may be about his sport, generally he is a responsible person who wants to live the other parts of his life in a meaningful way. Skiers are not too unlike their first cousins, the mountaineers. The late Senator Robert Kennedy, writing in the *National Geographic Magazine* about his experience climbing Mt. Kennedy, said,

> I returned with great respect for the men who climb mountains. They are not a footloose, carefree lot, haphazardly searching for thrills. For instance, of nineteen Americans on the 1963 Mount Everest Expedition, eighteen were college graduates; five held master's degrees, five were Ph.D.'s, and three were doctors of medicine. . . . The courage of mountain climbers is not blind, inexplicable, meaningless; it is courage with ability, brains, tenacity of purpose.

What a contrast to the kind of a skier referred to in Romain Gary's novel, *The Ski Bum,* a mixed-up outcast, a person without a country, so inbred that he is understood only by his own breed. The outlook ascribed to one member of this small strange minority was, "It simply didn't matter to a bum what he did below 6,000 feet. The only thing that mattered was not to get trapped in the glue down there."

Admittedly there are some skiers who head south in summer to find winter below the equator in Chile, New Zealand, or Australia. Some of these are international class racers, skiing all year round for a few years to keep up with the world's top racers. Some are ski instructors going where their profession takes them. Only a few are on year-round ski larks. Occasionally well-traveled, well-heeled recreational skiers try Chile's famed Portillo for one summer vacation.

I went to Chile myself in the summer of 1940 with three other Dartmouth boys and a friend from New Jersey. Although it was a great summer overall, with skiing the feature attraction, I found Chile to be an upside-down world in more ways than one. Not only were we reversing the seasons, but at Farellones we found a rope tow made of lightweight rope which never broke because whenever there was an overload, the two-cycle one-cylinder engine would hit dead center, balk, and then run backwards, taking the skiers, much to their surprise, down instead of up the hill. Also, where climbing was the uphill means of transportation, it seemed all wrong for Chilean señoritas to expect men to carry their skis. Most upside-down of all, powder snow skiing would last for over two weeks on the southern slopes, which in that part of the world faced away from the sun.

Another good way for young racers to avoid losing their touch and to get some intense training and coaching is to go west for the excellent summer ski camps at Mt. Hood, Mt. Baker, and Bend, Oregon.

However, most skiers by the first of May have not only left skiing behind, they have pretty much eliminated it from their minds. They do not brood, fret, or overly concern themselves with skiing; they even waste very little time talking about it out of season. Occasionally their thoughts may drift off to the wonders of skiing and how its challenges can be met. Sometimes they feel they have come up with a revelation—a brilliant, intuitive idea about improving technique.

Surprisingly, the commitment to one season makes the skier prone to appreciate all four. Nature's message certainly reaches the skier, and the serenity of winter, the feeling that it is the time when much of nature is asleep, heightens his longing to get on with nature's cycle. In late spring the skier welcomes rain, sensing how it is needed by the budding greenery. The approaching warmth of summer finds the woods in a new mood, bursting with all forms of life. The new-found heat of the sun seems good for all mankind.

Summer, whether skiers will admit it or not, is the time of the year when nature's richness is shared by the greatest number of people. Summer sports, of course, are in the limelight. For skiers, sailing offers the best adjustment to summer, since it requires facing the elements, this time in the form of the sea instead of the mountains.

Some of summer's simple pleasures, such as walking barefoot in a mossy wooded glen or at the water's edge on a deserted beach, are more intimate ways of enjoying nature than winter affords. As beautiful as a new snowfall can be, no one has the urge to walk barefoot in it. And, in summer, swimming in a clear cool lake or in the ocean's frothing surf, you can immerse yourself in nature, literally as well as figuratively.

The autumnal change of colors in New England is one of this country's most splendid sights. Skiers undoubtedly lead the vanguard of visitors who travel north in October to enjoy this spectacle. Then, as the gold of October gives way to the bleakness of November, the limbs of the trees are bare, colors subdued, and forms of life in the woods sparse. Winter's somnolence approaches. Still the clear cool air has a bracing effect, and as the deer hunter knows, nature has a harmony even in the muted period of late fall.

The skier's season is nearly at hand. Much as he knows what happiness the winter's snow will bring, there is some feeling that it is coming too quickly. The skier is not sure that he is ready to find the time, energy, and motivation to make his commitment to winter.

7

Woodstock-Personal Ski Resort

While at Dartmouth I had a separate skiing life centered in Woodstock, Vermont. This town offered by some margin the best skiing near Hanover, and it had many other charms, both natural and imported. Whenever there was no scheduled ski-team session for downhill or slalom, or whenever I had a weekend without a race, I would go to Woodstock, only eighteen miles away.

Leaving the campus on the Hanover plain, one drives a short way to White River Junction, a typical Connecticut River Valley industrial town. From a knoll about a quarter of a mile beyond the tracks of the railroad yard, a magnificent panorama of the White River Valley briefly comes into view. What follows is a wonderful assortment of Vermont countryside. The two-lane highway rises gently in the midst of heavy forests. Soon a bridge takes one over Quechee Gorge, a deep rocky chasm that seems as if it belonged in the more sharply eroded Rocky Mountain area of Colorado. The countryside then takes on the look of New England farmland, with fields bounded by stone fences and rows of trees. Some of the low-lying hills are wooded, some pastureland. Weathered farmhouses bear the traditional look of old Vermont homesteads. The variety of the route is simple and yet endless, its direction constantly changing, with the grain of the foothills changing too in its own pattern. The path of the road is determined by the valley of the Ottauquechee River, but the changes in direction of the hills defy a sense of order.

This is the nature of the open ski country of mid-Vermont, which makes such interesting ski-touring terrain. Recreational cross-country skiing may some day have its boom, since the popularity of downhill skiing is reaching such proportions that enjoyment of the serenity of winter is being compromised. Woodstock offers no end of touring routes, where skiers can break track and climb a hill for an entirely new view of the countryside. Then after a long glide down there is another hill to surmount.

Nearing Woodstock, one goes abruptly, with only the transition of a sharp right turn, from the state highway to the town's main street. Woodstock is so closely nestled among the hills that it looks as if it had been founded by a Thoreau who wanted to start a country town as remote from civilization as was Walden Pond. Actually, it was founded in 1765 by Timothy Knox, a Harvard intellectual who wished to settle in the wilderness. At that time the forests of maple, oak, and pine were so dense that it took one man a year to clear an acre of land.

The curves of Woodstock's main street also follow the course of the Ottauquechee River, as well as the shape of the overlooking foothills. The entire town plan adjusts to nature's terrain rather than having the conventional gridiron pattern. The village green, like the rest of the town, is free-form rather than square. But the real charm of the place lies in its variety of New England vernacular architecture. There are many splendid examples of Colonial homes, some of which were designed and built by their first owners, aided by their neighbors as a proof of good will. White clapboard houses are interspersed with brick ones, and even houses of later vintage, representing American architectural styles such as the Victorian with its mansard roof and the Greek temple, seem to have been creatively adapted to the scene. It is little wonder that Woodstock has been called one of the five most beautiful towns in America.

In the middle of town one takes a right turn at a T intersection just before the White Cupboard Inn, one of Woodstock's landmarks, and then a short drive down Elm Street, by the Congregational Church, another landmark, across a bridge over the river toward Mt. Tom, the pine-forested hill overlooking the town.

Prewar Woodstock had many ski lifts. Gilbert's, the first rope tow in America, was started in January of 1934. This was on a fairly steep hill in typical Woodstock countryside. Another lift was Pulsifer's, on the back side of Mt. Tom. And still another ski area known as Prosper's Hill operated for only a couple of years during the Woodstock prewar rope-tow boom. But the town as a ski resort is mainly known for Bunny Bertram's Suicide Six.

Bunny's establishment could be approached either by driving to the bottom of Six itself on the road to Pomfret, or by taking a narrow backwoods road up to Bunny's cabin on the other side of Six. On weekends we always went directly to the bottom of Six, knowing that the tow there would be running. During the week we would go up the back side. Toward the end of the narrow road the view opened up to a glen with Bunny's cabin set on a little plateau in the middle of a complex of rope tows. There was a beginners' hill somewhat below the road, with the line of the tow at right angles to the road, and a small slope leading to Bunny's cabin. Above that, going straight up, was another tow on the intermediate hill.

The entire layout was very primitive, quite different from the multimillion-dollar developments of today. A simple rustic-looking device, the rope tow left little mark on the countryside. It also had a very low sound level. The whirring of the rope, powered by an electric motor, spinning over automobile wheels on wooden poles, and sliding across the snow, did little to disturb the Vermont stillness.

Also, the winter rope-tow scene provided a better subject for painters than the modern steel-towered double chair lifts. Some of Paul Sample's paintings illustrate the charm of the rope-tow winter setting, and Tad Bailey, watercolorist and sometimes schoolmaster in Woodstock, did a classic caricature of Bunny's hut and the intermediate hill. Skiers were depicted in all conceivable poses, including falling, showing off, socializing, courting, and answering nature's call.

Bunny's cabin was a simple square structure of varnished clapboard with a large chimney a third of the way along the peak of the roof; it looked somewhat like a Cape Cod saltbox, except for its large well-proportioned windows. Bunny had a small apartment at one end of this building. The other two-thirds of the house consisted of an airy spacious room with a big fireplace and a small lunch bar. There was an unusual bench in front of the fireplace, made of a long plank loosely pegged at each end into two upright rockers. Bunny built it from plans in *Popular Mechanics,* and I have never seen another one quite like it. The bench, featuring both rocking and bouncing action, could hold as many as a dozen people across its length. Unlike the slopes outside, it was completely risk-free, and was one of the easy ways of meeting people at Bunny's.

The two interlocking slopes, beginner and intermediate, provided carefree, relaxing sport. But real drama was not far away, for at the top of the intermediate hill a walk of about one hundred feet brought one to the summit of Suicide Six. Approaching Six in this manner, the skier feels an inevitable buildup of emotion as he becomes aware of the steepness of the slope below. Six has often been compared to Tuckerman Ravine, since from the top the skier cannot see the bottom. Only after he has skied down to the steepest part does he have a complete view of the hill.

On the other approach, driving to the bottom of Six, one passes a whole succession of interesting hills, each of which looks long enough and steep enough to be Suicide Six, and each of which is topped by the next. When Six is finally reached, it has the effect of a climax, with skiers on the hill looking like ants moving so fast that they may come right into the path of the car on the road. Six is certainly very much of a hill. I consider it to be the best slalom hill in the East, because of both steepness and length as well as a built-in assortment of bumps.

Viewed from the bottom, the main part of Six appears to the left of the lift line. This is a broad rectangular-shaped slope, with its steepest grade near the lift line itself. The right side appears mostly wooded, and near the top two broad trails have been cut, leading into two steep head walls. Farther over to the right are several trails which branch out near the bottom into many other wooded paths.

From the top, one of our favorite runs was to ski down the intermediate hill toward the cabin, skirt the parking lot, and then go through a notch leading into a traverse on the bottom third of Six. This made an easy intermediate run of over three quarters of a mile, and was somewhat like spiraling down a Chilean volcano with John Jay, the famed ski photographer.

When the skier was in the mood, he could stop off at Bunny's hut and sun himself in a deck chair, for Woodstock's irregularly shaped hills offered good protection from winter winds, and sun was one of the area's main ingredients.

Skiing on Six itself, the runner is mainly conscious of the sheer steepness, the length of the hill, and the infinite variety of terrain. Six offers hummocks, an indented road which crosses the hill four times, a major slope followed by a flat transition, a smaller slope on the lower third of the hill, and a number of bowls with short shallow arcs. Someone could ski Six all day without following the same line twice.

There were some who thought that the name "Suicide Six" belonged not to the hill but to the tow. Rope tows have generally disappeared, belonging to an early and hardier era of skiing. Six was the toughest of them all. To hang on to rope tows, people had to use certain underdeveloped muscles they didn't know they had. The length of the lift line at Six was 1,850 feet, and the vertical rise 650 feet. Anyone riding this tow had the feeling of being pulled straight up into the air. But the most extraordinary aspect of the tow was not its angle of ascent, but the speed at which it ran. It took about a minute to go from the bottom of Six to the summit; this works out to a speed of over twenty miles an hour. There were some city-bred women for whom one trip up the Six tow constituted a day of skiing on the hill. On the other hand, there were always plenty of attractive outdoor girls who would ride up and ski down all day. On the tow the experienced Six skier would change his position, going from a grip with hands outstretched in front of him, to a pole-vaulting position, then to a crouch with the rope pinched between an elbow and a thigh, then to the full-nelson position with one hand behind the back.

No matter how many positions the skier used in going up Six, Bunny Bertram, who ran the hill in an authoritarian manner, always insisted on proper safety precautions. The skier's apparel was inspected closely. Anything loose like a scarf or a torn glove was ruled out, since it might get caught on the twisting rope. The straps on both ski poles had to be around the skier's outside wrist to minimize the chance of the poles' swinging over the rope and preventing the skier from releasing at the top of the hill. In addition, Bunny or one of his men would stand at the summit, electric starter button in hand, to stop the tow instantly if there was any trouble.

If the lift on Six was difficult to ride, there were still plenty of skiers who were up to its challenge. And the tow's capacity was so great that the wait for a ride was never longer than a few seconds. One of the most interesting records on Six was set by Harold Codding, now a ski shop owner in Reno, Nevada, who kept going for one hour, riding the lift up in the usual minute, then skiing down the hill in less than a minute, with an occasional 10-second stop at the top. Bunny, watch in hand, saw to it that he made a round trip every two minutes. At the end of an hour Harold had made thirty trips for a total vertical descent of 19,500 feet, and the approximate total distance he covered, allowing for swings out of the fall line, was about fifteen miles. This would be equivalent to the impossibility of ten runs on Mt. Mansfield in an hour.

One day in the winter of 1940 I was on the hill when Harold Hillman, the rugged downhill type of individual who was running the ski school at Six, set out to ski the equivalent of Mt. Everest, or 29,028 vertical feet. Skiing without stopping, he kept going at the rate of a round trip every two minutes for over an hour, to break Codding's record. But after about an hour and fifteen minutes at this pace, he gave up the idea and quit for the day. Of course, in a full day of skiing there were any number of us who could ski Six for forty-five runs, which is longer than going from summit to sea level on Mt. Everest.

Time trials on Six of a less strenuous nature than Hillman's or

Codding's, always provided a day of excitement. Attractive metal pins in the form of a figure six were awarded for negotiating the hill in stipulated times. The time required for a bronze six is not worth mentioning, since none of the initiates would have been caught dead wearing one. Silver sixes, awarded to women for a run of a minute and a half and to men for a 1-minute run were proof of a high-grade intermediate skier. Gold sixes were earned only by breaking the record on the hill.

Both at Choate and at Dartmouth I roomed with Richie Remsen, a man of many athletic accomplishments. Richie earned letters and numerals in four different sports at Dartmouth, played golf from a scratch handicap, and has on several occasions been a national squash doubles champion. He was considered by the girls to be a fantastic dancer, and as a clue to his personality, he took greater pride in this than in his prowess in sports. He scoffed at my skiing ability and made the claim that if he had one week to work on the sport, he would be my equal. He had such an opportunity between semesters of our sophomore year, and we drove over to Six together.

I proceeded to teach Remsen how to ski, shortcut method. His previous skiing experience was limited to a half-dozen days on toe-strap skis at Buck Hill Falls in the Poconos of Pennsylvania. On his second day at Woodstock, Richie amazed everyone by graduating to the big hill. It must be said that the naturalness of his technique, even his falling, was the main reason he could be pushed so hard. In fact, Richie, who became quite a Woodstock social skier, was later known for his unbelievable cartwheels on skis. He was not one to fight a fall, and at a given moment, like a whirling dervish, down he would go. The most characteristic feature of his fall was a momentary hesitation between somersaults, with his round moon face upraised, grinning from ear to ear. At the end of the week Richie had acquired good relaxed knee action over bumps, a powerful full stem, and one turn—a well-developed Durrance-type stem christie. Bunny, along with others, marveled at Richie's progress, and decided to hold a special time trial to see if someone could actually earn a silver six after skiing for only one week. Richie did not disappoint his coach or his following. Picking a fairly straight line, with occasional full snowplow checks, he covered the course in under 60 seconds—in fact, in less time than the original hill record of 56.8 seconds set in 1937 by Alec Bright.

As a Woodstock habitué, I had an interest in trying to break the hill record. The record at that time was held by Harold Codding, at 35.6 seconds, and I had been on the hill to watch his run. Someone figured out that he was descending at the rate of 18.2 feet per second, faster than the world's fastest passenger elevator, which went down at a speed of 16.6 feet per second in the Empire State Building. To give some idea of the pace of ski development in the late 1930's, this record had gone from 56.8 seconds in 1937 to 45.2 seconds in 1938, when it was once again back in Bright's hands, to Codding's record of 35.6 seconds in 1939.

The key to breaking the record on this hill was to be there on the right day, with the hummocks filled in by a good cover of snow. In mid-March of 1940, my sophomore year, we had a 2-foot fall of wet powder, and Bunny closed the hill for two days while he and his crew tramped it on snowshoes. As a result, the hill was probably in better shape than it has ever been. Word went out and on the following weekend a number of would-be record breakers appeared from nowhere. In two days the record changed hands several times, and on each run the line was farther away from the traditional arc to the right and closer to the fall line. Finally Jake Nunnemacher, Karl Acker—Pico instructor and coach of Andrea Mead Lawrence—and I all took a line through a narrow opening between some small spruces in the middle of the hill and ended up in a three-way tie at 33.3 seconds. Surreptitiously I went back on the following Monday and planned to move my line one notch beyond the spruces to take the straightest possible way down the hill.

Ordinarily the schuss is a section of a mountain which a skier works up to and only tries when he is very much ready for it. In a downhill, a turn, a bumpy transition, or merely a narrowing of the course may be worrisome, but while in the schuss, the skier enjoys exhilarating speed in the fall line.

That day the rope was stopped and held in the air so that I

could go under it and take a straight line down the hill. On a steep pitch past the clump of spruces, I found myself airborne in a crouch, with skis inches off the ground. Then there was a set of control gates off to the side at the top of the lower knoll, and the turn through the gates had to be completed on the flats, followed by a slight prejump before the knoll. Even so I had a 50-foot flight clearing the road, a few easy bumps, and then the finish—all to shave three tenths of a second off the record, for 33 seconds flat. This record stood until 1947, when Dave Austin, a Woodstock lad, broke it. In the early 1950's, Tom Corcoran, the Dartmouth skier who placed fourth in the 1960 Olympic Giant Slalom, brought it just under 30 seconds.

Like a megalomaniac, I went back again to Six a few days later, on the Thursday before spring vacation. The hill had a good hard crusty surface, almost but not quite sheer ice, and I foolishly tried to break my own record. You ski on ice very much the way you do on soft-packed snow, only more so, and there is no room for mistakes. As I headed for the knoll, I was late with my turn, and landed with my skis pointing in one direction and my body in another. The edges of the skis caught and I vaulted forward, chin-first, onto the crust, to have my face badly scratched and cut up. I was quite a sight when I arrived home for my spring vacation.

However, people, not records, give a ski resort its appeal. Woodstock is a very personal place and for some of us I am sure there will never be another ski area as personal.

First of all, there was our host, Bunny Bertram—not that he was genial or genteel. Bunny, who was carved out of the sinewy stuff of Vermont, had been captain of a Dartmouth winter sports team in one of the last years when snowshoeing was the big event. He was a fine-looking man, tanned and well-proportioned. Although he knew everyone, like a close-mouthed, inscrutable headwaiter in a fashionable restaurant, he was no glad-hander. There was no outward exchange of warmth, but we all loved him, and I am quite sure our affection was returned. He did have one habit that set him apart from his guests—he was always working away at a wad of chewing tobacco.

Bunny ran a good area. I have spoken of his concern for safety on the rope tows. He was on top of everything, and the place always had a clean Vermont look about it—except for tobacco stains on the slopes. His unbounded pride in Six was shared by all of us. He was convinced that the hill was more than the best slalom slope in the East; it was the best in the world.

Bunny also had a fine crew. Hal Codding, father of record-setter Harold, who among other duties handled the simple fare for lunch, maintained a great interest in the activities of the skiers. Then there was Ernie Dorn, who had a friendly greeting for everyone at the top of the hill. But our favorite was Pearl Gilbert, a bearded, somewhat seedy-looking Vermont character who sold tickets in the parking lot. He looked like an octogenarian, and was always clowning and pulling one-upmanship whenever he thought he had an amusing anecdote to tell about one of us.

I like to think that our young group who skied on the hill was not badly behaved. Woodstock meant fun to us. We were light and gay and sometimes even wacky, but we were no ordinary bunch of spoiled kids. There was at all times a fine relationship between the college youngsters and the Vermonters. Not only did we know Bunny's crew, we knew the high school boys and girls from Woodstock and their families—in fact, the entire Woodstock skiing community.

Often it seemed as if each person who skied Six wanted to add some special touch of style or color of his own. Len Woods, a tall thin Dartmouth skier, keen of wit and looking like Ichabod Crane, had a ski technique all of his own to offer the Six skiers. It was caller the "pelvic glide." Bungie King, of the Harvard ski team, was noted for the colorful vocabulary which he created for the sport. He takes credit for coining the word "boiler plate" to describe the slick icy crust caused by a thawing-raining-freezing cycle. "Pie" Truesdale was a great one for applying the nomenclature of sailing to skiing; as a determined intermediate skier he would take part in a practice slalom and want to know who placed "those damned buoys to starboard." Alex Salm would put on a real show when there was new snow on Six, performing graceful linked telemarks, even with the handicap of fixed-heel bindings. And what a rare treat to see Ralphie Townsend, a short man on unbelievably short skies which looked bowed like barrel-staves, racing slalom with skilled precision. Then there were always schoolboys like Joe Ward and Burt Porter who would find lines that took them down the steepest pitches and over the most bumps, all of which they handled with adeptness.

One of the most imaginative and least productive runs ever made on Six was a midnight trip down the hill in settlement of an argument. Seaman First Class Pie Truesdale, immaculate in new gob's uniform, was listening to Bunny expound on his favorite subjects—the steepness, charm, and lore of the big slope. There are some who say that the two men were drinking applejack. Inevitably the subject of the legendary road on Suicide Six was brought up—legendary because it couldn't be seen under heavy snow cover. Bunny felt personally wounded because Pie refused to believe that the road crossed the hill four times. He suggested to Pie that the two of them should drive the snowplow to the top of the intermediate hill, and then plow out the road to prove its existence to Pie as well as to other doubting skiers. The team of Truesdale and Bertram never did find the road, and its mystery remains for all who have never seen the hill without a snow cover. But the greatest mystery of all is how these ingenious fellows drove the snowplow down the steep hill in the dead of night without rolling the car over.

Very much in the spirit of Woodstock was a speed tow, which Bunny rigged up on the short slope in front of his cabin. A volunteer, often Nannie Nye from Chestnut Hill, would grab the moving rope, signal to Bunny, and hang on for dear life while the rope accelerated up to sixty miles an hour. At the top of the slope Nannie would let go, and shoot through the air for some forty feet. Nannie's father, who had been assured that she was a careful skier, was so horrified to see her pictured in a Boston paper performing this feat that he grounded her from skiing for two weeks.

About fifteen of us started one of the most informal organizations in the world of skiing. We called ourselves the Ottos, the idea being that each of us would go by the first name of Otto. Our one page bylaws stated:

> New members must meet the appropriate requirements of good fellowship and fantastic skiing established by the charter members. . . .
>
> The annual official meeting will be held each year in Woodstock over the weekend of the Fisk Trophy Races, and other meetings are to be held whenever and wherever convenient and appropriate for members to congregate for the purposes of skiing, drinking, or laughing.

Late Sunday afternoons when the muscles were too weary for serious skiing, a group of Ottos would gather for stunts on skis. It was particularly interesting when we had a new member to initiate. The better known and more eligible the prospect, the more extensive was the hazing. Serge Gagarin, born of Russian nobility, an old Choate skier, Yale ski team member, victim of leg breaks on some of New England's most famous trails, as well as fiancé of Otto Patty Moore, was given an especially hard time. The Ottos formed a giant stem with everyone's skis interlocking in a series of V's, and with each person hanging on to the waist of the one in front. Then we asked Serge, who was quite small, to ski in a crouch through the tunnel formed by our legs, as the giant snowplow made slow swings down the hill. In a style competition we gave Serge marks for performing telemark, open christie, parallel, and free-style maneuvers while skiing down the hill backward. He willingly took the rope tow *down* the intermediate hill, and was even ready to ride the speed tow backwards. However, at this point Otto President John Jay stepped in and congratulated Serge on his election to membership. Because of the war, the Otto Ski Club as an organization ceased to exist after its second winter, but all its members are still hardy skiers.

I had two Woodstock romances, both with Ottos. My junior year I was enamored of Nannie Nye, blond, pink-cheeked, vivacious, and extremely pretty. When the snow melted a Harvard hockey player took over, and eventually married her. He was later killed in the war, but today I ski with Nannie and her two children at Mad River, where her second husband has built a lodge.

During senior year Sis Bontecou and a friend rented a little house in Woodstock for the winter. Sis was a lovely looking girl, tall, slender, and graceful on and off skis. We were very serious about each other and thought we were the two happiest people in the world. Again, shortly after the snow melted, it was all over. We were both the same age, and yet because she was a more sophisticated mature person than I was, I tended to be in her shadow. Sis today is married to Reese Harris, the well-equipped cross-country skier of my Eaglebrook meet, and has two handsome children.

One of my last prewar memories of Woodstock was winning the Fisk Trophy Race, a competition I had entered for the fourth time. Later, back in the hut, Bunny broke out a bottle of champagne, and my Woodstock friends happpily toasted my victory on the hill I loved so well and had skied so often.

Postwar skiing to some extent bypassed Woodstock, the trend being toward bigger areas on bigger mountains. After a few tough years, Bunny finally sold the hill to Laurance Rockefeller. There is now snow-making machinery on Mt. Tom, plus a Poma lift. At the bottom of Six there is a large restaurant, and the rope tow that was so hard to ride yet offered more vertical footage in one day than any man was capable of has been replaced by a sturdy, efficient Poma lift. Skiers still take occasional runs down the back side, but the intermediate tow, the speed tow, and the beginners' tow are no more. Nonetheless, the sense of values offered by winter Woodstock is still there. And Woodstock's position on the ski map of New England looks bright, as it has become accepted as a fine place for a winter vacation.

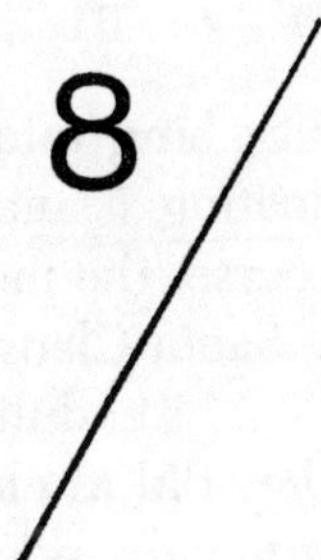

Ice, Snow, and Cold

When ice and snow take over the land, the scene is suddenly changed to a whole new world. Our interest in this world goes back to our childhood. How dramatic it is for a child to go to bed one night to familiar surroundings, and then wake up the next morning to the enveloping whiteness of the winter's first snowstorm.

Winter seems to belong to children. To toddlers romping around in the snow, the depth of the cover seems magnified by their Lilliputian proportions. Perhaps this is one reason why each generation tells the next about memories of days when snowstorms were more severe.

For children snow can turn a backyard into a true winter playground, better by far than a giant sandbox. Foremost, there is the fun of sliding in all its forms. Building activity can be feverish. Forts and crude igloos appear, as well as snowmen and other forms of sculpture. When the new snow is moist, the child can even roll a giant snowball.

Children seem to have a great interest in the lore of the far north. Eskimos have a culture as fascinating to children as any in the world, and the polar bear is perhaps the most intriguing of all animals. The true but unexplained story of the Lapland lemmings marching into the sea also stirs interest. And when a child eats floating island for dessert, he may imagine a huge iceberg. Of course, the most improbable and yet most cherished dream of all is Santa Claus and his reindeer.

Most adults continue to wonder at the mystery of snow, just as they did as children. For skiers this interest is magnified, and yet strangely, skiers know little about ice and snow.

On the shoulder of a mountain during a storm, a skier feels with a heightened sense of adventure that he is very much part of the mountain and storm. Enjoying the cocktail hour during a blizzard, he may look through the glass wall of a modern chalet into the floodlit endless procession of snowflakes, and wonder what started it, what keeps it going, and whether or not it will ever end. The next morning, before starting out in the waist-deep powder, he may wonder about avalanches and their unpredictable behavior.

It may, therefore, be interesting for the skier to learn something about snow, ice, avalanches, glaciers, and the mountain in its role as a snow maker.

A discussion of snow and ice surely starts with water. As we all remember from our school days, water is a simple compound, each molecule consisting of two atoms of hydrogen and one of oxygen which share electrons with each other. Its pure form—colorless, tasteless, odorless, almost transparent, and free from impurities such as bacteria and solid matter—exists only in the laboratory.

Life is not only dependent on water as a liquid, but also on water as a solid and as a gas. If we ever find life on another planet, we can be certain that water will be there in all three forms, and that the temperature range will be narrow—as it is on earth.

Of all water's wonders, the greatest is its existence as a gas. The restless water molecule, depending on what the physicists call vapor pressure, can go from a steaming kettle, or a sea absorbing the heat of the sun, into the air; from a cloud droplet into vapor and then into a nascent snow crystal, or even on a below-zero day, from an icicle into dry air.

It is not surprising that we don't take the weather for granted, for water in the atmosphere is precious. If all the water vapor, cloud droplets, and ice crystals were wrung out of the air at a given moment and spread evenly over the surface of the globe, only one inch of rain, or its equivalent in snow of about ten inches, would fall.

A quick inventory of the earth's water would reveal that 97.2 percent is the salt water found in the oceans, which cover over 70 percent of the surface of the globe. Fresh water in rivers, lakes, streams, and in the ground adds up to little more than half of 1 percent. Our great natural reservoirs of fresh water are the glaciers, especially the antarctic ice cap, which holds 2.15 percent of our total supply of water, more than three times as much as all of the fresh water in liquid form.

The process of water turning to ice is fascinating. As water cools it first behaves naturally; it contracts, gets heavy, and sinks. For this reason ice will not form on a freshwater pond until the temperature of all the water in the pond reaches 39° F. This is also the reason why the bottoms of the oceans are so cold, since cool water from the polar areas sinks into the deep troughs of the ocean's floor. But water's most unusual characteristic is that it expands when it freezes to 11 percent more than its original volume. Ice, therefore, being lighter and less dense than in its liquid state, floats on water.

When the surface of a lake is frozen over, the solid membrane preventing direct contact between freely moving molecules of air and freely moving molecules of water serves as a barrier between the cold air of winter and the latent heat of earth.

If ice were heavier than water, all bodies of water in cold climates would soon freeze solid. During an Ice Age water everywhere might freeze, even the great oceans. Life, at least in its higher forms, could not exist under such conditions. Therefore, water's peculiar property of being lighter in its solid form than in its liquid form has played a decisive role in maintaining life on this planet.

A much less known characterstic of freezing is that it is a purifying process; similarly, a chemist purifies a substance by crystallizing it. As water freezes, it rejects foreign matter, small particles, and even bacteria. Ice formed over flowing water across the boulders of a brook is purer than the water in the brook. But even though bacteria tends to be rejected as part of the freezing process, it may be found in ice and snow, and can survive temperatures far below the freezing point. In artificially formed ice the impurities become trapped and are driven to a cloudy core. Colors such as green, dull yellow, and purple are caused by particles suspended in ice. Ice is weakened to the extent to which it is impure. Salts, in minute quantities, tend to be rejected and spread to lines of cleavage where ice can sometimes be split with a knife.

Sea ice, which forms in the polar area when the water temperature reaches 28.6° F., is partially freed of brine. Salt crystals are further rejected by temperature change, since the impure part of sea ice has a much lower melting point than the purer mass of ice. In the far north, Eskimos keep track of sea ice which has gone through two summer seasons to use for melting into drinking water.

The purest ice tends to be a deep blue. River men claim to be able to tell when a river like the Saint Lawrence will freeze by the appearance of this color. Glacial streams, unless they carry a vast amount of glacial till which makes them white, also tend to be a deep blue. The first ice on a clear pond, if formed on a still night, is almost completely transparent. Because of an optical illusion this is known as black ice.

Of all the forms of water, that which comes from the sky as part of the weather process most captivates the curiosity of man. The atmosphere continually recycles water. The sun, as the prime source of earth's energy, directly or indirectly causes the evaporation of ocean water which as invisible vapor is transmitted into the air. Similarly, lakes, streams, and damp ground as well as breathing plants, transmit water into the air.

Water vapor remains invisible until it reaches the magic moment of condensation, the dew point. This usually happens as an air mass is being cooled, since as air becomes cooler it can hold less and less water vapor. At the dew point, or a relative humidity of 100 percent, invisible water vapor is transformed into minute cloud droplets.

As one example of conditions preceding cloudy weather, a

warm air mass sometimes moves up the slope of a cold wedge, and as the warm air is cooled, clouds are formed from which even rain squalls may result. This is an explanation of weather formation at its simplest. The many different ways that fronts can meet each other and create storms is a subject in itself.

The mountain, too, exerts its role in weather. Air moving up a slope loses heat as it rises. When the air cools enough to reach the saturation point, clouds will begin to form.

An extraordinary fact about weather is that air masses do not mix unless they are similar in temperature and moisture content. Thus, on a windy day one can watch a large white cumulus cloud move across the sky without becoming mixed with clear dry air and losing its identity.

Rain is normally caused by the collision of cloud droplets. But since cloud droplets are minute, 1 million of them must be coalesced before a raindrop is formed. These droplets are suspended in the air much like tiny dust particles which can be seen in a shaft of sunlight. As they are whipped around by air currents, larger particles move more slowly and tend to collide with smaller ones. It can readily be appreciated that this is a slow process. Because the cloud droplets are sometimes held in an almost perfect state of suspension, a warm rain cloud can be said to be quite stable. Attempts thus far to seed rain clouds and artificially create rain have been uneconomical.

There is only one type of major rain-producing storm which takes place without any ice formation. Rain squall clouds formed by trade winds are trapped by a temperature inversion and produce rain for the warm latitudes of earth. But perhaps as much as 90 percent of the rainfall is somehow initiated by the formation of ice crystals, snow, or even hail. Thus, in New York City a good heavy rain in either January or July probably starts as a snowstorm in the upper air. For as we shall soon see, if the moist rain cloud is stable, the supercooled snow cloud is unstable.

Of all the weather's mysteries, the creation of the snowflake—correctly known as the snow crystal—seems to defy the laws of logic. The largest form of the single snow crystal is the most perfect form, a flat hexagon with delicate symmetrical branches. First sketched in the early seventeenth century by the great philosopher-mathematician Descartes, these crystals, one thirty-second to one-half inch in size, are big enough to be seen by the naked eye. A snowflake actually consists of a conglomeration of snow crystals.

Wilson A. Bentley, a native of Jericho, Vermont, a town just west of Mt. Mansfield, first made the world conscious of the snow crystal. Known as "Snowflake" Bentley, he developed a technique for taking photomicrographs of snow crystals with a simple microscope and bellows camera. He began this photography in 1886, and during his lifetime took six thousand pictures, some of which appeared at various times in periodicals like the *National Geographic Magazine.* Over a year before his death in 1931 he had the satisfaction of seeing three thousand of his photographs published in book form.

Bentley, like many of the individuals who have contributed to man's knowledge of snow and ice, was not a scientist. His photographs were slightly retouched in order to put them in profile against a black background. Also, he was very selective, generally photographing only the most perfect six-pointed stars. As a result, many skiers today are under the misconception that almost every "snowflake" is a geometrically perfect hexagon. Actually, these perfectly formed flakes are in the minority. However, almost everyone knows that no two snow crystals are identical twins, and this information is due to Bentley's discoveries.

Today an outstanding scientist of snow is the Japanese Ukichino Nakaya. In his work he has provided much practical information about characteristics of snow and snowstorm. His classification tables have shown the types of snow crystals falling during a snowstorm, as percentages of the total fall of snow. Also, he has measured a snow crystal's rate of fall, which is a shade faster than one-half mile per hour.

Most of his studies were done in a low-temperature laboratory at Hokkaido University, where he successfully reproduced all the types of snow crystals found in nature. Through the means of a snow-making apparatus, he was able to control atmospheric pressure, humidity, and temperature as well as flow of air. He succeeded in making snow crystals grow on the fine hair of a rabbit. Within a period of fifteen to thirty minutes he could grow a fully developed hexagonal crystal. These crystals usually showed some distortion because they grew in a fixed position on the hair, as opposed to the natural crystal which grows around a small nucleus and falls freely. The air temperature in his snow-making chamber was usually around 0°F., but the temperature of the water droplets was always much higher. Similarly the temperature of the air in a cold cloud is somewhat lower than the temperature of the cloud droplets themselves.

As a result of Nakaya's studies, it has been possible to estimate the types of weather conditions responsible for the formation of different snow crystals. During natural snowstorms the same type of snow crystal is rarely produced continuously. Snow crystals normally fall through atmospheric layers where conditions of saturation, temperature, as well as pressure may vary. But since the development of a snow crystal—from a microscopic nucleus to a full-blown geometrically perfect form—cannot be continuously observed in the middle of a snowstorm, Nakaya's studies of the artificially grown crystal have been most significant. For instance, he noticed that minute cloud droplets disappeared before coming in contact with the nascent crystal. The disappearance connoted the moment of truth when the droplet, through a difference in vapor pressure, was transformed into a gaseous state, with the water molecules assuming the frozen latticed structure of the snow crystal.

Practically all of Nakaya's work had to do with ice and snow crystals after their nuclei had been formed. Perhaps even more interesting is the work of Vincent J. Schaefer, since most of his observations and experiments have dealt with the actual point of nucleization.

Vincent Schaefer is a scientist from Schenectady, New York. Much of his great contribution was made during and after the war when he was associated with the General Electric Research Laboratory. In some of his work his associate was Dr. Irving Langmuir, the Nobel Prize winner for chemistry. Both men were pioneer skiers in the early 1930's.

During the years from 1943 to 1956 Schaefer spent much of his time during winter making observations of snow clouds from the summit of Mt. Washington, which has a well-deserved reputation for the worst weather in the world. For days at a time he would be immersed in the supercooled droplets of a snow cloud. Sometimes he would be above a layer of clouds which were generating snow crystals and spewing them on the slopes below. Watching chilled water droplets freeze solid in noncrystalline form, he could witness the formation of rime on the sometimes glazed structures of the Mt. Washington observatory. He also saw the crystalline beauty of hoarfrost in all its variety, where patterns are formed by the sublimation of water vapor from chilled droplets. Although much of the direction of his research during the war years was toward military objectives, such as reducing the formation of ice on aircraft and creating clear air for planes through cloud modification, he was even then farsighted enough to sense the possibilities of making artificial snow.

In the summer of 1946 Schaefer made his most important discoveries through experiments conducted in a very simple cold chamber, which contained an open-topped freezer space measuring about six cubic feet. This space had black walls lit by a diagonal bright narrow beam of light. The temperature in the center of the open freezer unit was maintained at about 5° F., and because of the tendency of cold air to sink, the air inside was quite stable. Schaefer would make a cloud by blowing several exhalations of his moist breath into the box, or by passing a warm wet towel through the chilled air. Thus the supercooled droplets of the snow cloud were artificially generated. He made many attempts to make snow through introducing different types of airborne dust. Occasionally crystals could be seen to form and fall to the floor of the freezer. However, he knew that either he would have to find mineral dust having a crystalline structure similar to ice to serve as nuclei, or he would have to introduce some element at –40° F.

A little known fact of science is that the true freezing temperature of water is not 32° F., but –40° F. Pure water in an absolutely still state can be brought down to –40° F. before it freezes. Since water does not exist in its pure form except in the laboratory or perhaps in the cloud droplet, it normally crystallizes on some impurity, such as a speck of dust, and turns to ice at the temperature of 32° F.

Thus, in the high cirrus cloud which we can see on a clear day at any time of the year in any part of the world, ice crystals form without nucleization, because of a temperature aloft at below –40° F. Schaefer therefore sprinkled small particles of Dry Ice which were far colder than –40° F., actually –109° F., into the cold box. Within less than ten seconds the supercooled cloud produced ice crystals, which in the brilliant beam of light were easily identifiable. The water droplets tended to scatter light uniformly, mostly in a forward direction. The ice crystals, however, because of their flat geometric form, sparkled and twinkled as they tumbled. It could also be witnessed that the ice crystals grew at the expense of the supercooled water droplets, since each crystal was surrounded by clear air. In later experiments, Schaefer, like a magician, was able to create ice crystals by waving a metal rod which had been chilled to –40° F. through the air. The extraordinary aspect of his studies was that once a trail of tiny white crystals had been created, the growth of the crystals proceeded with tremendous speed, increasing a billionfold in volume within a few seconds. The mere presence of ice among supercooled droplets creates a chain reaction. In theory Schaefer determined that a single pellet of Dry Ice about a half-inch in diameter could create enough nuclei to generate 300,000 tons of snow.

The experimental studies in the open-topped freeze box thus indicated that snow making was a practical possibility. On November 13, 1946, Schaefer took off in a small Fairchild monoplane to fly into a supercooled snow cloud at 14,000 feet in the vicinity of Mt. Greylock. This cloud had a temperature of –1° F., but contained no trace of ice crystals or snow. A 4-mile stretch of the cloud was seeded with six pounds of Dry Ice particles, half of which were distributed from a mechanical dispenser on the floor of the plane, with the rest being scattered into the slipstream from cardboard containers held out of the cockpit window. Within five minutes a section of the cloud had been modified into a deep, almost clear trough, and snow crystals were falling, having been created at the expense of the water droplets. Although the snow disappeared through sublimation as it passed through the dry air below, the experiment was a success. Later that winter cloud seeding produced snow on the ground.

The fact that for the first time man had controlled the weather and created precipitation stirred the imagination of the world. Vincent Schaefer was followed by a great many other would-be weather makers, many of them no more than opportunists. Inevitably there were many failures, some ballyhoo and even some lawsuits connected with snow making.

One of the problems of snow making is that it is difficult to control where the snow will fall. Fred Pabst of Bromley once employed a snow maker who succeeded in dumping several inches of snow at Pico Peak, about forty-one miles away. In New Mexico Dr. Langmuir once did some cloud seeding which appeared to have influence over weather patterns throughout the country, even in New England.

A –40° F. temperature in the snow cloud and the resulting ice crystals may be the key to the change in weather, for in the true snow cloud the same chain reaction that was effected in Schaefer's freezer chamber occurs in a widespread way. Once ice crystals are introduced into the unstable cloud made up of supercooled droplets, more crystals are formed and "all hell breaks loose."

Interestingly enough, –40° F. is also –40° C., this being one point where the two scales meet. This temperature is sometimes called the Schaefer point.

Through recent studies with the electron microscope we now know that infant ice crystals grow ice whiskers which are extremely fragile. The rupturing of these whiskered crystals apparently has a great influence on the fantastic multiplication of ice crystals in the supercooled cloud. As snow crystals collide with one another, they create bits of debris which become the ice nuclei of new snow crystals—one of the ways that snow crystals can be formed. Perhaps as part of the crystal growth pattern, a damaged hexagonal snow crystal which has lost one of its six points has, like the salamander, the ability to regenerate its lost member.

Schaefer, like Bentley, has been interested in photographing the form of a snow crystal. He has also developed a technique for making plastic replicas of its crystal structure. Schaefer's many visitors from all over the world are given two rare treats: the freezer box is in a state of readiness for the cloud-seeding experiment; and the plastic replicas provide visitors with a microscopic view of the delicate geometry of snow.

Schaefer and Nakaya were part of the three-man committee which has classified snow crystals. There are seven basic types: needle crystal, columnar crystal, plane crystal (the famed hexagonal and stellar types), combination column and plane, column with extended side planes (Bentley called this the "collar-button type"), rimed crystal, and irregular snow particles. But to give some idea of how complex snow crystal forms are, within these seven categories there are another thirty-seven regular variations, one of which is the pyramid type in the far north. And if, sadly, the beautiful symmetrical hexagonal crystal, which has become the symbol of snow, is in the minority, so also are the deformed ones which defy the laws of ice crystal form.

There is, alas, no neat bit of reasoning to explain the growth of snow-crystal structure. We know much about the genesis of the common snow crystal; we have also been able to observe the artificial growth of various types, but we still know very little about ice crystal habit.

There have been various theories put forth. Does it spin like a descending leaf? We know that the crystal gives off heat as vapor sublimes to form its ice structure; does this heat of crystallization set up a minute whirlpool in the surrounding air? Is there some molecular telegraph system which determines its growth? None of these theories has any substance. The last was treated by Nakaya, who said that there were too many millions of molecules involved for a molecular telegraph system to work. Nevertheless if each snow crystal had its own computer to trace out an original design, as well as its own nervous system to send the molecules where they should go, nature's artistry could not be improved.

Perhaps we should give millions of children models of water molecules as toys with which to develop hexagonal designs. Then some young genius might come up with the true theory of ice crystal growth.

As exciting as the snowstorm is to the skier, snow in the air has little utility for him. It is snow on the ground which really counts. The Eskimos have distinguished between snow that is falling and snow that has fallen with a word stem—*ganik* for the former and *aput* for the latter. The Eskimo even has a whole vocabulary of one hundred words for ice and snow on the ground.

New snow can reflect up to 87 percent of the light from the sky. But light can penetrate through snow to a depth of up to twenty-four inches in dry snow and ten inches in wet snow. And if snow seems white it is because light is so fractured by individual crystals that the eye is unable to discriminate the fine shades of the rainbow which bounce off a single snow crystal.

Along with most of the sky's light, most of the heat from the air is reflected by snow. Very little heat penetrates the snow. Likewise very little of an extreme cold spell penetrates the snow cover. Even after several days of zero weather, the temperature inside a snow bank may be only a few degrees below freezing. Animals and plants make great use of snow's insulation. Strangely enough, a man in distress from extreme exposure rarely looks to the snow as a place of refuge.

The quantity of snow crystals which rest on a given piece of ground defy calculation. One observer estimated that in a 10-hour storm a million billion crystals fall in a single acre. Schaefer in one of his papers stated that 5,750 crystals reach a square meter of ground every second during a blizzard.

There is a tremendous discrepancy in the specific gravity of snow. Six inches of moist new snow equal one inch of rain, but so do thirty inches of dry snow. On an average, a 10-inch snowfall is equivalent to one inch of rainfall. So-called wild snow, being about 98 percent air, can flow off a shovel as if it were some kind of unearthly liquid.

Snow on the ground continues to undergo change, some but not all of which is related to temperature. Within one hour after a fall of two feet of light snow, it will settle one or two inches. The fine structure of the individual snow crystal begins to break down through sublimation as the water molecules race around to find new havens.

When a skater glides across ice, the pressure as well as friction of the blade melt ice crystals, providing a thin film of water as a lubricant. On an extremely cold day the skating is slower because the blade cannot melt much ice and is retarded by the friction of steel in direct contact with the grain of the ice. A ski going over snow slides effortlessly when the pressure of the ski melts the points of the snow crystals. Experiments conducted with a fuchsine dye sprinkled on snow reveal red streaks from where the ski melted minute amounts of the snow. So a ski, like a skate, rides on a water film, and the role of ski wax, at least in below-freezing temperatures, is to prevent water from refreezing on the ski bottoms.

One of the most stirring and dramatic aspects of snow is the avalanche. The stem of the word, from the French *avaler,* meaning "to swallow," is expressive of the skier's fears of what may happen to him. There will be no pretense here of providing a guide for avalanche dangers, for a definitive discussion of this subject requires great knowledge and experience. The Ski Club of Great Britain has put out a remarkable small portable handbook, *Ski-Touring and Glacier Skiing,* which should be indispensable equipment for any party bound for Alpine slopes. For general reading on the subject, Seligman's *Snow Structure and Ski Fields,* originally published in 1936, has no equal.

The slope which is about to let go is like some stressed-concrete structure badly designed by an architect who had a sense of aesthetics but no engineering ability. The slope, like the building, may be beautiful to look at. However, if a sidewalk superintendent had watched the building throughout its construction, he would have been aware of some of its flaws. Similarly, if the skier had observed the slope before and during the buildup of the snow layers, he might have some idea of which layer was unsecured. The important rule then, when skiing off the beaten path, is to rely on local knowledge, which usually means having a good guide who knows where and when there is danger.

There are four basic forms of avalanches—dry-snow, wind-slab, wet-snow, and ice avalanche—but many are combinations of these forms. And the most treacherous is the dry-snow avalanche, which paradoxically, does not seem as if it could produce such awesome power, since it is usually made up of light powder snow.

One of the best descriptions of a dry-snow avalanche came from an observer who on a certain day in March of 1898 took notes on an avalanche at Glarnish in Switzerland. This one started high up on a 44-degree slope; within a period of one minute and twelve seconds it had covered a distance of 4.3 miles at a speed of 217 miles per hour. It had such momentum that it crossed a valley 1.2 miles wide, traveling several hundred yards up the other side, before falling down again into the valley. Powder-snow dust from this avalanche settled seven minutes after the slide itself had subsided.

Dry-snow avalanches travel at an average speed of seventy-five miles per hour, and rarely under fifty miles per hour. They are preceded by a pressure wave which has sometimes been known to fell hundreds of acres of trees that were untouched by the avalanche itself. In the Wallowa Mountains of Oregon, air pressure knocked down a wooden bridge that was one-half mile away from the avalanche.

The dry-snow avalanche starts with snow moving along the ground. As it picks up momentum, turbulence under the avalanche causes it to become airborne. With each particle of snow suspended in the air the avalanche behaves like a heavy gas, ten times denser than normal air and moving with very little friction. The dry-snow avalanche drags a mass of air with it as its central core moves with fantastic speed.

This type of avalanche kills more people than any other type. Sometimes rushing into an Alpine valley, it knocks down buildings that have stood for hundreds of years. For the powder-snow skier it represents a great hazard because the moment of peril can coincide with the moment of supreme satisfaction. At times this type of avalanche starts six hours after the end of a snowfall, when the tips of the hexagonal crystals lose their sharp points. At other times it occurs on the first clear day after a snowfall, or even one or two hours after a hot sun has been beating down on the slope.

Sometimes there is a warning: Sun balls form as surface grains become heavy and slide down, packing together until hundreds of snowballs run down the slope. Sometimes as a skier is crossing a slope the snow from above the ski track slides downhill across the skis as unstable fluff. The shadow of a cloud going across a slope can create a sudden drop in temperature, causing the slope to freeze and contract slightly. A dry-snow avalanche can be triggered off by snow falling from the tree branches or by a few rocks which have become detached by frost and finally dislodged by the heat of the sun. Even the vibration of a sound or of wind or of skiers walking nearby can cause the slope to let go.

If the dry-snow avalanche is unpredictable, at least the wet-snow avalanche can be plotted with some certainty. For as Seligman stated:

> In the low-lands the great spring avalanches come down year after year in the same well-defined tracks—in fact the avalanches have names according to the track they fall in—and for this reason the wet avalanche, although responsible for greater volumes of snow than the dry, is more calculable and therefore less deadly to the skier.

The wet-snow avalanche is brought on by rain or continued thawing or both. The first effect of moisture in the snow is actually to increase the cohesion between the flakes. However, when the snow becomes fairly saturated, the particles tend to slide apart, and a lubricant on an under layer of crust is provided. As one writer on snow, Corydon Bell, says, soon it behaves as if it were "alive with weirdly crawling grains."

The movement of the wet-snow avalanche is slow, having an average speed of seventeen miles per hour. In its pattern it often consists of large snow boulders which roll down the hill, leaving a striated track. As it goes out into the valley, it breaks into several freewheeling remnants which leave curved tracks.

The wind-slab avalanche takes place on a lee slope over which a gradual deposit of moist yet cold drifted powder snow has accumulated. Gradually a rooflike structure is built up, which is held in a precarious position by its edges and by occasional contact with the snow underneath. However, because of settling, much of the loose snow below the wind slab is sometimes separated from it by one or two inches. The slope has a dull chalky look, much less rippled than wind crust. To the unknowledgeable skier, a wind slab has an illusion of solidarity. The first warning is a sharp feeling that the slope is suddenly sinking, followed by hollow booms or cracking noises. Sometimes a crack appears at the ski tips and then a fracture line zigzags out of sight. Suddenly the whole slope goes, and breaks into large blocks.

The fourth type is the ice avalanche, which is generally caused by ice or crust breaking away from a steep rock terrace high up on the mountain. The ice avalanche tends to be a summer phenomenon, and it is usually more hazardous for the alpinist than for the skier.

Once caught in an avalanche, there are a few steps a skier can take to try to survive. He has little hope of being able to ski out of an avalanche, or even to outrun one. First, he should try to get rid of his ski equipment, especially his poles. If near the edge of a wet-snow avalanches, he can often roll out of the slide area. In any avalanche it is important to try by means of a swimming motion to stay on top of the snow. And when the avalanche starts to slow down, a desperate effort should be made to free oneself, and at least provide an air space for breathing.

There is no set rule on the number of hours someone may be buried and still be found alive. In light powder snow the chances are best, although here there is danger of suffocation because of the lungs' filling with the billowy snow. Wet snow tends to seal off air and inhibit breathing by holding a man as if buried in concrete.

When an avalanche strikes, the most important responsibility for members of the party who are free and clear is to observe the victims' paths and to mark the approximate area where they may have come to rest. Sometimes some small part of a skier or his equipment may be seen; sometimes a muffled sound can be heard. Once an initial search has been made without success, some member of the party should go for experienced help.

Avalanche rescue is in its infancy. Probing with slender steel shafts known as sounding rods is still one of the most accepted ways of systematically searching an area. In the Alps much progress has been made with Alsatian dogs (German Shepherds), often flown in by helicopter with their handlers. These dogs are trained for rescue by finding their masters, who first lie in an open hole, and who then are gradually covered with snow. Once the dog has accepted the idea, it is easy to train him to pick up the scent of a buried stranger. These rescue dogs work in pairs, since one dog can only search for half an hour at a time. But in a half hour the well-trained dog can cover one hundred square yards, an area that would take a team of twenty men four hours to search using the sounding rod method.

In ski areas where avalanches are a frequent threat, preventive measures include throwing explosive charges or firing with a lightweight recoilless cannon. A ski patrolman may even be assigned the nasty job of knocking away a cornice while anchored from above by a rope or linked ski poles to another patrolman.

Some day powder-snow skiers may carry special equipment to enable them to mark their location and to assist their breathing if they are caught by an avalanche. The avalanche cord, in use already for about a century, consists of fifty to one hundred feet of trailing red line, and is still helpful as a marker for victims. In some areas each member of the avalanche patrol wears a lighter-than-air balloon tied to his belt by a short line.

However, what we really need are some James Bond types in frogman equipment to prove that a man can be harmlessly buried alive by an avalanche. Standard equipment for the powder-snow skier in the future then might consist of some electric audible device, a fiber-glass plate over the diaphragm to enable free breathing, and something like a gas mask to permit the skier to absorb air from a large surface of porous snow.

For we should remember the well-documented survival of two women, a 13-year-old girl, and two goats, who were buried in a barn one day in March of 1775 by an avalanche. Ignazio Somis, a professor of physics at the University of Turin, reported that the three people and the two animals were alive after being under fifty feet of snow for thirty-seven days. Snow, of course, in its natural form consists mostly of air.

But snow can undergo vast change and become solid blue ice, impervious to air. This process may be witnessed in all glaciers. The raw material of the glacier is snow, but snow which does not survive one session is of no use to the glacier. Snow which has lasted from late spring to the next winter as a mixture of ice granules and water is known as firn snow. When further consolidation has taken place and the crystals have grown together, we have glacier snow or névé. True glacier ice is over one hundred feet below the surface of the glacier, a solid monolithic material capable of plastic flow.

Like avalanches, glaciers are awesome: With the avalanche there is the fear of instant burial, with the glacier of the world's slow engulfment. Most glaciers start on high mountain slopes, sometimes spreading down into the valleys. But at one time the great ice sheets almost covered entire continents. In the half million or so years of man's existence on earth he has been fighting severe cold for more than half the time. Only 10,000 years ago New England's Green Mountains were being shaped by glaciers. There is no major mountain of the world which has not had its profile carved by the action of ice.

Today we are conscious of a warming trend in the world, and one of the most accurate ways of telling whether the trend is continuing is by watching for the advance or decline of glaciers. The Greenland ice cap is melting, and the snow line in Greenland is now three hundred feet above sea level. The famous Rhore Glacier has retreated three miles, but there are some places, like the Cascades, where glaciers are growing. In many areas the total amount of snowfall has more effect on glacier growth than the average mean temperature.

A glacier has really two parts, an outer rigid layer and an inner moving layer. The outer part is called a zone of fracture, where ice steps appear and crevasses open up as the glacier descends over a steep or convex slope. The inner layer is its great moving mass, known as the zone of flow. The crevass sometimes extends through the zone of fracture up to the zone of flow, where it is sealed.

John Burroughs, the great naturalist, while visiting what is now Glacier Bay National Monument in Alaska before the turn of the century, gave us this marvelous description of the Muir Glacier:

> We were in the midst of strange scenes, hard to render in words, the miles upon miles of moraines: the towering masses of almost naked rock, smoothed, carved, granite-ribbed, that looked down upon us from both sides of the inlet, and the toppling, staggering front of the great glacier in its terrible labor throes stretching before us from shore to shore. We saw the world-shaping forces at work; we scrambled over plains they had built but yesterday. We saw them transport enormous rocks and tons on tons of soil and debris from the distant mountains; we saw the remains of extensive forests they had engulfed probably within the century and were now uncovering again; we saw their turbid rushing streams loaded with newly ground rocks and soil-making material; we saw the beginnings of vegetation in the tracks of the retreating glacier; our dredgers brought up the first forms of sea life along the shore; we witnessed the formation of the low mounds and ridges and bowl-shaped depressions that so often diversify our landscapes—all the while with the muffled thunder of the falling bergs in our ears. We were really in one of the workshops and laboratories of the elder gods, but only in the glacier's front was there present evidence that they were still at work. I wanted to see them opening crevasses in the ice, dropping soil and rocks they had transported, polishing the mountains, or blocking the streams, but I could not. They seemed to knock off work when we were watching them. One day I climbed up to the shoulder of a huge granite ridge on the west, against which the glacier pressed and over which it broke. Huge masses of ice had recently toppled over, a great fragment of rock hung on the very edge, ready to be deposited upon the ridge, windrows of soil and gravel and boulders were clinging to the margin of the ice, but while I stayed not a pebble moved, all was silence and inertia.

Glaciers and avalanches are great physical manifestations of the power of snow and ice. But life can exist everywhere, even in the severe cold of the high mountains, the far north, and the antarctic ice cap. The extraordinary thing is that plants, animals, and men can adapt to extreme cold.

A trip up a high mountain, whether near the equator or in the temperate zone, is like a quick trip to the arctic. One climbs from plains to hardwood forests to evergreens at the edge of the timberline. Near this line dwarfed evergreens huddle behind protective ledges like a skier in a storm. Branches tend to grow on the lee side of the tree. Sometimes the clipped top of the stunted tree represents the average height of the winter snow, for it is the snow's protection that enables the tree to survive the arcticlike cold near the mountain top.

On the summits of some of the high California mountains stunted foxtail or bristle-coned pines, up to 4,000 years old, are the oldest living things on earth. These remarkable trees have a dense, brushlike arrangement of needles, and sharp tips on their cone scales. Of course, the evergreens generally survive at higher elevations than the hardwood trees, mostly because they conserve strength by not having to grow new leaves each spring.

In the high Rockies amid the lichens growing on the rock terraces there are over three hundred species of flowering plants, all but two of which are perennials. Sixty-five of these species also grow in the tundra country of the arctic. One of the truly remarkable plants is the snow buttercup, which can survive even if the snowbank where it is buried does not melt in the summer season. Although it needs sunlight to produce the starches necessary for growth, the plant can survive one summer without it because of tremendous stored energy. The plant's cells are so minute and its fluid so full of nutrients that it is as resistant to freezing as is an automobile radiator adequately protected with antifreeze.

The animals of the far north have adapted beautifully to the extreme cold. One of these adaptations is their white color. Even the wolf of the high arctic is pure white. In part this adaptation evolved so that the animals would be less conspicuous against the polar whiteness. Color is also a consideration in the conservation of heat, for in the long arctic night there is less heat radiation from a white object than from a black one. In addition, the cells of

Stowe News Bureau

A 1938 view of Mt. Mansfield's profile, complete with the old Toll House, headquarters for the original Sepp Ruschp Ski School, authentic wooden station wagons, and ridge-top hickory skis.

Adrian N. Bouchard

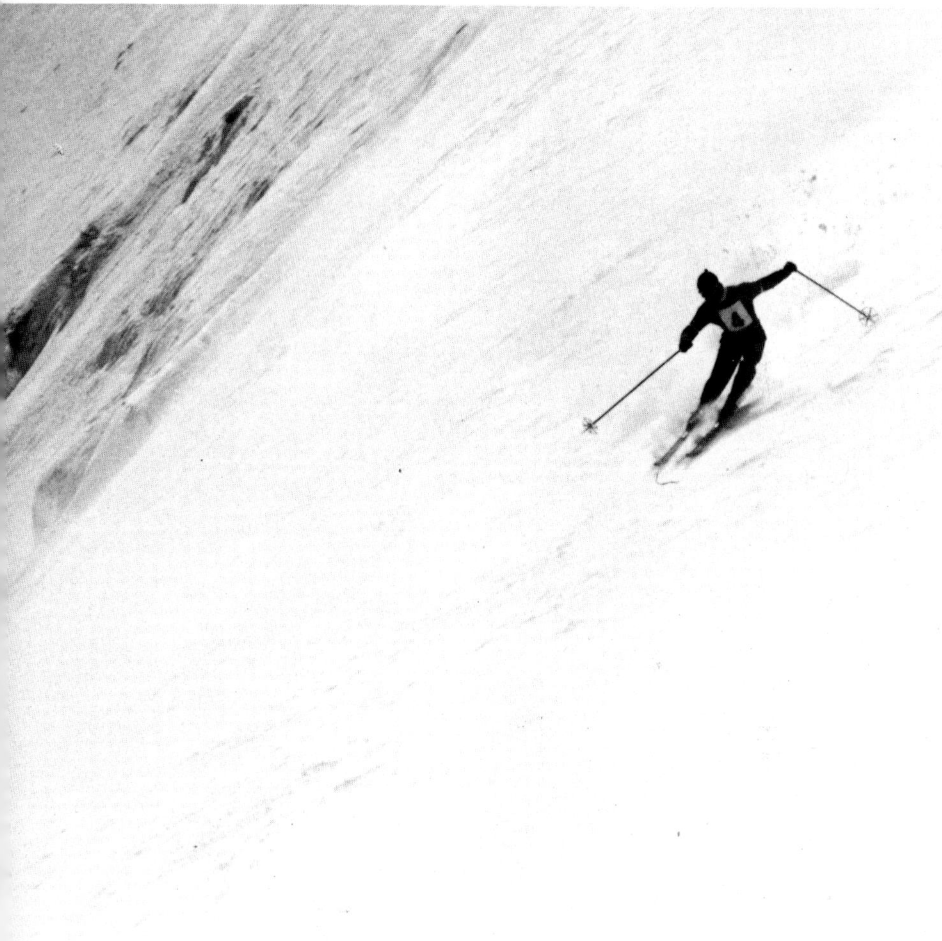

Left. View of Tuckerman Ravine from Lion Head, showing the Left Gully, and over fifty skiers enjoying the bowl on a sunny spring day. *Above.* Toni Matt, in a historic American Inferno photo, April 16, 1939, making his check turn a second or two before his famed schuss of the Head Wall. Single slalom pole is a guide flag only, marking entrance to ravine—no mandatory control gates on true Inferno course.

Adrian N. Bouchard

Above. Dartmouth 1941 captain Charlie McLane, of unorthodox fame in Alpine skiing, shows classic Nordic style in the sliding step of cross-country racing. *Below.* Blindfolded Harold Hillman gives wine-bottle ski lesson to 1941 apres-ski group at Bunny's cabin, Woodstock, Vermont. Author in upper right with friend Nannie Wilder.

R. Meservey

Left. The number-one hill of rope-tow skiing days, Bunny's Suicide Six. *Top right.* View from Tuckerman Ravine Head Wall, emphasizing steepness of terrain. *Below.* Bob Mesevey starts the year off the right way, the parallel way, skiing on early snow in front of his home in Hanover.

R. Meservey

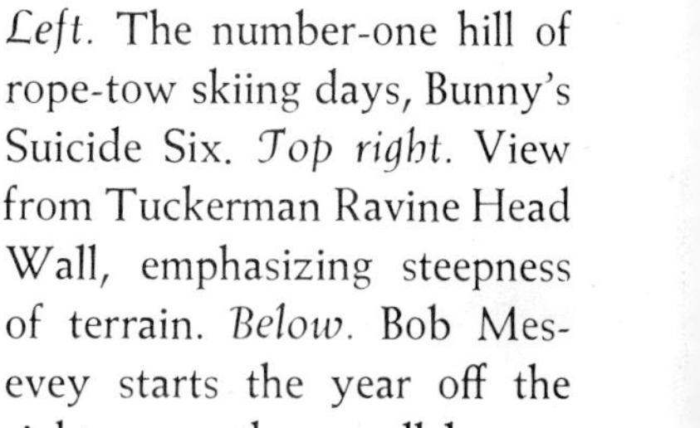

Sidney N. Shurcliff

John

Top right. Pinkham Notch, spring 1933: uphill transportation had not yet started but Tuckerman Ravine was going strong; also, the rumble seat lessened the necessity for the invention of a ski rack. *Top left.* Ski fashions at Mont Tremblant, 1940.

Right. Richie Remsen's spectacular falls add to the fun of Suicide Six. *Below.* Marilyn Shaw, 1949 National Champion, poses cheerfully after spill in deep Mt. Mansfield powder.

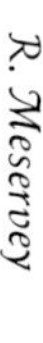

R. Meservey

R. Meservey

Adrian Bouchard

Thee great personalities of the American ski scene, Walter Prager at top left, Dick Durrance top right, and Stein Eriksen below.

Aspen Skiing Corporation

Margaret Durrance

Dick Durrance in steep fall-line skiing in unbroken powder. Only ski pole hoops and details of costume date this photograph, Alta, 1941.

R. Durrance

Above. Picture taken of author while in the Navy. Mt. Rainier early-winter snow, October 1943. *Below.* The camera never lies. A cold courtship, Christmas week, 1945, the author and wife-to-be Barbara in period ski costume at the top of Mt. Mansfield.

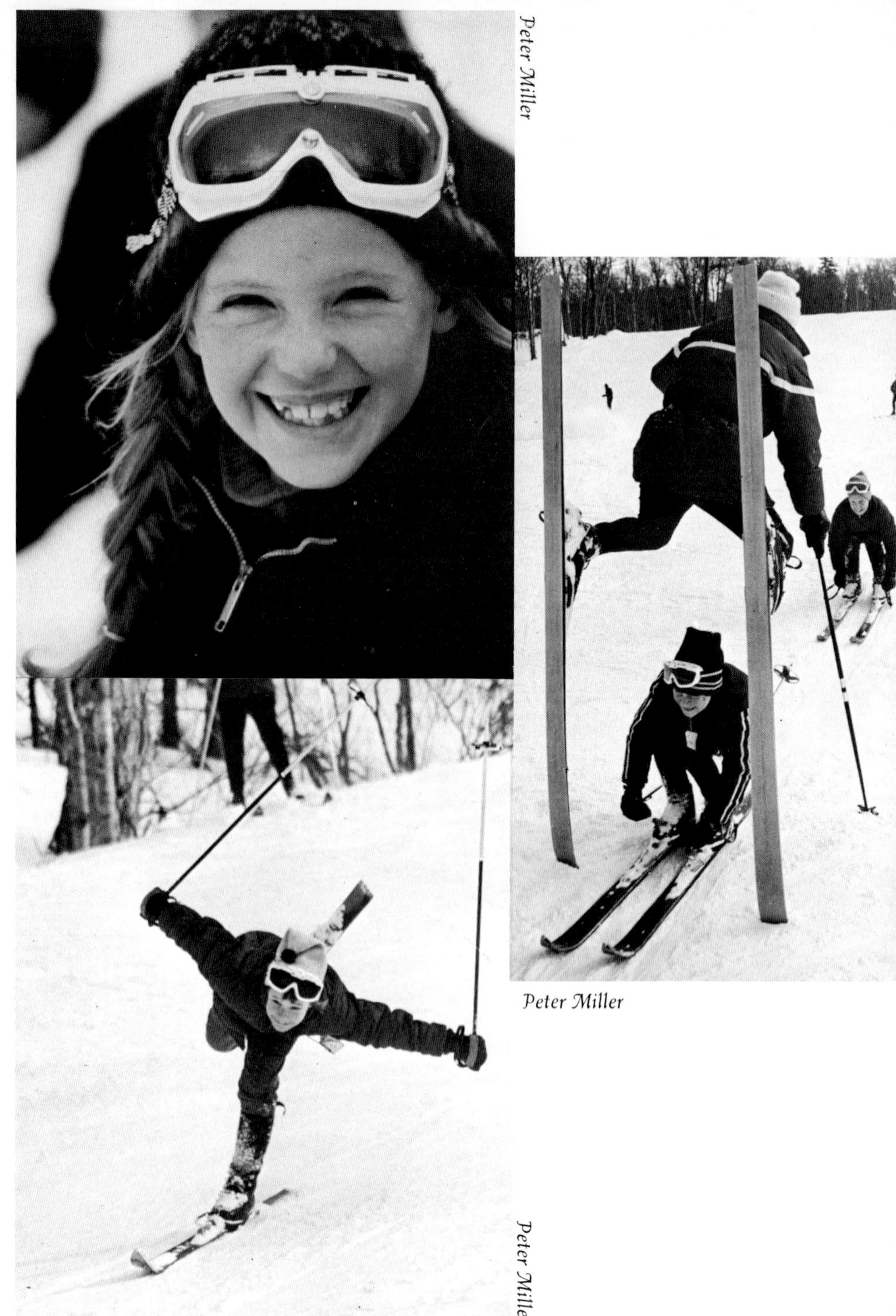

Peter Miller

Peter Miller

Peter Miller

A young happy face and antics on skis reflect the pleasure youngsters find on ski slopes.

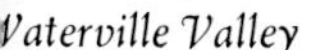

Vaterville Valley

Above left. Tom and Birdie Corcoran, husband-and-wife winners of a veterans' race on Mt. Tecumseh, New Hampshire, in mid-April of 1966. This was billed as the last of the walk-up races, having taken place the year before the start of Waterville Valley, of which area Tom is the president and general manager. *Right*. Robert Gluck, St. Anton ski instructor and star of the chapter "European Adventure." *Below*. Olympian Brookie Dodge skiing over a small snowslide in the Right Gully of Tuckerman Ravine, his boyhood backyard.

Adams Carter

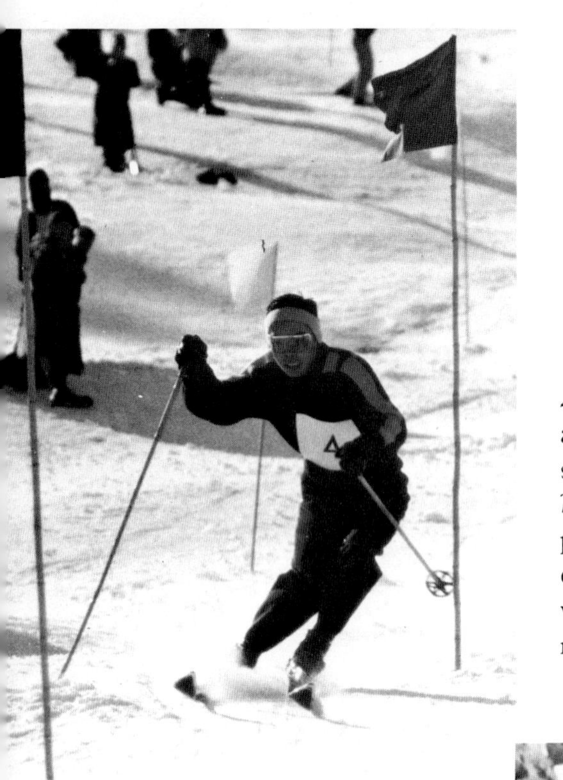

Left. Dartmouth's Chick Igaya, skilled and colorful slalom star, winner of a silver medal in the 1956 Olympics. *Below.* Toni Sailer shows his slalom prowess. Olympic gold-medal winner of 1956, he was undisputably the world's greatest skier until Killy repeated his feat in 1968.

GMP Sports Ltd.

Wide World Photos

Jean-Claude Killy winning the giant slalom in the 1968 Olympics at Grenoble. He shows the mental attitude and racing style that earned him the title "the world's greatest skier."

Studley Studios

Above. One of today's international stars, the Austrian Hubert Huber, steps up to his high line for the next turn in a giant slalom race at Vail. *Below*. With pose and a determined expression, the Norwegian Terje Overland shows perfect downhill technique as he holds his tuck while airborne at over sixty miles per hour.

Frank Bering

white hair or white feathers are filled with insulating air. Another result of adaptation involves a reduction in projecting body parts. The arctic fox has a round head and short ears, quite different from the slender pointed nose and long ears of the red fox. And dense fur, two to three inches thick, is helpful, as is a layer of fat accumulated for the beginning of winter. All the animals of the far north are capable of sleeping in comfort at the lowest temperatures which prevail.

The mountain men of the high Andes and the Himalayas are the most specialized of all humans on earth. These people have short, well-rounded bodies, with abbreviated extremities, which provide the least opportunity for heat loss. They have barrel-shaped chests, with tremendous lung capacity, and the small pockets of the lungs known as alveoli are always wide open. The 130-pound Andean Indian has six quarts of blood whereas the same man living at sea level only has five. Even the blood is specialized, with a high proportion of red corpuscles, which contain the hemoglobin that catches oxygen. But even for these well-adapted Andean and Himalayan men there is a practical ceiling for existence. The highest center of habitation is Gartok in Tibet at 15,200 feet. At 18,000 feet atmospheric pressure is one half that at sea level.

Even though all of us can adapt to high altitudes, there is an elevation at which a gradual physical deterioration takes place. Experiments conducted in the Himalayas at 18,765 feet, where the highest house in the world was built, indicated that men cannot live indefinitely above 18,000 feet. After a period of time, each day at such a height rapidly brings a man closer to death.

One of the most unusual civilizations on earth is that of the 52,000 Eskimos of the arctic. Almost half of the Eskimos live in Greenland, where four fifths of the land mass is occupied by the ice cap. Theirs is a true culture of survival, for the struggle to exist is a full-time job. They have an extraordinary knowledge of the vagaries of winter weather and of the intimate habits of the arctic animals, which are the Eskimos' main source of food.

The Eskimos hunt the polar bear, not for food, since they say its meat tastes like human flesh, but for its skin, which they use for making their version of warm-up pants. The polar bear is one of the most dangerous animals on earth, and can travel at tremendous speed, even on glazed ice. Its claws are so sharp that it can climb the steepest ice pinnacle; it has been sighted swimming in open water more than one hundred miles from land. It is also an uncannily skillful hunter which takes great pains to hide its tracks.

Both the Eskimo and the polar bear are highly dependent upon seals. The Eskimo catches most of his supply during the short period of smooth snow-free ice, when it is possible to move up quietly on the seal's blowhole. The polar bear waiting for a seal at its blowhole cleverly hides its black nose behind its huge white paw.

As dangerous as the polar bear can be, it is sometimes killed singlehandedly by an Eskimo with either a harpoon or a knife. When hunting with a harpoon, the Eskimo carries an extra one because a speared polar bear instinctively rolls to break off the wooden-shafted harpoon. When hunting polar bears with a knife, the Eskimo pretends that he is running away from the bear; just as the bear is about to pounce on the Eskimo, he wheels and stabs the bear in the heart.

A whole book would be necessary to describe the Eskimo, with his marvelous cold-and-sound insulating igloos and his remarkable mobility with dog-teamed sleds and kayaks.

Man's struggle for existence goes on in Siberia too, where the pole of cold of the northern hemisphere is in Oymyakon, a town of 3,500 people. Actually located three hundred miles south of the arctic circle, in winter it has a clear, dry, almost windless climate. It also had the lowest temperature ever recorded in the northern hemisphere, –96° F. Strangely enough, during the summer when the sun shines twenty-four hours a day, the temperature can go as high as 100° F.

The reason for the existence of this town is a large animal farm where silver foxes are raised; there is also trapping in the surrounding area for ermine, muskrat, sable, and various types of fox. In winter the town throws off an almost continual fog from human breath, heated buildings, and smoke particles. Buildings have to be anchored on piles extending twenty-four feet into the permafrost.

These piles are buried after holes of temporary mush have been created with steam hoses. The windows of the houses collect individual canopies of ice from the freezing of moist warm air. When a man is out driving, he ignores a flat tire, for his hand can become frozen to the tire rim.

One seventh of the earth's surface is made up of permafrost, half of which is in Siberia. An average annual temperature of less than 23° F. is necessary to keep the ground frozen throughout the year. In some areas severe cold is estimated to have continued for 100,000 years. Man has drilled as deep as 2,000 feet into permafrost. Untold millions of tons of fossil, plant, and animal remains are buried in the frozen soil, and Soviet scientists have dined on mastodon meat. Pure black fossil ice has been discovered which when melted turns to a clear liquid. Perhaps some day we will find an advance hamlet of primitive man buried intact like a lost Atlantis under the cover of frozen soil.

The one continent where there is no record of man's existence is Antarctica. The only thing there on two legs is the penguin, so there is little wonder that it walks proudly. There is not even a blade of grass on Antarctica. Virtually the entire continent is covered with a massive ice sheet—nearly two miles thick in some places—which contains almost 6 million cubic miles of ice, 86 percent of the world's ice. If the earth is undergoing a warming trend, there is no evidence of any melting in Antarctica. The lowest natural temperature ever recorded was −132° F. in the middle of a blizzard in Graham Land. So who says it's too cold to snow?

Despite all the recent geological expeditions to Antarctica, not much is known about this continent. However, the little that has been discovered is astounding. Algae have been found imprisoned in frozen ponds. Brilliant red-hued lichen have been found on rocks everywhere. Bacteria found in snow have endured temperatures of nearly 100 degrees below zero, ready to carry on their primary function of cell division within an hour after being thawed. Coal exists in plentiful supply, proof of earlier vegetation and a warmer climate.

Life is even more abundant in Antarctica under the sea. During the long daylight of summer, continuous sunlight creates an ocean rich in nutrients. Also, the cold water of the Antarctic Ocean holds more oxygen than warmer water. This results in a prodigious growth of plants and animals. Perhaps some day hungry people may be fed by protein from krill, a crustacean about as big as a small shrimp existing in untold billions in antarctic waters. Nuclear power can provide a continued source of electricity and heat in Antarctica, and transportation by air is no problem. But when man takes over Antarctica in a permanent commercially feasible way, life there will no longer be an adventure. Certainly it is the one continent on this earth where man cannot survive as a noble savage in his natural state.

Here we have taken a look at a separate world of snow, ice, and cold. The skier is linked with this world principally through his enjoyment of it, but sometimes through a situation where he is confronted by the necessity for survival. He may be lost on a mountain, caught in a severe storm, or have a near-miss with an avalanche. It is then that he wishes he were a better match for that world.

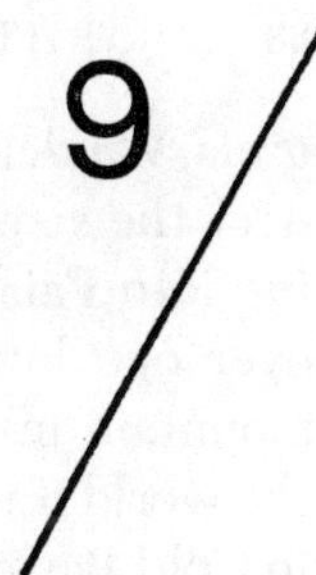

War and Postwar

Having deliberately chosen the Navy over the ski troops, I went into uniform feeling that I had turned my back on skiing for the duration of the war. Yet as my naval career evolved, I did manage to have some interesting experiences on skis.

After my graduation from Dartmouth in May of 1942, following a slightly accelerated semester, I went to Midshipmen's School, which was mostly drudgery and by far the dullest aspect of the Navy. A small group of us selected for PT boat school spent two wintry months near Newport, Rhode Island, on Narragansett Bay. I found out quickly that ocean spray has a very special sting when it hits a watch officer on the bridge of a PT boat, forging through choppy water off the New England coast in January. We also had to face the cold during classroom sessions, which took place in drafty, poorly heated Quonset huts. Another student officer, Joe Coons, and I would huddle around the kerosene space heater during every break. Skiing must be a warmer sport than it gets credit for, or I probably never would have shown interest in it.

At the completion of the course, Joe Coons and I, the two chill-ridden ensigns, were ironically assigned to Aleutian duty. In February of 1943, the two of us flew out to Seattle, where I skied over the weekend at Snoqualmie Pass. I met a girl from Seattle, Virginia Vanderbilt, and then had an interesting flight up to Alaska over the snow-covered caribou country of British Columbia. Flying into Fairbanks, we had a magnificent view of Mt. McKinley, over one hundred miles away. At 20,320 feet it is the highest mountain in the northern hemisphere, and one of the highest in the world if measured from its base. Before proceeding by steamer to Cold Bay on the Aleutian peninsula, we stopped over at Kodiak, where Al Lindley, a Naval officer and well-known skier, arranged for me to ski with some Army troops. They were skiing more for recreation than for military training, but recreation was certainly important for men stationed in these desolate Aleutian Islands. The tips on skiing I passed along seemed greatly appreciated.

At King Cove we found our boats on a spit of land alongside a small hamlet of 150 people. This spit ran between two large hills which poked out into the water, both of which were snow-covered and one of which was steep enough for a championship slalom course. I managed to get a pair of white Army skis at nearby Cold Bay station, and skied every day the weather was halfway decent. It was quite unusual to be able to ski right down to the edge of the sea. By the end of March two of the boats, PT-24 and PT-27, had been repaired and we were under way to points to the west. I found some fair skiing at Dutch Harbor, but the other islands such as Adak and Amchitka were too flat. Besides, since it was later in the spring the snow was left only in patches, with the islands taking on their usual bleak, tundra-covered look.

Our two boats were badly damaged near Adak while we were operating in a particularly rough sea kicked up by a high wind. We were unable to find a speed at which the boats could move without being battered, and they started to fall apart, with the seams in the plywood decks opening up underneath us. After making a few patrols off Kiska in newer boats Joe and I were part of a group ordered to take PT-24 and PT-27 back to Seattle for major overhaul. So in the month of June we had a thrilling trip across the Bay of Alaska and down through the famous inland waterway in fjord country between the off-shore islands and coastal mountains of Alaska and British Columbia. For anyone who loves mountains it is breathtaking to see the snow-capped peaks rising out of the water, and glaciers extending right to the ocean's edge.

At Seattle our boats were scheduled to be on the ways for a number of months. As it turned out, we were there from July through October. I looked up Dick Durrance, who was doing photographic work for Boeing Aircraft Corporation. Through Dick and Virginia Vanderbilt, the girl I had met briefly on the way out, I got to know quite a few of the skiers in Seattle.

We had great fun water-skiing with Dick and Don Amick on Lake Washington. Dick managed to maintain his characteristic Durrance downhill crouch on water-skis. And his legs had such power that when crossing the wake of the boat, he could jump from the upside of one wave over the trough and onto the downhill side of the next wave.

Seattle seemed like an extremely good place for skiers to live. The volcanic cone of Mt. Rainier, white-capped with its twenty-seven glaciers, is a stirring sight, and many passes in the Cascade Range feature ski slopes with a huge annual snowfall. Driving in almost any direction out of Seattle, one sees forests of Douglas firs, tall and graceful, the most stately of trees.

The first weekend in October I had an interesting experience. Four of us went up to Mt. Rainier to ski on the back of Paradise, where a large field of corn snow was left from the previous winter. On Saturday we enjoyed several hours of skiing on the fast, manageable, springlike corn. That night, staying in cabins quite a distance down the mountain, we were pelted by a heavy rainstorm, and gave up any thought of skiing the next day. In the morning it was still raining hard, but someone looked at the thermometer, to discover the temperature in the low forties, which meant that there was undoubtedly new snow falling in the upper elevations. We drove up the mountain, and sure enough, as we got near Paradise Lodge, the rain turned to snow. Wet as it was, it was coming down hard enough to put a white covering on the unfrozen ground. We elected to climb to the top of Paradise and ski on the slope we had been on the day before, knowing that we would find six to eight inches of new snow over a base. The skiing was indeed excellent. And to encompass two seasons in one weekend, skiing Saturday on the last of the snow from the previous winter, and Sunday on the first snow of the approaching one, was quite a thrill.

In early November, newly outfitted PT-24 and PT-27 were loaded on a tanker bound for Middle Lock in Pearl Harbor, where there was a fairly large PT base used as a staging point for outgoing squadrons. After being there a short time, we began to feel like a couple of strays, for whom the Navy had no plans. We were used for training destroyer and plane crews in antitorpedo boat maneuvers, and we were sent around the island of Oahu to give coastal defenses searchlight drill.

I was anxious to get on with the war, having been on duty for about a year without seeing action or even being involved in any activity that seemed at all purposeful. While stationed in the Pacific I met quite a few submarine officers who told some intriguing tales. Early in the war, submarines had a major but largely unrecognized role in crippling the Japanese shipping arm, as well as in sinking many naval vessels.

Finally I wrote an official letter to the Bureau of Personnel to request submarine school at New London. This was then the only proper way to apply for submarine duty. At the same time I met a lovely girl by the name of Evanita Sumner, whose father was an ex-Annapolis man, prominent in business in the islands, and friendly with Admiral Nimitz and the submarine chief, Admiral Lockwood. Somehow I sensed that Evanita's father might easily be more influential than my letter in getting me into submarines. Every time I saw him I made a great point of discussing my interest in submarines. Looking back, I must have been out of my mind to want to change jobs. We had pretty soft duty in Pearl Harbor, the Hawaiian Islands are beautiful at any time of the year, and unlike most men stationed out there, I had a girl whose company I thoroughly enjoyed. But as I said, I was restless.

One evening when I went over to pick up Evanita, her mother met me at the door and said that they were having a party for the officers of the submarine *Gudgeon,* and that if Evanita and I had no definite plans, we were welcome to stay. Knowing my keen interest in submarines, she was not surprised when I accepted the invitation. The *Gudgeon,* just back from a successful patrol, was at the time one of the four or five top boats in the fleet. The officers were a great group, and it was a fine party. I had no chance to monopolize Evanita, but this I had expected. And as liquor, wine, and food were offered liberally, spirits rose accordingly.

Very much in evidence at the party was an illustrious Naval officer named "Dusty" Dornin. An ex-Naval Academy football player with an impressive war record, he had been exec on the *Gudgeon* before becoming skipper of the *Trigger,* another top submarine. I had been told that he was something of a hell-raiser ashore. If true this was obviously not a blot on his career, because his next assignment was to be flag lieutenant for Ernie King, Admiral of the Fleet and Commander in Chief of the Navy in Washington.

At the height of the party, Evanita's father told Dusty about my interest in submarines. When Dusty inquired about this, I told him emphatically that I wanted submarine duty and that I had sent a letter to BuPers requesting submarine school at New London. He then fired this question: "Are you just interested in going back to the States, or do you really want to get into submarines?"

Without blinking an eye, I replied that I wanted to get into submarines. He then said, "Meet me at ComSubPac tomorrow at noon, and I'll see what can be done."

Since we had all had a few drinks the night before, I was almost surprised when Dusty hailed me at ComSubPac the next day. He immediately took me into a command room, where I met about five or six submarine skippers gathered around a long table. Introducing me with a flourish, he luckily was not challenged in some of the sweeping statements that he made about me. The only factual material he offered was that I was a Dartmouth skier and a prospective submariner who was bored with a PT boat career. By the time Dusty had finished his pitch, the skippers were fighting over me. The argument was settled very quickly, because Dusty's classmate, Sam Loomis of the *Stingray,* had a boat leaving in exactly twenty-four hours. "That's the boat for you," Dusty said decisively.

How I managed to be released from my chain of command,

pack my gear, write letters home, and say my good-byes to my shipmates and to Evanita, all within twenty-four hours, is a story in itself. There was one personnel officer attached to ComServPac who tried to abort my scheme by going to his captain and pointing out that this was not at all in conformity with regulations. The captain blurted out, "Where is this young man! I want to see him!"

On entering the captain's office, I found to my surprise that he was on my side. He was thoroughly dressing down his personnel officer for standing in the way of anyone who wanted so much to be in submarines. For it turned out that the captain greatly admired the work being done by our submarines. He wanted to know whether I needed transportation and what he could do to help me get aboard the *Stingray* before she departed at 2 P.M. that day.

I made it to the *Stingray*, and Joe Coons was there to wish me well. I had not been aboard for more than half an hour before we shoved off. So on March 10, 1944, at 1420 Navy time, I was under way on the U.S.S. *Stingray*, my first trip on a submarine out on war patrol. Except for one stop at Midway, we were at sea for fifty-three days. Twenty days after leaving Pearl Harbor, while on station off the northern Marianas, we made a successful night surface attack on a fair-sized Japanese Maru, during which I had the excitement of a topside battle stations watch.

But the *Stingray*, despite the fighting sound of her name, did not have an impressive war record. She was in the Philippines at the time of the first Japanese air strikes, and in early January, 1942, bagged the fourth ship sunk by a United States submarine in World War II. We made seven war patrols, but only on the first was our primary mission to make torpedo attacks on shipping and men-of-war. As an older boat, the *Stingray* was relegated during her last year of war duty to special missions, rescuing naval aviators shot down off Japanese bases, taking coastal photographs, landing guerrilla troops, and contacting or delivering special agents. Yet I enjoyed submarines immensely. I don't ever again expect to be so much a part of a team or to have quite the same pride in being a member of an elite group.

It may seem odd for someone who loves skiing and the open spaces of the mountains to end up in the confined quarters of a submarine. This was a volunteer service during almost all of the war, and men who felt uncomfortably confined in an elevator or a crowded room naturally did not even consider submarine duty. There were remarkably few instances of men becoming hysterical during the pressure of depth charge attacks. There was even surprisingly little evidence of growing irritation or uneasiness among the men on long arduous patrols.

Possibly the psychological makeup of the submariner is not unlike that of the astronaut. The latter cannot be bothered by claustrophobia, since he must adjust to the confinement of the space capsule. But he, like the submariner, cannot on the other hand have the fear of open spaces, or agoraphobia. The astronaut leaves the earth behind and pioneers the openness of outer space. The submariner heads out to the loneliness of an enemy's ocean and pioneers the uncertainties of the world below.

As I have pointed out, there is some common ground between the rhythms of the sea and the rhythms of the mountains. While traveling at sea, a man meets the elements face to face, just as he does while skiing on a mountain in a snowstorm. Being on a submarine at sea is an adventure, even without action with the enemy.

A surfaced submarine is surprisingly graceful. Its sleek bullet-shaped pressure hull knifes through the water with ease, and its lightweight superstructure, which alone is visible, gives it a tenuous existence as a surface craft. In heavy seas, when the conning tower is rolled over by a sea breaking from abeam, the submarine seems to hang, as if unable to return to an upright position. When the bow plunges under green water, the submarine seems about to make a crash dive, but long before the sea breaks in front of the conning tower, the bow suddenly thrusts its way out of the water with great power.

At night on a phosphorescent sea a porpoise can jump, and create a luminous wake that looks surprisingly like a torpedo homing in. Waterspouts are common in the Pacific with sometimes four or five in sight at one time. Another phenomenon occurs when the submarine discharges static electricity from the earth at such a rate that cold blue flames, St. Elmo's fire, dance along the extremities of the ship, along the periscopes, and along the up-pointed barrel of the forward Oerlikon gun. Of course, the extraordinary aspect of being in a submarine in the enemy area, whether surfaced or submerged is the confidence that your presence is not in any way known. When it is surfaced at night, the low-lying hull of the submarine, with its superstructure painted a light gray-blue, blends in well with the horizon, which, by contrast with the blackness of the sea, appears relatively bright. Underwater, the stealth of the submarine is notorious, but so great is the confidence of the crew that even when depth charges are dropping, the attitude is, "They'll never find us. They have no idea where we are."

During an all-day dive the smoking lamp would usually be lit for two 15-minute periods. I have always been a nonsmoker, but if ever I was tempted it was as I observed the pleasure cigarette breaks gave my fellow submariners. For the first and last time, I wondered if I was missing something.

While on submarine duty, I missed two winters of snow, and I probably thought less about skiing then than at any time in my life. In fact, I was so absorbed in what I was doing that I took the absence of skiing in stride.

The *Stingray* came back to New London from the Pacific just as the war ended in Europe. Being an older submarine, she was scheduled for use as a school boat. On my first weekend pass I went up to visit Barbara Crane, a senior at Smith College, whom I had met while home on leave from my Seattle tour of duty in the summer of 1943. I had borrowed a set of blues from a fellow officer, who warned me that the pants zipper was quite temperamental. Before I got off the train at Northampton, I discovered that the zipper had become completely inoperative in the open position. I was not too concerned, figuring that I could buy some safety pins in any one of a dozen stores in Northampton. Little did I know that safety pins had become a war casualty, and were not available for sale anywhere.

Immediately after I greeted Barbara, I had to explain my predicament and ask her if she could find a safety pin. This was an embarrassingly inauspicious way to get started again with Barbara, a tall beautiful girl who had excelled both in her studies and in campus activities at Smith. Since she became my wife within the next two years, and a good marriage makes bad copy, her role in the book will be largely confined to her occasional head-on collisions with my other life—skiing.

My first leave was spent, not surprisingly, in the mountains near Franconia, New Hampshire, where I visited my old friend, Sel Hannah. A former captain of the Dartmouth ski team, Sel was running a big potato farm. He put me to work out in the field harvesting potatoes, which could be a fairly tedious hand operation. But after being at sea for so long, I liked the feeling of digging my hands into the earth, as well as of being surrounded by Mt. Lafayette, Cannon Mountain, and farther off, the Presidential Range. The evenings were fun too, since Sel makes such a colorful drinking partner.

At Christmas Barbara and I, along with a group from New Jersey, headed for the postwar reopening of Stowe. The trails were crowded and the snow cover thin and icy. Since Christmastime skiing in the East is on a hit-or-miss basis, the Eastern skier generally is so glad to be on skis again that he is thankful for what he gets. However, for me this was no mere seasonal resumption of the sport. Skiing had been out of my life for too long. I wanted to pick up the joy of skiing from the point where I left it, and I was frankly looking for much more than Stowe could provide at that time. A picture of Barbara and me near the Octagon at the top of the mountain documents that the sun was out, but to judge from the expressions on our faces, it was a miserably cold day.

On January 14, 1946, I again became a full-fledged civilian. Very shortly thereafter I flew west with the idea of getting in some real skiing along with looking over job prospects in Seattle, Salt Lake City, and Denver. In Seattle I stayed with a family named Rolfe who had already been hospitable to me when I was with PT boats. One day Peter Garrett, former Yale ski star, and I went to Stevens Pass in the midst of one of the incredible heavy wet snowstorms which the Pacific Northwest features. Seattle did not turn up a promising career, and I went on by train to Salt Lake City, where I immediately headed for Alta.

Alta probably offers the best skiing close to a large city. After leaving the flats of Salt Lake City, one starts up sharply eroded Little Cottonwood Canyon. And in less than an hour from downtown Salt Lake City, one can be in Alta ski country. The transition is hard to believe, particularly since Alta is a true Alpine wonderland, replete with steep open snow bowls, two impressive peaks, Mt. Superior and Mt. Baldy, and best of all, powder snow in plentiful supply. Alta's only drawbacks are avalanche danger and the shortness of the runs.

Many of the ski areas in the West owe their start to some factor completely unrelated to skiing—for instance, the availability of a steep slope on a highway crossing the Continental Divide, the presence of a railroad spur line going into the mountains for some industrial need, or as in the case of Aspen and Alta, the existence of an old mining town or camp. Alta possessed a rich silver lode, and the mine was on a boom basis for the first ten or fifteen years after the Civil War. Frequently the abundance of snow was a problem. Constant avalanches caused large loss of life and extensive property damage. In 1874, sixty lives were lost in one slide alone, and the main mine shaft was completely demolished. But man is persistent, and despite the danger people were always available to work the mines. Only the demonitization of silver and a dry-up of the richest lodes curbed the mining activity.

Today at Alta the avalanches continue to threaten skiers. However, the National Forest Service carefully controls skiing activity, sometimes shutting it down completely and other times merely closing certain runs. There is probably no ski area in the United States where avalanche studies are undertaken with such vigilance. The approach is both scientific and practical, the practical aspect being important because the variety of factors causing an avalanche means that no two cases will have identical conditions.

Shortly after arriving at Alta, we were snowed in for over two days, with the famous light Alta powder reaching waist-high. Although not yet hit by an avalanche, the Lodge looks like a sitting duck. Avalanches from various directions have even come right up to the door. During this storm we were shut in by snowslides on the highway, but the main problem was a prevailing wind direction which interfered with the ventilation of the chemical toilets. Since Alta is located in the watershed for Salt Lake City, it must control its own drainage and waste.

When the ski slopes finally opened up again, I had a chance to ski with Dev Jennings, Dick Movitz, Bud Philips, and George Macomber, all racers who were to figure importantly in skiing over the next several years. But I realized that I was so out of shape that probably never again would I consider myself one of the top racers.

After a week of skiing I was at least starting to ski fast and really enjoy it, but my practice was to be cut short. On one run down the main lift line, I was skiing the top section, doing a few long-radius high-speed turns in the fall line. Unknown to me, another skier was about fifty yards to the side, going almost as fast. Some alert people on the lift watched, out of fear that there might be a collision. At the top of the steep section known as the face we went around opposite sides of a cluster of spruce trees, broke away from the fall line, and veered toward each other. When I saw the other skier he was less than ten feet away, bearing down on me at a 90-degree angle. Instinctively I straightened up—not the smartest maneuver—and he hit me squarely with his shoulder on my left thigh. We bounced apart as if an explosion had taken place, and tumbled down the length of the slope.

The ski patrol treated me for a broken femur and put my leg in a traction splint. I too thought it was broken, for whenever I was jolted by the toboggan a nerve pain raced up and down my leg. The other man, after resting for a couple of hours, was back on his skis that afternoon. In an Army hospital in Salt Lake City X rays indicated that the bone was in one piece, but I had such a bad charley horse that I stayed in bed for a couple of days before being released on crutches to fly home. This accident ended all prospects of job-hunting in Salt Lake City and Denver, as well as plans to ski at Aspen.

When my leg was well enough for me to walk without limping, I accepted a job in retailing with Gimbel Brothers in New York. Since then business has never taken me into skiing, and today I am a marketing man working in the cosmetics field for Shulton Inc.

In the winter of 1947, less than two years after I got back from the Pacific, Barbara and I were married, and naturally headed for a three-week skiing honeymoon at Sun Valley. True to form, I decided that I would enter the Harriman Race. The second day we were there, the Warm Springs Run, site of the downhill, was open to competitors. Near the top, some of the racers seemed to be informally sideslipping, packing the course they had skied three days earlier in the Olympic tryouts. I joined them for a while, and then, anxious to familiarize myself with the course, skied on down the trail, which needed work before it could be run fast. On my next trip when I came upon the same group of racers at the top of the steilhang, I realized they were packing the course all the way down, as requested by the race committee. As I slowed down, planning to come to a complete stop, Jack Reddish, then the number one boy in downhill, thrust out his poles in front of my legs to stop me, and made some angry comment about my skiing the course when everyone else was packing it. Although I had many friends among the racers there, including Bob Blatt, Steve Knowlton, and Colin Stewart, I suddenly felt like an outsider. It was a lonely feeling to know that at least one racer thought that I was trying to take an unfair advantage. But even with an advantage I was no threat to these fellows, who had been racing all winter and training hard for selection on the 1948 Olympic Team. I was now a weekend skier, one of the newest arrivals at Sun Valley, looking over a trail which I had only skied recreationally in 1941.

Later that day I was skiing with Barbara through the Rock Garden, on the other side of the mountain. Because she was still unsure of herself on skis, and not quite ready for the steep Middle Canyon part of the mountain, I put her on the number two lift to let her ride down and bypass this section. While I was skiing over the mogul-studded area of the Canyon, I had a rather bad twisting fall, straining my ankle. Barbara, riding the lift down, saw the fall and also saw me lying still on the snow afterward. It was obvious to her that I had been hurt and that there was nothing she could do about it. She was doubly frustrated when my rescuer turned out to be my old Woodstock girl Sis Bontecou, who came gracefully swooping down the Canyon to take care of me. Sis helped me up, brushed me off, and escorted me slowly down the mountain, while Barbara continued to ride helplessly down on the lift.

The strained ankle kept me off skis for a couple of days, and handicapped me only slightly for a few more. It should have abruptly ended any thoughts about skiing in the Harriman Race. But I did have moments of insanity. The day after the accident as I was hobbling along in the lobby of the Challenger Inn, I was stopped by Charlie McLane's father, "Judge" McLane, who inquired about my ankle. I said it was nothing and that I might still be able to race in the Harriman. With a rare tone of severity in his voice, he said, "Even if your ankle is all right, someone on a honeymoon shouldn't be thinking about racing."

As it turned out, I watched the races from the bottom of the steilhang, taking some dramatic color movies of the racers negotiating the schuss, the most difficult part of the course, in a fast, long S-turn. Edi Rominger, a Swiss, was the winner, beating the great Toni Matt by a few seconds, and bettering Dick Durrance's legendary 1940 run by thirty-four seconds. A 1948 Olympic team was picked from that year's crop of American racers, but none of them was to become a first-rate international skier. The 1948 showing for the men was perhaps the poorest American effort in any Olympic or F.I.S. Alpine competition.

The girls were the ones to watch. At Sun Valley, Georgette Thiollière of France, who skied in a stylish outfit topped by a fancy turban, was then the finest woman skier in the world. She had such confidence in her winning margin that she was able to ski for show, demonstrating the grace that Frenchwomen are known for. There were two American girls also worth watching. One was Gretchen Fraser, who placed second behind Georgette at Sun Valley, and who was to ski brilliantly the following year at St. Moritz, earning a gold medal in the special slalom—the first medal won by an American in Olympic Alpine competition. Another girl worth watching was Andy Mead, who was then fourteen years old. She already had the mark of a champion, and in 1952 was to win two Olympic gold medals.

For Barbara, Sun Valley was in many ways the perfect place for a honeymoon but in others it was off the mark. In those days Sun Valley was definitely the "in" place to ski. Aspen had not yet become popular, and Vail, Squaw, and Jackson Hole were nonexistent as ski areas. We had magnificent weather, in the stage setting of rounded foothills and big mountains. We had all the comforts of a skiing vacation, as well as the pleasant companionship of another pair of newlyweds, Nan and Dix Leeson from Philadelphia. Barbara's skiing progressed rapidly, as the first long ski vacation always does wonders for a skier in the early stage of development. Perhaps because it was our wedding trip, I was a little more patient and understanding than usual in my role as her instructor.

My low point in this regard had been on the way back from Stowe on our Christmas ski trip the year before, our first trip together, when we stopped at Pico Peak for a couple of runs before heading south. Barbara, exhausted after a series of sleepless nights in a girls' bunk room at the Green Mountain Inn, fell several times on the first run, and it seemed to me that she was not making any effort. On the second run she took another fall in a place which, to my eyes, did not look difficult. She lay in the snow for a few seconds, and in one of my most unfortunate outbursts, I commanded, "Damn it, Barbara, get up fighting!" That was the end of our day at Pico, and we had an uneasy trip home, with Barbara giving me the silent treatment.

So under the Sun Valley three-week formula of long sunny spring days, open slope skiing, and a new spouse for an instructor, who showed, briefly at least, that he was capable of being appreciative and interested, Barbara became handy on skis. Before leaving she was able to ski all the slopes and trails with good form and in a somewhat relaxed manner.

Barbara was actually slower to adjust to the après-ski life at Sun Valley. It seemed as if I knew everyone, and she often thought the company was pretty fast. Everywhere we turned there were famous skiers and people completely at home in the ski world. Barbara herself was not often ill at ease, but being newly married to an expert skier, she sometimes thought the ski world a tough nut to crack. But Barbara mastered all the challenges of Sun Valley and in the last week she was even at home with Sun Valley night life.

In the years ahead, I was sometimes a rather frustrated ex-big-time racer. I followed racing very closely, continuing to participate for several years in top races in the East, but I was rarely satisfied with my performance. I remember being fifth once in a slalom on the Taft slalom slope at Franconia and occasionally I placed tenth or eleventh in a downhill. I could enter a New York Interclub Race and win it, but I never deluded myself into thinking that this was a real accomplishment.

As a weekend skier only, I was pretty much of an outsider among the racers. For instance, I did not always have the best equipment. At Sun Valley I was skiing on a pair of laminated Splitkein skis which were almost indestructible, but which had no resiliency. Since I had no real pride in these skis, I did not take care of them. One day I was skiing down the top of Baldy, trying to go fast, on bottoms whose lacquer surface had worn down to bare wood. Walter Prager, my old coach, was watching me from the lift. The snow was quite wet, and as I crossed the shadows of the trees, I was alternately thrown backward and forward by the difference in the snow consistency. I was embarrassed that Walter should see me struggling awkwardly on unwaxed skis.

In 1948 I purchased a pair of Attenhofers with new plastic bottoms, modified ridgetops, a flexing action forward of the foot which gave a planing effect, and stiff tails which held well on hard snow. They were fast racing skis and helped me quite a bit in competition that winter. I was next talked into buying third hand from Peter Estin a pair of Northlands that were specially designed for Steve Knowlton for the 1950 F.I.S. Downhill. They were heavy, thick, 7-feet 3-inch skis with edges that were both offset and angled away from the Lucite bottoms. These skis wanted to go straight, and could only be turned easily when a speed of thirty miles per hour had been attained. However, I actually tried to use them in two slalom races, with a conspicuous lack of success.

Rapid changes were taking place in technique. For a while the Allais French style was the favorite, consisting of a forward driving action with the body, with the shoulders somewhat square to the skis, but still aiding the turn. This French technique was beautiful to watch when properly executed, but I never really had the opportunity to learn how to do it. Meanwhile the Austrians were at work on a new turn which was to become the accepted parallel turn for the whole world of organized skiing, from racers to ski schools. In its early form this technique was recognized more by certain style traits than by its basic movement. What stands out in my mind is the upright body position, with elbows bent and pointed outward, and the noninvolvement of the shoulders, with even a shoulder-duck or shoulder-reversing when running slalom gates. Through the years I had often skied with Austrians, particularly at Stowe, where each year the ski school imported some of the best-known racers and instructors. But a few scattered days of instruction each winter were not enough to convert me. Besides, in the early 1950's the Austrian technique had not quite evolved into the simplicity of the modern wedeln-type turn, with its reverse shoulder and body angulation. The net result for me was very little change from my prewar style of skiing. The youngsters coming along inevitably patterned their style after the best skiers on the hill, and I became aware that my style was old-fashioned.

For conditioning I did a little running each fall and a sparse selection of calisthenics. More important, once the season got under way, I skied almost every weekend of the winter, still managing on the few homebound weekends to go up for the day to the nearby Catskill resorts. Because of the endurance and basic strength still in my leg muscles, I could ski a regulation downhill with a 2,000-foot drop and a mile and a half course with sufficient reserve. However, the quickness of reaction was missing on tough bumps or sharp turns. It was hard to get used to going in races without a fine margin of control.

Moreover, I always compared myself to youngsters racing for college teams, rather than to other weekend skiers with family-job involvement, of whom there were few still racing. Admittedly I did hit the weekend circuit pretty hard, and some of my friends wondered if skiing wasn't continuing to dominate my life. The answer to that was that I have never once had an employer complain about my skiing. All days off have been on legitimate vacation time. However, it would not be quite honest to say that Barbara has never complained. With a growing family it was impossible for her to make every weekend jaunt, so in any given winter I had a good number of bachelor ski weekends. Even though she would occasionally chastise me for neglecting family responsibilities, she rarely stood in the way of a ski trip.

In 1952 I entered my last Eastern Alpine championship. The downhill took place on the Wildcat, the familiar trail where I had earned my A rating freshman year at Dartmouth. Barbara, who was expecting our second child within a week, had stayed behind in New Jersey. Sure enough, the baby was born on the morning of the downhill, actually before the race started. As a practical joke, Barbara toyed with the idea of trying to get the news to me at the top of the mountain before my run. But I was having lunch after the race at the Pinkham Notch hut when a telegram arrived announcing the birth of a second daughter, Gretchen. Ralph Miller, winner of the downhill and then a freshman at Dartmouth, was sitting across the table from me. He was highly amused to think that someone still racing could be the father of two children, and particularly that he would be racing the very day one of them was born. I called Barbara, and true to form, reminded her that I was supposed to go in the slalom the following day. In a firm tone she said, "No, you'll be visiting me in the hospital tomorrow."

Bungie King once said that for each child you add twelve seconds to your time in the downhill. With two more additions to the family in the next three years, for a total of three girls and one boy, I faced the prospect of racing the Wildcat or the Nose Dive with a 48-second penalty. This would have been more like an end-of-the-day run than a racing effort.

Fortunately a new category was being started—the veterans' racing class. There was some experimentation with the age bracket. At first it was for skiers thirty-two and over, and when I became thirty-two it was raised to thirty-five. A few years after I reached thirty-five it was lowered to thirty-two. Today the starting age for veterans is twenty-seven, the theory being that a few years after a racer leaves college, he soon settles back to the same plateau where most of the better veterans find themselves. Veteran competition opened up a whole new horizon for me, and in a chapter yet to come we shall discuss the fun of this racing circuit.

10

Racer on the Course

In any sport in which performance can be measured in units, such as time or distance, a participant can compare himself directly with the world's best. In skiing the discrepancy is probably greater between the intermediate and the Olympian than in any other sport. In golf, for example, an intermediate player having a good day might shoot a 90 at Pebble Beach, while Jack Nicklaus in a tournament might have a 69. On the famous Stratofana race course at Cortina in Italy, a race might be won by Karl Schranz in under 2 minutes and 40 seconds. To put an intermediate skier on a 2-mile course as difficult as this would be sheer folly. To ski it no-stop no-fall he would have to be at the peak of condition. Then, fighting speed all the way, and zigzagging all over the course, he probably could not get down in less than twelve minutes, which would be four times as long as Schranz's run. The intermediate skier, if he could accomplish this, would be extremely proud of himself, and yet he would be nowhere as close to the champion as the intermediate golfer was.

This gap can be narrowed if skiers know more about the racer, his equipment, his conditioning, the way he thinks, and the way he skis. Even the newcomer to the sport should know something about the racer. The novice must concern himself with kick turns, the snowplow, and the correct way to fall and get up, but he will soon leave these basic matters behind. Only by knowing the racer can the average skier set his standards. After all, in golf the par figures for a course give the player something to strive for. There is much in a racer's form which applies to all skiing. For instance, the hotshot on a steep slope, going fast, knows exactly where he is, while the average skier is lost among the moguls. However, it is of greatest importance to remember that skiing is the most imitative of sports. A skier should pattern himself not just after an expert on the hill or a graceful instructor, but after the international-class racer.

We should therefore take a close look at the racer and some of his outstanding characteristics. Physically he is in a state of conditioning comparable only to the Olympic-caliber track and field man. Keeping in shape is a year-round necessity for him. A racer like Billy Kidd does calisthenics every day, and he fills in with all sorts of other activities such as road work, mountain climbing, bicycling, and running through a forest dodging trees as if they were slalom poles. When the racer steps on skis at the beginning of the season, even if he missed the summer skiing south of the equator or at a ski camp out West, he is still in far better shape than the average skier is at the peak of his midwinter form.

The racer's first day on the boards is apt to consist of a whole morning's session of slalom running, followed by open slope skiing, where he skis the entire mountain in nonstop style, making giant slalom turns all the way. In the early weeks of a racing season he is most pleased with himself after a leg-burning session, during which he holds a full egg-position crouch on the longest route down the mountain, for he knows that sore, aching muscles are a step toward toughness and stamina.

As he approaches top form he is inwardly obsessed with the power in his leg muscles, conscious as he skates off to a start that he has a reserve of power sufficient to face any of racing's challenges.

His lungs are so good that he is seldom very short of breath. And at the top of the steepest slope, he shrugs his shoulders and arches his back, realizing that even the strength in his back muscles helps him relax about the prospect of a fast run.

His pride in his ski equipment is also very personal. His skis, bindings, boots, poles, and even his clothing have been selected with great care. His skis, which are probably on loan from a ski manufacturing company, may only have been used a half-dozen times, and yet they are tuned up with a file and waxed each day. Before a race this filing and waxing procedure may require two hours. Since skis today are so specialized, he will change his skis each time he shifts from slalom running to giant slalom or downhill. In the matter of clothing the racer can be building his ego step by step as he dresses himself, convincing himself that there is even something special about his long underwear and socks.

For when the racer is on the hill, he has the impression that he, his skis, and his clothing all combine to create one animate being pitted against the mountain. Skiing generally is an individual sport, far more personal than almost any other, and racing is the loneliest sport of all. The skier has only his wits, his well-tuned muscles, and his equipment to meet the challenge of the course. The skis are responsive to the skier both because of the leather-to-leather union made possible by the long-thong binding wrapped around a tight-fitting armor-plated boot, and because of the skier's familiarity with the feeling of 210 centimeters of ski under his foot. He feels as light on his feet as if he had on a good-fitting pair of sneakers. There is a sense of lightness, too, about his snug racing tights and jacket with knitted stretch inserts. The only bulk is his crash helmet, which he has come to accept as part of the equipment needed to face the mountain.

A hotshot racer can be spotted by his ease of movement, sometimes by the manner in which he springs out of a car in the parking lot, often by the way he briskly straps himself into his long-thong bindings, then skates over to the lift line in one graceful gliding motion, and always by the way he carves his turns on the hill.

When the racer is practicing slalom endlessly hour after hour, he tries to imagine himself in a race as he hesitates a few seconds before starting down through the gates. With a sparkle in his eye and a look of excitement on his face, he begins only when he is ready to attack the practice course. When practicing for a downhill, he does not need to prod his nervous system. There is such a methodical buildup toward speed that in the final practice run there is the fullest feeling of exhilaration. Even skiing the mountain for fun does not permit the luxury of skiing without an objective. The more difficult the conditions the more aggressively he skis, and the more fun he is to watch. As he makes the first couple of runs on the most dangerous trail on the mountain, he will work out a plan for mastering the most difficult sections on a later run. Sometimes he will spontaneously take an unbelievably steep section straight, and at the bottom test his acrobatic powers by making a sharp fast turn over bumpy terrain.

I remember well the most spectacular open slope skiing I have ever seen. In January of 1955 I was skiing down the National Trail at Stowe, a steep 100-yard-wide swath down the side of the mountain. As I stopped, just below the intersection with the Lift Line, I saw a skier go by, skiing fast in long swings. There was something unmistakable about his style. What I was looking at was my first view of the new so-called international racing technique. As the skier went on, he was always upright, his hips seeming to be a pivot point. In his turns he was in a comma position, with the drive in his feet and knees, his upper body pointed down the hill, and his shoulders and hips seeming to move counter to the direction of the turn. It was smooth, fast skiing in a superb-looking style. This skier continued on down about three eighths of a mile, stopping at the top of the last long pitch where the National joins the Nose Dive. I skied down after him, and as I got near recognized Tom Corcoran. I congratulated him on his smooth run and asked where he had picked up his new look. Before he could answer, another skier standing nearby shouted, "By God, here he comes." Even before looking up I knew that it was Chick Igaya, Dartmouth sophomore from Japan and one of the world's leading slalom specialists, who was on the hill that day.

He existed as a black dot, skiing fast under the lift. Instinctively we moved off to one side of the trail, waiting at the top of the pitch. This was our signal to Igaya that the slope below was clear, and that we expected a good show. If Corcoran had been going at forty miles an hour, Igaya was going fifty, which is dangerously fast skiing over an unprepared course. As he approached he did not slow down, made a half turn at the top of the pitch, and took it mostly airborne in a long steep traverse to the left, touching only the tops of the bumps. The sound of the air rushing by his body as well as the sound of his skis slapping the crests of the bumps dramatized the speed of his schuss. At the bottom near the woods on the left he made a right turn in three or four inches of untracked snow and continued straight on down the last pitches of the Nose Dive. The group of bystanders were not disappointed; most spellbound of all was Corcoran, white as a sheet because of what he had just seen. Corcoran, after all, was the caliber of skier who should be able to equal anything Igaya had done, but he was not at all sure he wanted to duplicate this mad performance.

When all of us had recovered from the shock, we skied down the slope, examining Igaya's tracks. They were interrupted, 18-inch, single-skilike sections on the crests of the bumps, sometimes forty feet apart, marking his path down the schuss.

Two years later I met this bright Nipponese skier at cocktails one afternoon at Top Notch in Stowe. I told him that just once I had seen him ski when he seemed to be going fast even for Igaya, and described the run for him. He remembered it right away, and admitted that he was plenty scared. Igaya was never a first-rate downhill skier, more because of his small size and slight build than because of any lack of personal courage, and must have been trying to prove something to himself when he made that inspired run.

The racer's entire drive is focused on preparing himself for proficiency in the art of racing. As much as he loves to ski and to be in the ski country, the real sweetness of life is victory. The sense of attainment is unbelievably high for the racer who has faced up to his fears, worked out a plan of attack, and then put together a medal-winning performance.

One of the most marked differences between the recreational skier and the racer is in mental attitude. If the racer has an edge in conditioning he has an even greater advantage in mental toughness. The average skier, worrying too much about the physical challenges of skiing, seems unable to think his way through these challenges. The racer knows that unless he has prepared his mind for the mastery of the mountain, all of his training and practice will have been in vain.

In the end the racer conquers his nervousnes, even making it work for him. The loneliest moment in the lonely sport of racing is the prerace jitters period. This is the part of racing that no one likes and everyone wants to get through as quickly as possible. There is no way for the outsider to reach the racer when he is alone with his thoughts. He is absolutely incommunicado. If he speaks it is only by reflex, for his mind is at work trying to think positively about the race ahead. The skier knows that the only information useful to him would be new revelations about the state of the course. Yet he is leery of revising his plan because of information passed along to him secondhand. Experience tells him that he can rely only on what he has seen for himself. Nor is he in any mood to be mollycoddled by well-meaning friends. He knows that only self-control can keep his nerves calm enough to provide split-second reflexes and skilled judgment. Yet he must never be so relaxed that he loses the benefit of his fighting spirit.

Perhaps the skier's most important sustenance during his hour of prerace trial is his ego. It is characteristic of racers to have tremendous inner confidence. The better the racer the more boundless his ego. It is a reflective, somewhat introverted ego rather than the boastful kind, but it can be disdainful of competitors and not above gamesmanship. Sometimes the racer will take great delight in exhibiting to others what he can do best, such as holding a sharp hairpin on a steep icy slope. Or he will talk calmly about an airplane turn on a downhill course that his fellow racers are worried about. He knows too that he must be able to put his competition into perspective, and that his only problem is to ski right up to the outer edge of his ability. If he can truly be master of his own destiny he knows that he can win the race.

To comprehend fully the way the racer must discipline his mind for the contest, one should review each of the three Alpine events. For all three, the racer tries to control his worries and have his equipment in readiness several days ahead. Since the three events are all quite different, some racers ski better in one than in another. Certainly the racer must prepare himself for each event in slightly different ways.

For the downhill he actually has more than a day to develop his plan in full. In this event the skier is permitted, even required, to run the entire course in a nonstop full-speed fashion. The usual procedure is first to run the course in sections and to get the feel of the slope and the turns, and to adjust to the speed of the course. The objective naturally is for the racer to work out a plan so precise that he can ski as if following a 12-inch-wide painted stripe all the way down the course, leaving it only when airborne.

The downhill, by Olympic standards, must show a vertical drop of 2,468 feet. Often the drop will be more like 3,000 feet over a distance of approximately two miles. The average speed is usually over fifty miles per hour. Strangely enough some of the easiest courses are the fastest.

To win a downhill the racer must be able to concentrate on his profile and try to hold the French egg position throughout. At speeds over sixty miles an hour, a wind check, standing upright with arms outstretched, can reduce speed by one-third within a short distance. Turning at such speeds is no problem; only a slight shift of weight to one ski is sufficient to produce a change of direction. There is no need for pronounced weighting and unweighting, heel thrust, or body angulation. The faster the speed, the easier it is to start the turn, but at high speed the real skill, as with any turn, is to hold it and finish it properly. The racer's problem in the turn, as well as on the straight stretches, is to ride his skis with his weight properly positioned. Even on sharp turns there is no full commitment to the turn, because the skier never knows when a sudden jolt will throw him off balance.

At the top of the course the racer has to make his mind believe in the plan that he has made, and to direct his body to carry it out. The racer does not dare think in terms of a fall, let alone of a crash. He knows that he has already faced all the real challenges of the course in his final practice run, when his mind came to grips with any imagined dangers. Positive thinking has now taken over and the skier is ready for speeds of sixty to seventy miles an hour, bumps, pitches, and tricky turns.

From watching the forerunners and the first few skiers on the course the racer can sometimes, for the few seconds that they are in sight, estimate snow conditions on the parts of the course, farther down, which are unseen. Also, after starting he immediately gets a feel of the course which transmits important information about how fast and how icy it is going to be. As he "finds himself," on his first few somewhat deliberate turns, his mind races ahead to what is approaching. His eyes look down the course to a point as far ahead as he can see. He seeks speed, he wants speed, and he feels that his pace is too slow. He wants to be farther down the course, up front where his thoughts are. His muscles are resilient and his legs work with ease over small bumps. Generally, his reflexes take care of what is at hand, while his mind is concerned with what is ahead. He has the poise to hold his egg shape when airborne, reaching for the ground only at the last second. Where a prejump is necessary his timing is precise, so as to avoid a long flight curve. In a troublesome section he forgets his egg shape and rides it out, avoiding checking while making a recovery, avoiding it completely if he can. In places where he has planned to check he does it quickly and effectively, rather than gradually and halfheartedly.

He knows above all that most races are won in the flat sections, and he enters such parts of the course with great care from the highest possible line. Attuned to the way his skis are tracking, he keeps them flat and riding easily. He is ready at all times for trouble, and takes acrobatic recoveries very much in stride. He concentrates more than anything else on keeping low, well over his skis, and avoiding a fall. At such speeds the avoidance of a fall is paramount. He knows, too, that a fall can happen anywhere—often more likely to occur in a safe place than at one of the trail's danger points. His mind never relaxes its grip, and is not blurred by the way the trees go by. He knows precisely where he is and what he is doing every second, even when he is flying off blind drop-offs. He permits his concentration to relax only as he crosses the finish line; he knows then that he has skied a no-fall run. Sometimes, too, he has skied the course so well that he senses he will be the winner.

In the slalom it is not very often that the course is set the day before the race. Even when the course is available, the racer looks it over somewhat casually, for his mind is trained to study it the morning of the race. The slalom must, however, be studied with utmost care. If downhill racing requires a dogged concentration, slalom requires a keen concentration. The good slalom runner inevitably knows his course so well that he mentally runs through it several times before the race, and for weeks later he can remember the exact configurations of the gates and the colors of the flags.

The slalom, by Olympic standards, must have a drop of 617 feet and include generally over sixty gates, with the flags set apart by a uniform distance. Of all the three events, the slalom requires the greatest practice and the highest proficiency in technique. The racer must ski with rhythm, both as a function of his style and of the way the course has been set. When the racer can watch a forerunner ski most of the course he has an opportunity to adapt his prearranged plan to unanticipated peculiarities of the course. As the racer approaches the starting gate, his nervousnes, although different from what it was before the downhill, is just as intense, for in some ways he will need even more judgment than in the downhill, particularly since he will be skiing the course for the first time. Ideally, when the racer is on the course he can sense the rhythm the course setter had in mind. A tight slalom in the fall line can sometimes remind one of the cohesiveness of a Mozart composition. From just skiing the first few gates, the racer can catch the rhythm for the entire run. In the 1960 Olympic slalom at Squaw Valley, Ernst Hinterseer, the Austrian gold medal winner, was mentally three or four gates ahead of himself all the way down the course. Every good slalom runner always knows where he is and completes his turns early.

If a downhill is often won on the flats a slalom is sometimes won in the fairly easy open gates which require sweeping turns and enable the racer to pick up speed. Yet it is the closed gates and hairpins that test precision slalom skiing. In the flush the skier is engaged in disciplined wedeln skiing, generally opening up on speed for the last few gates of the flush. The technique of the slalom racer is very much in evidence in a good run. The speed, the adeptness, the anticipatory work with the poles, with both hands generally ahead in readiness for setting up the turn, are admirable to watch.

Perhaps of all the slalom racer's tools the most effective is the edge check, which allows him at all times to be on the fastest possible line and yet to hold back speed where necessary. But to win slalom races, the racer must ski beyond the point of control. He has trained himself to do this, and he is skilled in scrambling, always driving forward down the course. His style is that of the modern parallel turn. His feet are apt to be fairly close together, his body position is the comma, his driving knees and feet reflect heel thrust, and as he ducks slalom poles, his shoulders neatly reverse. He works hard every inch of the way, but rarely loses his rhythm. The winner generally has the mark of a champion all the way. Even when he falters he recovers quickly, and he makes the spectators think that no one in the world could have gotten more speed out of the course.

A giant slalom is sometimes erroneously compared to a downhill, being thought of as a controlled downhill race. Certainly in its inception it was an attempt to provide a truly safe downhill. Today the giant slalom is as unique as either the downhill or the slalom. However, it does remain safer by far than either the downhill or the slalom. Since in the giant slalom the racer rarely goes over thirty miles per hour, speed in itself is no hazard. In the slalom, speed is about fifteen miles per hour, but on a relative basis speed is high in proportion to tight intricate holding turns, and racers can get hurt when they "crash and burn" and catch their ski tips on slalom poles in awkward ways.

The giant slalom is laid out in graceful sweeping turns. Unlike the slalom, which gets its rhythm from the course setter, who imposes the order of the flags on the contour of the hill, the giant slalom is laid out in such a way that it accedes to the contour of the mountain. A good giant slalom course is thus very much an outgrowth of a steep, variable, interesting slope.

The vertical drop, by Olympic requirements, is 1,234 feet, but more often it is something like 1,600 feet over a length of about a mile. There are thirty to fifty gates, most of which are open—that is, laid out at right angles to the fall line rather than parallel to it.

In the giant slalom each turn must be accomplished with a carving action. Merely to ski a smooth race and hold the best line is not enough. The skier must work, poling constantly, sometimes finishing a turn on an inside ski to hold the highest possible line, sometimes skiing for the next gate in the classic manner for a high turn well above the gate, sometimes desperately heading straight for the gate and at the last minute stepping up to the high line and making the turn on one ski. The skier goes from one turn to the next without any respite, yet occasionally for only a second he will go back into the egg-shaped position. Because of the changes in the contour of the slope each gate must be skied in a slightly different way, and the skier must be adaptable, adjusting his style to each turn. Sometimes on a banked downhill turn, he lets gravity do the work for him.

The giant slalom requires a higher state of conditioning than either of the other two events. It is a long race—in terms of time usually as long as the downhill. There are no breathing spells, for the racer works hard to accelerate his speed each second he is on the course. The giant slalom is a tremendous test of natural ability, and now and then the event will be won by a relative newcomer to the sport, like ex-hockey player Roger Staub, who won a gold medal in 1960 at Squaw Valley. The giant slalom after all is the only completely unrehearsed event, the downhill run being worked out with care and precision by skiing the actual course, and the slalom run being rehearsed in the sense that a winning performance is the result of interminable practice sessions which have given the racer the confidence and skill necessary for victory. The victor in the giant slalom may therefore be a more natural athlete than the winners of the other two events.

As previously mentioned, the skis required for these three events are highly specialized. Since the French downhill victories on Rossignol metallics at Squaw, led by Jean Vuarnet, the metal ski has been supreme in downhill racing. Prior to that time the metal ski was the exclusive property of the recreational skier, as none of its forms had the holding power on turns necessary for racing. The modern downhill ski, a fairly heavy, stiff metal ski that is slightly longer than the standard ski, has good holding and fantastic tracking power. It rides bumps well, flexing forward of the foot in an almost sinuous manner. It is a wide ski with very little taper under the foot. And like all racing skis, it has a fast polyethylene-type running surface with narrow hidden edges.

The giant slalom ski, of metal or fiber glass, is not as stiff as the downhill ski. It has more flexibility and camber, and narrows somewhat under the foot. An average size skier might use a 220-centimeter length in the downhill, 210 in the giant slalom, and 205 in the slalom.

For the slalom, the laminated wood ski has recently been replaced by fiber glass. A slalom ski must react quickly and have tremendous holding power. A stiff, narrow ski, it tapers in a fairly pronounced way under the foot so that the minute the skier goes to his edges, the curvature of the side of the ski puts him in a turn. Its stiffness is mainly in the shovel and tail, for it flexes fairly easily in its middle section. On sharp bumps the slalom ski can be a liability, as the stiffness in the tip gives it a tendency to ram into a bump instead of riding over it.

After studying the physical and mental makeup of the racer, as well as the three Alpine racing events, the skier should also know something about the great racers of all time. Earlier in the book we have seen how Dick Durrance, the finest American racer of the prewar era of skiing, dramatized the sport and attracted newcomers to it.

More recently, Buddy Werner was America's outstanding skier. I never knew Buddy personally, and yet I knew him the way several million American skiers did—through his warm friendly smile and his unblemished good sportsmanship. On several occasions at Stowe he smiled directly at me as if I were an old friend. Buddy Werner, as the leading Alpine skier from his country, felt the whole weight of national honor resting on his shoulders. In a country like Austria, any one of the team of four skiers was good enough to win an international event. Buddy was absolutely fearless and pushed himself beyond the margin of control. Skiing the fastest line in the fastest possible way, he pioneered the use of the flat ski at high speeds. Often he rode with his weight back to make his skis plane more and go faster. In countless races Buddy

Werner was the fastest man on the course up to a certain point. What happened then is well known; sometimes his spill was a dramatic eggbeater that put him completely out of the running; occasionally he would make one of his famous recoveries—even bouncing back on his feet after somersaults. In the 1958 F.I.S. Downhill at Bad Gastein, after a fall in which he lost a ski, he made a sensational finish, coming down the last schuss on one ski, water-skiing style. When he did stand up, he usually would win over the best skiers in the world. Among his victories on the European circuit were the Grand Prix de Chamonix Downhill in 1956, the Lauberhorn Combined in 1958, and the Hahnenkamm Downhill in 1959. His victories in this country are too numerous to mention.

The last time I saw him ski was in the post-Olympic races at Stowe in 1964. In his last practice run for the downhill at the fastest point of the course, going down the Corridor on the Nose Dive, he purposely took off on a bump and gave a cry of exhilaration. On the following day I watched him win the slalom quite handily, beating Olympic medal winners Billy Kidd and Jimmy Heuga. Buddy Werner will never be forgotten, his style and the dramatic sadness of his death in an avalanche accident assuring him an eternal place in our hearts.

America has not produced a champion of worldwide renown. The great skiers of all time are the three who have been double winners in either Olympic or F.I.S. world championships, and the two who were triple winners. These five skiers are also the most exciting ones. The double winners are the Frenchman Emile Allais, the Italian Zeno Colo, the Norwegian Stein Ericksen, and triple winners are the Austrian Toni Sailer and another Frenchman, Jean-Claude Killy.

The name of Allais has been important on the ski scene for over thirty years. Allais looks like a Frenchman, or at least like a handsome continental. He is the first double winner of the F.I.S., which predates the Olympics, going back to the first official championship of 1931. Allais won the downhill at Chamonix in 1937 on his home course by the remarkable edge of 13 seconds, in the winning time of 4 minutes 3.4 seconds. He went into his second run of the slalom with such a tremendous margin that all he had to do was stand up to be assured of the combined world title. Not only did he stay on his skis, but true champion that he was, turned in the best time recorded for that run, and won the slalom in addition to the downhill and combined. Since there was no giant slalom event that year, his victory, like Sailer's in 1956 and Killy's in 1968, was a clean sweep. He went on to win the 1937 Arlberg Kandahar, the oldest of the Alpine championships, dating back to 1928, and usually considered the unofficial world's championship in years when the F.I.S. or Olympics are not held. The following year he won the combined in the F.I.S., which was held at Engelberg in Switzerland.

Allais, more than any other great skier, has been personally identified with a system of teaching. He was an originator as well as the prime mover of the French style of skiing. As we have seen, this method of skiing, like the Arlberg, was based upon rotation, yet it was a refinement, with minimum counterswing and the outside shoulder driving onto the downhill ski but remaining almost square to the ski. There were innovations with the French style, too, such as the ruade or heel-lift—an extremely useful way of making a quick turn on a steep slope—and the first streamlined schuss position, with the upper body bent over and the hands and poles held behind the back, almost like the position of a swimmer's racing start, except that the hands are close together.

Allais may have been the first racer to perfect the prejumping technique, so important in the modern downhill. Sir Arnold Lunn, writing in the British Ski Year Book about the Arlberg Kandahar at Murren, Switzerland, in 1937, says, "It was most interesting watching him take the big bumps on what is now known as Bob-Run Slope. He seemed to give a little jump before getting to the bump, instead of allowing the bump to throw him into the air."

Allais also deserves credit for leading the battle against the stem. His excellent book, *Méthode Française de Ski Technique,* published in 1947, just as the French technique was becoming the most talked about style of skiing, does not show one picture of the stem until page 87. There is then one illustration of Allais looking very unhappy demonstrating the snowplow as a braking maneuver, and on the following page pictures of the full snowplow turn. Much to his credit, there are no other pictures of the stem in any of its forms. He thereby denies the existence of the stem turn and the stem christie as necessary steps toward correct parallel skiing.

The best French racers have usually skied with grace and verve, Allais more than any of them. He was the American Olympic coach at Oslo in 1952, and some of the members of that team think he was the greatest racing coach we have ever had. He was so much of a racer himself that he easily earned their respect. Sometimes when the boys were practicing for the downhill, hurtling along at top speed, Allais would surprise them by pulling alongside and shouting some bit of advice. When Allais was down at Portillo in Chile during the summer of 1952, he was observed skiing according to the new Austrian method, while his compatriots in the ski school still skied the French way. He was not one to ignore a good thing when he saw it, even if he had to turn his back on the style he initiated. Among his many accomplishments was his success in convincing the French government to start a ski resort at Courchevel, now one of the leading ski areas in the Alps. Even today it is a rare treat to watch the great Allais on skis.

Zeno Colo has also won his share of titles, twice winning the Arlberg Kandahar, winning the Olympic downhill at Oslo in 1952, besides winning both the downhill and giant slalom F.I.S. events at Aspen in 1950. Colo was known as the Italian woodchopper. During World War II, he had been interned at Murren, where he developed into a championship skier. However, there was not a trace of the Swiss style in his way of skiing. His style was his own. In a crouch with his feet apart and both hands forward at all times, he was very much forward over his skis. Looking somewhat like a defensive guard plunging across the scrimmage line, he did not have a really graceful basic position, yet in motion he was so light and rhythmic that he was still graceful.

The men's downhill at Aspen in 1950 was held on the Spar Gulch run, which for that era was a tremendous test. The first schuss down into Spar Gulch over crosswaves and humps was enough to scare even the most seasoned racers. Then there was a series of dams to be prejumped, a tricky transition featuring a sharp S turn from the left to the right side of Spar Gulch, and an exceptionally difficult spot across the V center of the gulch. On the right bank of the gulch there was a punishing washboard section, created by the racers sideslipping on hard snow in their practice runs. Then there was a fairly easy stretch along the center line of the gulch. Near the end of the course there was a dramatic drop-off coming after a high-speed catwalk which bent gradually to the left around the shoulder of the mountain. The drop-off was called Niagara. As the skiers sailed off the end of the catwalk, it was as if they were being shot from a gun. At the bottom of Niagara there was a difficult turn to the left on the flats and a schuss across bumpy terrain to the finish.

The course was a nemesis for four out of the five Americans, with only George Macomber running without a fall, and tying for twenty-first. The most famed racer to come to grief was Henri Oreiller, nicknamed "Hank O'Reilly," the Olympic Gold Medal winner of the 1948 downhill, who missed his prejump at the dam in the upper Spar Gulch just below Tourtelotte Park. Some bystanders swore that he cleared 180 feet before landing in a tangle. Future world champion Stein Eriksen spilled twice, and the great Canadian downhiller Ernie McCulloch was also upended. Among the more notable airborne accomplishments was that of the young Austrian Christian Pravda, who after being a little off in his timing at Niagara soared for about one hundred feet, holding his skis together in flight like a jumper, and landing with the ease of a cat dropping out of a tree.

Colo ran fast and steady. On the Spar Gulch dams he had near-perfect timing on his prejumps, and stayed very much on the ground. He also had very little air under his skis at the difficult S turn from the left to right side of Spar Gulch, and went into his two turns without any noticeable skidding. True to his style he was low on his skis all the way. Just before going off Niagara he went into a momentary full snowplow, and accomplished the difficult drop-off without faltering. Farther down he allowed himself the luxury of soaring off the road crossing the last pitch. His winning time was 2 minutes 34.4 seconds, more than a full second ahead of the great French veteran, James Couttet, who had won the F.I.S. Downhill in 1938. Colo's average speed over the difficult course was fifty-three miles per hour.

The giant slalom at Aspen was laid out by Dick Durrance over some of the same terrain as the downhill. One of the most difficult spots was again the treacherous lip at the end of the catwalk. The course was Zeno Colo's meat and he won handily.

In the 1952 Olympics in Norway Colo is reputed to have tried the downhill course only once and then gone back to Oslo. Needless to say he still won, beating slalom champion Othmar Schneider by 1.2 seconds. There was one very difficult fallaway turn, and Colo was the only one to take this on the correct line, his skis never leaving the snow. Zeno Colo then retired from international racing at the age of thirty-three. He was definitely the hero of downhill races, and also won his share of slaloms. Downhill skiers generally are better at slalom than slalom specialists are at downhill racing. Personable and colorful, Colo was always a popular figure, and a great sportsman with a minimum amount of show-off.

Stein Eriksen today is known as the great stylist, perhaps the most impressive-looking man on skis. You hear the expression over and over again, "Nobody skis like Stein." He was probably the first man to ski slalom with the reverse-shoulder style. During practice for the 1950 F.I.S. at Aspen his style was a revelation to all racers, including the Austrians. Yet his magnificent form was taken more as a personal idiosyncrasy than as a new style of skiing applicable to racers and recreational skiers. In his own country at one time he was considered a maverick—actually somewhat ridiculed because he worked incessantly at his "idiotic" style, even skiing at night under lights outside of Oslo. His countrymen wanted him to stand up in races and his new style seemed to give him an unsteadiness. He had more success perfecting his famed forward somersault on skis, as well as his acrobatic feats on the trampoline, for which he attained early recognition.

In 1952 Stein proved the merits of his style when he won a gold medal for Norway in the giant slalom. In the 1954 F.I.S. at Aare, Sweden, he became the undisputed champion of the world by winning the slalom, giant slalom, then nearly taking the downhill, where a quick spill robbed him of victory. The gold medal in this race went to Christian Pravda. Stein won the combined event by a wide margin.

The key aspect of Stein's skiing is the tremendous amount of reserve power he has throughout the turn. His shoulders go to fully reversed position and the hips are the pivotal point, with the upper body in comma position like a poised counterweight. Stein's long sweeping turns are surely the most beautiful sight in skiing. No matter how bumpy or icy the slope, Stein, refusing to accede to difficult conditions, still does the same high-speed sweeping turns. He has been nothing short of inspirational, drawing newcomers to the sport in droves, and spurring veterans on to more graceful efforts.

A spectacularly handsome man, Stein is one of skiing's best-dressed and most glamorous figures. He has been the director of several ski schools, which always have had well-organized, well-balanced classes. As a teacher he manages to be all over the mountain, so that each person feels he is getting some attention. He is particularly good with children, aware of the thrill they get from talking to him. During the East's meager winter of 1965 before Stein took over at Snowmass, there were two big attractions for Sunday afternoons at Sugarbush. One was Stein's exhibition somersault; the other was a slalom race in which Stein pitted himself against all comers. In the race anyone coming within 5 seconds of Stein was to be given a medal. The average length of the slalom was 30 seconds, yet no one came very near him. Only one medal was awarded—to one of his ski instructors, a Frenchman who had been trying to beat him all winter. On some runs on the ice prevailing that winter, Stein looked as if he were endowed with supernatural powers.

Toni Sailer's claim to skiing greatness is well established. This man was nothing short of a genius on skis. His triple win at Cortina in 1956 is what he is rightfully remembered for. Almost forgotten, however, is his double victory in the 1958 F.I.S. at Bad Gastein, where he won the downhill and the giant slalom. He took second in the slalom, and of course won the three-way combined by a big margin. In his last two years of competition he was virtually unbeatable in the giant slalom, his outstanding event.

It is significant that Toni was so good at giant slalom. His fantastic athletic ability and his adaptable style made him an absolute demon in the race. Pictures show him responding to various gates in different ways, but he was always like a tiger, forward on his skis, beautifully balanced, and ready for anything. If there was something striking about the way he stood on his skis, there was something even more notable about the expression on his face. Toni always looked as if he were enjoying himself, almost as if he were playing touch football. Certainly no somber serious champion, he fully understood that to win he must be relaxed enough so that his entire body would react to the skis, the slope, and the speed of the course. Toni's reflexes were always keen, and his ability to recover from a near fall in the downhill often left spectators breathless.

No discussion of Toni Sailer would be complete without reviewing his accomplishments at Cortina. Injuries had prevented Toni from qualifying for the 1954 F.I.S. at Aare, Sweden, but he went into the 1956 Winter Olympics at the top of his form. He was already the record holder on the difficult Stratofana downhill, which was to be the course for the Olympic downhill. Fortunately for him, the first race scheduled was the giant slalom, a race he knew to be his best event, since the previous year he had won five out of the eight that he entered.

Toni raced eighteenth, and before his turn came, his three other Austrian teammates had preceded him with good times, Molterer and Hinterseer holding first and second best times. So when Toni went down the course, an exceptionally long sixty-gate giant slalom, he was able to ski without any special pressure either to take risks or to have a no-fall run. His time was incredible—3:00.1—against the great Anderl Molterer in second place at 3:06.3.

In the slalom the conditions could not have been more difficult. The two courses, one set by President Otto Menardi of the F.I.S., and the other by Fred Roessner, involved a total of 178 gates set on a steep slope, the Col Druscie. This slope had been sprayed with water for several days to freeze it, but it had frozen in varying degrees, with the surface in some places consisting of rough lumps of ice. On top of this, the weather was foggy the day of the race, and the racers could only see a few gates ahead. To give some idea of how tough conditions were, the three first Austrians to go down the course, Josl Rieder, Anderl Molterer, and Othmar Schenider, each easily among the best ten slalom skiers in the world, all fell on their first run. This time the pressure should have been on Toni, but as was his custom he skied according to his plan. He raced magnificently and finished in 1:27.3, the best time—two-tenths of a second ahead of the French Adrien Duvillard, and three-tenths of a second ahead of American Brookie Dodge.

Toni studied the second course, a ninety-two-gate slalom, with great care. It was faster than the Menardi slalom, but had several critical spots, including one dangerous hairpin turn. He had three and a half hours before the second run started, and he used them well. At the start, according to Toni, about twenty people gave him advice, and although he pretended to listen with interest, he had already decided how to ski the second slalom and made no change in his overall plan. He won the second run, too, ending up with 1:47.4, with Chick Igaya, Japanese slalom star, second at 1:48.5. Igaya was also second for the two runs, but he was over 4 seconds behind Toni.

The downhill, like the slalom, was run under the most adverse conditions. The course was icy and dangerous, strong winds had blown the snow in drifted stretches, and this snow, although dry, had a heavy consistency that was difficult to wax for. The weather was bad, too, with the temperature a few hours before the start between nine and eighteen degrees below zero at various places on the course. And there was a wind storm, with gusts coming from all directions. Toni and his teammate Anderl Molterer decided that the race would be won by skiing with care and that the winning time would be well over Toni's record of 2:46.2. The combination of ice and drifted snow, coupled with fearful moguls on the last quarter-mile corrugated section above the finish, would make it difficult for any racer to ski without falling. This time Toni was slated to be the third Austrian to go down the course, with Rieder wearing number 2 and Schuster number 8. Toni's starting number was 14, and before his turn word reached him that Austria was in trouble again, with both Rieder and Schuster having fallen. Just as number 9 went into the starting gate, Toni broke a strap while getting into his long-thong bindings. There was some scurrying around; the Austrian coach did not have an extra strap, and finally the coach of the Italian team gave him the strap from his own binding. This experience might have upset a lesser man, but again Toni knew how the mountain should be skied that day, and he was prepared for the challenge.

The start of the Stratofana course is on a 45-degree schuss between two mammoth rock towers. Toni skied the entire course with good judgment, getting all the speed he could out of most sections, and skillfully checking at the danger spots. There was a perilous iced path crossing the course, and he checked carefully before this spot. On the final corrugated stretch he was filmed rebounding from one ski to the other, as if fighting for his balance. Incredibly, he never fell. Toni's winning time was 2:52.2—6 seconds more than his 1955 record. Molterer also had an excellent run, turning in 2:56.3 for a bronze medal. Toni's third gold medal was certainly won under the most dangerous and difficult conditions. Out of ninety runners only seventeen finished the course without falling, and what was even more staggering, among the top twenty-five seeded racers, nineteen crashed.

So Toni did what no one else had done by winning all three Alpine events in world competition. Since the speed of the slalom has increased to the point where in order to win a racer must go beyond the brink of control, fate plays an increasing role, and the trend in this event is away from dominance by one skier.

I saw Toni ski at Stowe several times. In 1956, a few weeks after Cortina, I was up at the Octagon just before the start of the International Downhill. The faces of the ring of racers around the fire in the center of the room looked as grim as usual before a downhill. Suddenly the twin swinging inner doors burst open and in walked Toni. With all eyes in the room on him, he stamped his feet to shake off the snow with such confidence, such exuberance, that he reminded me of a flamenco dancer. Another year I watched him study a giant slalom course at Stowe, and again I could sense the tremendous assurance of the man.

Surely Toni knew all there is to know about how the mind must master the physical challenges of skiing. He could look at a course and relate it to the way it would be as he skied down. His poise while racing was evidence that he completely understood the course. If it might be said that he made no great contribution to technique, it should also be stated that he was at all times trying to be himself. He was not absorbed in technique, either his own or anyone else's. Most racers are so concerned with trying to put themselves in a technique mold, so worried about keeping up with the advancement of the sport, that they never find themselves.

Toni liked being the world's best skier. As a well-tanned handsome idol of the crowd, he enjoyed in every way being Toni Sailer. And he was the first to have a triple Olympic victory.

Of course, at Grenoble, in 1968, Sailer's feat was repeated by Jean-Claude Killy. And what manner of man, or superman is Killy?

Like Sailer, Killy was raised in ski country, where he learned to ski as a toddler off the roof of his house in Val d'Isère. Like Sailer, he became a hero of the whole ski world, but even more than Sailer, Killy is a hero among nonskiers too, especially among young people, who consider him a "cool guy." Large for a racer and certainly for a Frenchman, Killy is almost six feet tall and weighs 170 pounds. His neatly groomed look has brought dignity to long hair and sideburns. And Killy, photogenic in a different sense from Sailer, has an expressive face that somewhat resembles David McCallum's, of "U.N.C.L.E." fame. Killy has also contributed a rare stage presence to the ski scene. When talking with reporters, he speaks as though his lines might have been written for a champion by a first-rate scriptwriter. His interest in automobile racing has added to the picture.

If Killy was relaxed both on and off skis, behind the scenes every last detail of his racing career was well taken care of. He was the product of an organization without ever becoming an organization man.

His coach, Honoré Bonnet, took over the French national ski

team in 1959, when the Austrians were walking off with all the skiing honors. Bonnet gave the French team a regimentation it needed, and yet as a Frenchman he understood the need for fun and relaxation before races. Bonnet did not believe in year-round skiing, and yet he set high standards for conditioning, placing emphasis on yoga exercises to relax muscles. Killy used the bicycle for muscle and mind tune-up, going on downhill high-speed bike runs as a test of speed with precision.

Bonnet deserves much of the credit for the development of the egg position, and the new technical refinements of racing turns. Also helpful to Bonnet was his ability to organize. In late November training, members of the French team could run as many as 450 slalom gates a day, since up to twenty helpers would be standing by to pick up the gates as they were knocked down by the racers. In nonstop predownhill runs the French skiers would be timed along each section of the course. On the morning of a race, snow temperatures were taken with a rectal-type thermometer to remove most of the risk from waxing. During the race, intelligence was transmitted instantly back and forth by means of walkie-talkies. For Killy, there was even a racing stand-in, Michel Arpin, who was a former member of the French team. Michel skied in a style similar to Killy, and used the same length skis and even the same size boots. Killy, who went through boots very quickly, always had Michel breaking in a new pair for him. Michel worked closely with the French ski manufacturers and helped to design and discover skis that were just right for Killy. The great superstar never had to think about any phase of equipment; his well-waxed, edge-honed skis would be ready for him on the morning of the race. In addition to being racing serviceman, Michel was also Killy's friend, confidant, and trusted advisor.

Under Bonnet's organizational genius, the Frenchman started winning right away, taking a gold and two bronze medals at Squaw Valley in 1960, and earning more world championships at Chamonix in 1962 and Innsbruck in 1964. However, it was at Portillo in the summer of 1966 when the Austrians were stopped cold, with the French showing unquestioned supremacy in winning eighteen out of twenty-four medals.

In his early years Jean-Claude Killy was just another expert skier on the French team. Guy Perillat was then the star. Still, in the Olympics at Innsbruck in 1964, Killy came within a second of Bonlieu's gold medal run in the giant slalom, and won several big races in the spring of that year. At the beginning of the 1966 season he won the first couple of races, but then Billy Kidd came over to Europe, and for five or six weeks was the world's best slalom and giant slalom skier. At Portillo Killy won the downhill, his first big victory in that event, but it was a short course, and extremely fast. He won in 1:34.4, skiing at an average speed of sixty-four miles an hour. He then set out to win the world's championship in the F.I.S. Alpine combined, and he conservatively settled for a fifth place in the giant slalom and eighth place in the slalom, which was all he needed. On this basis he was now a world champion, but not yet one of the all-time great skiers.

In 1967 a new event was created, the World Cup of skiing. This determined the top skier of the year on the basis of point score in seventeen races which covered all three events. In 1967 World Cup competition it was Killy all the way. He accumulated the maximum possible number of World Cup points, winning twelve of the sixteen races that he entered, and getting a second, third, fourth, and one d.n.f (did not finish) in the others. No man had ever dominated racing to this extent. He won every downhill he entered, and he actually had eight straight skiing victories in this country when the season ended.

So as the winter Olympics opened in 1968, the big question was, would Killy be able to repeat Toni Sailer's grand slam? Unlike Sailer, Killy was under pressure to win all three. Victory in just one or two races would be for him a disappointment, yet he was faced with brilliant competition, racing against specialists like the 6-foot 4-inch, 220-pound German, Franz Vogler, in the downhill and the Austrian Herbert Huber in the slalom. And in the slalom there was the trend toward the all-or-nothing type of run.

The Olympic downhill at Grenoble was a short course, just barely in excess of the F.I.S. requirement of an 800-meter vertical drop, with nine radical changes of direction, each one followed by a difficult drop-away which tended to pick up chatter marks.

In the practice nonstop run Killy came up with the best time. The next morning, following his custom, he skied a mile or so down the side of the mountain to gain the feel of his skis and break in his wax. He thought he would be skiing in soft snow, but the slope turned out to have an icy surface under a dusting of snow. The result was that he lost most of his wax. He knew then that he would have to go all out on the difficult tight upper stretches of the race. He skied the first few control gates in giant slalom style, aiming at each gate and then at the earliest possible moment cranking in a sharp turn by skating to his inside, uphill ski. He handled the rolling bumps on a section known as *Les Bosses du Coq* with easy knee action. On one difficult downhill turn his body balance shifted from one ski to another over a surface rough with chatter marks. As he went into the two big rolling bumps of the *Col de la Balme,* where Moose Barrows made his ill-conceived flight, he wind-checked on the first bump so that he could pre-jump the next and land with perfect timing on the downhill side of the second bump, for the fastest possible outrun. Near the end of the short flat which followed, he was timed at 1.1 seconds faster than anyone else. On the last part of the course he lost most of his margin because he was going over warm moist snow with almost waxless bottoms, yet he beat his teammate Perillat by 0.08 second, to win the first gold medal.

The giant slalom was the first two-run giant slalom ever held in the Olympics. On the first day the hard and icy course, with seventy gates laid out over rolling terrain, glistened in a bright sun. Killy decided to burn up the course for the first heat. He skied in classic giant slalom style, turning high, accelerating, making a technically perfect run, and at the end of the day's competition he had the impressive lead of 1.2 seconds. On the second day conditions were different. Snow during the night had provided a new soft surface, and a heavy fog three hundred yards down from the start restricted visibility to only two or three gates ahead. Killy's job was now to ski carefully and protect his lead. On this run, Billy Kidd posted the best time, but for the two runs Killy's victory was by a comfortable 2.22 seconds, and he had won a second gold medal.

In the slalom fog again was thick. And because the two courses were laid out on not too steep a slope, they were the kind of slaloms where hundredths of a second would be important. The Lord above was kind to Killy, since a break in the fog occurred as he was waiting in the starting gate. Like a true champion he took full advantage of the clear course to gain a lead of 0.3 second over the Austrian Alfred Matt. Fourteen skiers came within a second of his time. For the second run the fog was thick for everyone. Under the circumstances Killy had a good run, but because of the bad visibility, he held back to some extent and could not be certain that no one would catch him. There were two skiers who did beat Killy's total time: the Norwegian Haakon Mjoen and the great Austrian skier Karl Schranz. The Norwegian sensed that he had missed gates in the fog, and was shortly disqualified. Schranz had missed the same gates, numbers 17 and 18, but he was given a provisional second run because he had seen the shadow of a spectator crossing between gates 20 and 21. Later the race jury ruled that since Schranz had missed gates earlier than the point of interference, he was not entitled to his second run. Also, pictures of Schranz taken during his short-lived moment of glory show what might be interpreted as a look of concern on his face.

So Jean-Claude Killy, in winning his three gold medals, probably takes the unofficial crown from Sailer as the all-time king of skiing. Killy behind the scenes was a champion too. As a true sportsman as well as an interesting personality he was well liked by all the racers, especially the Americans. He and Jim Heuga are great friends, and Penny McCoy told me after the 1968 Olympics, "If it couldn't be an American, there's no one I would rather see win."

Killy as a competitor could be concentrating with mathematical precision, or relaxing, as the situation required. He admitted that he could fall asleep instantly the night before a race. "I go pouf," he said. At the top of a slalom course, in mentally running the gates, he could imagine the clock ticking away, and almost know where he was going to be every second on the course. Bonnet said of him, "I can tell by his eyes if he will be good. If I see that Killy's eyes are cold and flashing just before the start, I will not have to worry. He will do something wonderful."

And Killy said of himself in a starting gate, "It never occurs to me that I will not be first."

On the course Killy sometimes skied with such dedication to speed that he appeared violently opposed to style. He contrasted vividly with one of the best Austrians of a slightly earlier era, Egon Zimmerman, who during slaloms in the early 1960s would make his turns in perfect feet-together angulated wedeln style, as if doing a commercial for the Austrian ski school.

In a slalom Killy seemed to go radically from one type of turn to another, skiing in a wide stance without any apparent rhythm and on the verge of an eggbeater fall all the way down the course. Killy knew more about the outer limits of control than any other racer. Skiing right to the brink but no farther, he always had recovery within his grasp. But Killy, despite not looking pretty on the slalom course, was technically the world's greatest skier. For instance, he mastered two new types of turns, one of which is *avalement,* meaning "swallowing" (of the hill). In the *avalement* the skis are unweighted by being thrust forward, and the turn accomplished by steering with the feet. The racer, like an intermediate skier on fast skis, is left sitting back as if his skis have run out from under him, only he has the power in his muscles to recover. Also, he is ready to push himself forward with both poles if necessary. The other turn is the "jet turn," where an edge set is used as a momentary angulation without any braking, followed by a rebound with a natural unwinding of the body. This produces an almost effortless change of direction, as if the turn after the edge set had been accomplished without any technique.

In a downhill Killy skied in a modified egg position, slightly out of the crouch so that his knees could ride the contours softly. Riding the bumps hard would have slowed him down. At sixty-five miles an hour on a difficult turn Killy could shift his weight quickly by instinct to his uphill inside ski, almost at the exact instant that the downhill ski was about to wander. He could even do this with *avalement,* sitting back on one ski, and thrusting it forward. In one downhill race at the choppy steep finish when he was low in a tuck, his right ski seemed to be going dangerously astray. And he was seen to correct this near-fall situation without even coming out of the tuck.

In a giant slalom Killy could pole harder and faster at the start than anyone, picking up the good part of a second before reaching the first gate, and then skiing in easy sweeping turns, always taking his gates close, stepping up to his high, fast line.

The objective in any racing turn is to accelerate rather than to skid and lose speed. Killy managed to start his turn early, clip the gates close, and use his wide stance position to push off one ski or the other whenever possible. Whether in a skating step, or stepping uphill to a faster line, usually one ski was in full contact with the snow for perfect sliding action.

Therefore, the answer to Killy versus Sailer is that Sailer may have been the most natural skier of them all, but Killy's commitment to speed was so complete that had the two ever raced against each other under equal conditions, Killy would have found a way to go faster than Sailer.

Perhaps the great exhition of all time will take place some day before a world championship race when all five of the double and triple medal winners forerun a race. The race itself would be an anticlimax to such a presentation by these skiers. Somehow I suspect that Allais might steal the show, because his age would make his style so impressive.

11

Stowe

The White Mountains of New Hampshire are so named because they culminate in the Presidential Range, whose above-timberline slopes in the winter present a proud white profile visible for hundreds of miles on a clear day. As is apparent from earlier chapters, I have a personal involvement with the leading mountain in the Presidential Range—Mt. Washington.

In Vermont, the mountains running north from the Massachusetts border are called the Green Mountains. In character, they often seem more like high rolling hills than mountains. Nevertheless there is a knife ridge to the Green Mountains extending for more than one hundred miles from north to south which is sharply defined from the air. This range culminates in Mt. Mansfield, which at 4,393 feet is the highest point in the state of Vermont. Mansfield has some above-timberline glacier-scarred granite terraces, and certain features in its profile that remind one of an elongated human face, complete with forehead, nose, and chin. Yet Mt. Mansfield, even though higher and more rugged by far than any other part of the range, does not lose the character and feeling of the rolling Green Mountains. In midwinter when the top of Mansfield appears white, this is not because of extensive snowfields, but because the trees are frosted with ice crystals.

Halfway up the mountain the trees are almost green, and then in graduations they are increasingly coated with ice. At the top they are bent with snow, merging into the short rock-studded snowfields at the summit. So Mansfield is still a Green Mountain, even though completely frosted at its summit. And my personal link with its green profile is at least as strong as my link with Mt. Washington's white profile.

When Stowe first became a skiing community, it went under the billing, "There's always snow at Stowe, you know." There is some truth to this folksy advertising slogan, since the mountain topography of Stowe actually has a snow-making effect on the weather. As the prevailing westerly winds, sometimes from the southwest, cross Lake Champlain and are forced over Mt. Mansfield, colder temperatures at the upper elevations cause condensation which during winter results in snow. In truth this weather pattern generally applies all along the Green Mountain range, and has much to do with Vermont's thriving ski industry. However, often when the warm moist air from the southeast moves into New England, all the Eastern snow country is pelted with rain—yet on the mountain at Stowe snow is falling. Of course, Stowe can have its share of rain, too, followed by dropping temperatures and inevitable "granular surface." The town now has a new title, "Ski Capital of the East." I don't know whether this change occurred because of a cautious Yankee desire to avoid lawsuits when it rained, or because of the new claim's increased appeal.

Stowe does offer excellent skiing, and in some ways may be considered one of the finest ski areas of the world. Actually two mountain ranges are separated at Stowe by the rocky cleft of Smuggler's Notch. The eastern range is topped by Sterling Peak whose north and south sides have separate systems of slopes, trails, and lifts. The south side is known as Spruce Peak, and the north, under separate ownership, is known as Madonna Mountain. The western range is dominated by Mansfield itself, whose northeast side is covered by a network of trails and lifts.

Stowe, being in the northwestern part of the state, also has a long snow season. From mid-November to mid-December skiing is spotty. But a good fall of snow on or before Christmas Day is a certainty, although often the holiday cover is not equal to the hordes of skiers who descend on it. The January thaw rarely takes away the full cover, and for most of the weekends through the season, Stowe can offer as much or more than the other New England ski areas. Generally the snow gets more and more reliable right up to the final weekend, which for the Mt. Mansfield lift occurs at the end of the third or fourth week in April.

But more than the snow, the variety of terrain as well as the sheer drop of some of the runs has earned Stowe the reputation of the ski capital of the East. The Starr, the National, and the Goat Trails compare favorably, except in length, with the steepest runs at Chamonix, St. Anton, and Aspen. Also Mt. Mansfield has long been known for the Nose Dive, perhaps the best downhill trail in the East. But Stowe is more than just a present-day ski community. It is a New England town with a typically rich historical tradition.

Vermont, one of the least populous states in the country, was the last New England state to be settled. In part this was because it was the only state without a sea coast. Vermont, not being one of the original thirteen colonies, had an indefinite status before and after the Revolutionary War. In fact, Vermont was started as part of a questionable real estate operation. Benning Wentworth, the Royal Governor of New Hampshire for the thirty-five years leading up to the Declaration of Independence, ceded townships called "New Hampshire grants" to speculators in the area. Of course these grants were in direct violation of Wentworth's royal charter. And New York's claim on this land was at least as well founded as New Hampshire's.

One of the townships granted by Governor Wentworth was Stow, named after a town in England spelled the same way. The 6-mile square tract was granted in 1763, but it was not until 1793, two years after Vermont had joined the Union as the fourteenth state, that anyone actually settled in Stow. In that year Oliver Luce, pulling a stubby wooden hand sled filled with a few personal possessions, made the snowy trek from Hartland to what is now the village of Stowe. Today some of his descendants still reside in Stowe, and the hill where he settled is now known as Luce

Hill. It is the site of the Trapp family lodge, the first American home of the von Trapp family, whose story inspired "The Sound of Music."

Luce was followed very shortly by other settlers, and by the turn of the century there were forty-six families in Stowe. During the War of 1812, when the cannonading of Plattsburg was heard in Stowe, the town was big enough to send 150 volunteers, none of whom saw action because the British were defeated before the Stowe contingent could cross Lake Champlain. By contrast, 236 sons of Stowe saw service in World War II. Most of the growth of Stowe took place prior to 1850, and since then the population has hovered under 2,000.

If the population has been relatively stable, the means of supporting it has changed drastically. The early settlers derived income from the sale of potash salts, which were made by evaporating lye obtained from the ashes of burned hardwood. At that time there was a big market in Europe for these salts, which the settlers could manufacture from the trees they chopped down in clearing their land. Through the years both farming and lumbering have been the mainstay of the Stowe economy. One thriving local industry during the mid-1800's was the manufacture of starch, made from a coarse-grained potato from Stowe. At one time there were five starch factories in operation. In the 1880's a large tannery had a successful business, with a capacity of 72,000 calfskins a year. Stowe's hardwood forests have been a valued natural resource. At the turn of the century the town was an important producer of butter tubs, over 100,000 of which were manufactured a year by four firms. A violin shop was a short-lived venture, ending with a fire in 1923. A very successful item was a wooden package resembling a book that contained Vermont maple sugar. It was labeled "The Sweetest Story Ever Told." Today a firm by the name of Shaw turns out a line of wooden gifts called Stoware. Farming continues to be important, particularly dairy farming. Nevertheless Stowe is not nearly so dependent on agriculture as it was thirty years ago.

Among the industries in Stowe that failed was the electric railway linking the two rural communities of Waterbury and

Stowe, which are ten miles apart. The railway, in use from 1897 to 1932, was a Toonerville Trolley type operation, in receivership from 1907 on. One visitor who rode the trolley on one of its last trips described it as so decrepit that it generally had to take two or three running starts before building up enough speed to make the first hill out of downtown Waterbury.

Of course, today the tourist business is the number one industry in Vermont. And for Stowe, summer and winter resort operation is by far the biggest source of income, with skiing making winter more profitable than summer. Fittingly Stowe's first settler, Oliver Luce, was also the first to take in paying guests. The Green Mountain Inn, which is still doing a thriving business, providing fine accommodations and exceptionally good Vermont cooking, first hung out its sign in 1833. The largest hotel ever built in Stowe was the Mt. Mansfield Hotel, opened for business in 1863, and located on the south side of Main Street on the site of Shaw's General Store, facing the mountain. The town became more and more aware of the opportunities in the resort business, and the Summit House was built in 1858 on top of the mountain, just beyond the "nose," and operated until 1957. The Toll Road was completed to the halfway house in 1856, and was finished to the Summit House in 1870. It was laid out by a man named Byron Russell, who knew the mountain and its contours so well that the road has been changed very little through the years. The job of designing the road was not much different from the task faced today by Sel Hannah, who skillfully carves out mountainsides into ski trails. The first recorded descent of the Toll Road on skis took place in 1914, when Nathaniel Goodrich, Dartmouth librarian, skied the entire 4½-mile road. But the Toll Road, still used by novices, and by many other grades of skiers on icy days, was undoubtedly the nation's first ski trail, available almost fifty years before it was actually skied on.

The town's foresight was also evidenced in a plan to capitalize on the scenic possibilities of Smuggler's Notch by putting a carriage road through the notch. Smuggler's Notch, in addition to being one of the most picturesque mountain passes in New England, with its huge towering rock cliffs, is of historic importance, since during the War of 1812 rovers used it as a secret passage for contraband goods. The first appropriation of $100 for construction of the carriage road was authorized in 1862. By 1873 a total of $1,300 had been spent, and in 1893 the road was finally completed. Today the road has a hard surface, but when I last drove over it about ten years ago, it was still an unimproved gravel road. I remember that a tremendous boulder which had fallen from the cliffs on the Mansfield side of the notch had been left in place, with the road broadened so that traffic went on either side of it.

The town at one time had ten covered bridges, more correctly known as arch bridges. Before the existence of motor-driven conveyances, the roads were opened in winter by means of snow rollers, drawn by teams of four to six horses, which packed down the snow for horse-drawn sleigh traffic. The same snow rollers may be seen today, pulled by Sno-Cats, packing down slopes for skiers after a snowstorm. One of the most interesting items on the Stowe budget in preautomobile days was the expediture of from $8 to $37 for "snowing" the covered bridges so that horse-drawn sleighs could slide along with ease. There is only one covered bridge still standing, located in Stowe Hollow.

Stowe today is not by any means as quaint as Woodstock, but is all the same an interesting town with a view of the mountain from many points on the main street. If the town somewhat lacks a sense of unity, it does contain striking examples of New England architecture. A fine watercolorist, Walton Blodgett, made a good living painting views of Stowe, one of which hangs in our living room. The graceful 171-foot spire of the Community Church lends charm to our watercolor, which depicts a sheepskin-bundled man walking down the main street of town, with the long shadows of the January sun slanting across the snow. The church is said to have been patterned after the architecture of Christopher Wren.

In contrast, the Catholic Church of the Blessed Sacrament is a contemporary structure designed by an architect who was a student of Rouault. It is located on the farm where Brother Joseph Dutton was born, the man largely responsible for the development of the leper colony on the island of Molokai in Hawaii. In 1908, sixteen United States battleships, on instructions from President

Theodore Roosevelt, altered their course around the world to fire a salute to Brother Joseph and his lepers, who stood on the shores of Molokai.

Stowe also takes great pride in Edward Martin Taber, an artist, writer, and poet who loved nature, much like Thoreau. He came to Stowe for reasons of health and died in 1896 at the early age of thirty-three. His painting of Mt. Mansfield is owned by the Metropolitan Museum in New York and a book called *Stowe Notes* contains most of his writings. His essays on the months of the year are much more extensive for the winter than for other seasons. Perhaps he recognized winter as Stowe's special season. Also, his descriptions of early snows, the first November thaws, the depth of midwinter snow, and the beginnings of spring fit into the pattern of the typical winter of today. Had this man lived longer he might have distinguished himself in American literature, for his prose has a unique quality. Here is a paragraph on a tool which has played an important part in the development of Stowe:

> The axe is in itself the most inviting weapon, an exceeding handy tool. The environment is so charming, and there are pleasures connected with it that result from the work itself, as of the echo that wakes the wood on every stroke of the axe, a sound that satisfies the ear, neither too harsh nor too loud, but full of a certain primitive music, ringing, conclusive.

Another paragraph deals with ice harvesting, an industry which did not end until 1956:

> They are taking the ice out of the pond, and the clear, green-blue, peacock-blue cakes, shot and veined with light, present a sight as rich and satisfying as if they were indeed of the so-called precious minerals.

Here Taber writes about town government:

> I am a citizen of this State, you know, so, to act the part of a good one, I go to town meetings and vote as my conscience dictates. Party is not considered at these elections; personal spleen influences the voting slightly, but in the main the farmer's common sense (which is vast) governs, and good men are chosen.

Stowe's pride is compounded of a rich history, somewhat typical of many New England towns, and its position as "the Ski Capital of the East." Its continuous winter sports program dates back to its first Winter Carnival in 1921. Scheduled skiing events were then limited to a "ski obstacle race" and "sensational exhibition ski jumping" off the new 60-foot jumping trestle. This tower was designed by Fred Harris of Brattleboro, founder of the Dartmouth Outing Club, and John Carleton, a student at Dartmouth who was famed for his forward somersaults off ski jumps.

In 1926, Craig Burt of the Burt lumber firm took his 10-year-old son and a friend up Mt. Mansfield on skis. Because the snow was very deep that winter, the group took six hours to reach the top. The trip down the 4½-mile Toll Road took twenty-five minutes, but only six minutes from the halfway house to the foot of the mountain. In 1932 Roland Palmedo and José Machado, founder and charter member, respectively, of the Amateur Ski Club of New York, visited Mt. Mansfield on a scouting mission for the club. The same two boys who had conquered the mountain six years earlier served as guides for the New Yorkers. After taking a careful survey of Mt. Mansfield and its terrain, Roland and José wrote a report which had the style and excitement of an explorer's account of a newly discovered peak in a remote part of the world. They concluded: "Apparently Stowe has been little visited by skiers from the outside world, except for an occasional party from the University of Vermont or Middlebury College."

In general they enthusiastically recommended the area, but felt its terrain would be unsuitable for the "most adventurous skiers." Little did they know what manner of steep trails were soon to be carved out of the mountainside.

In the early 1930's a C.C.C. Camp was set up with the Ranch Camp as a base. Charles Lord, an engineer and a skier, was in charge of this group, and under his direction a ski trail system was cut out in the woods. The Bruce Trail, the first used for racing on the mountain, was also the first cleared. This was followed by the Nose Dive, the Chin Clip, the Perry Merrill, and the Lord Trail itself. The Nose Dive was ready for the 1934 winter, but because of many stumps, it could only be skied when the snow cover was over 3-feet deep.

In 1938 Roland Palmedo persuaded a group of American girls, who had been racing in Europe for several years as a team managed by Alice Kiaer, to come for a race at Stowe. Some of these girls, such as Clarita Heath, Grace Carter Lindley, Marion McKean, and Betty Woolsey, had become well-known skiers in the F.I.S. Races and the Arlberg-Kandahar. Some of the girl skiers in the United States were beginning to wonder why these Americans never skied in their own country. When the elite group arrived at Stowe they were appalled at the primitive stage of skiing in this country. The road to the mountain was not plowed all the way in. The girls had to walk almost a mile to the base of the mountain before they climbed the Nose Dive. After the race Grace Carter Lindley told Roland it was high time for American skiing to get organized, and that the most important move was to build ski lifts. Four years earlier, when she first skied in Europe, the Alps already had over seventy mountain railways, fifty of which were aerial tramways. Roland, agreeing with her criticism, soon organized a group to finance a lift on Mt. Mansfield.

Like most infant organizations, the ski industry faced many problems—one of which was that the best ski terrain on the mountain was state-owned, and could not be purchased. However, after studying the state law, a Burlington lawyer named Wiltsie Brisbin found a clause that stated, "if it was deemed to be in the public interest, state-owned land could be leased to the public." It was determined that if a lift company built skiing facilities on state property and then gave them to the state, the state in turn would lease them to the lift company. Accordingly a group of fifty stockholders invested money in the new venture. Many of them were members of the Amateur Ski Club of New York, including Lowell Thomas, and some of them were natives of Stowe, including local businessmen Gail Shaw and Craig Burt.

The risk was great for the stockholders, since they had just given away property for which they had in effect paid a large sum of money, in return for a questionable lease extending over a ten-year period. Also there were many delays, because a number of elected state officials had the responsibility of determining if building a lift on Mansfield was truly in the interest of the public. Nonetheless, after raising a total of $101,200, the lift company opened a chair lift for business in the 1940 season, with no indebtedness but with virtually no cash position and a few bills outstanding.

A few weeks after the lift opened, the success of the venture was assured. It should be noted that the stockholders had taken the risk not so much to profit financially as to contribute to the sport of skiing. Strangely enough, even today much of the money invested in Eastern ski businesses is an affair of the heart. Since the addition of new areas has more than kept pace with the number of skiers, operators have been faced with intensive competition as well as with the uncertain New England winters. But the Mt. Mansfield single chair lift has proven a good investment.

Today Stowe handles a tremendous weekend load of skiers. Mt. Mansfield has a double chair lift alongside the original chair, a new gondola, and two T bars. Spruce Peak has two more double chairs and a T bar. Also on the north side of Sterling Peak there is another major area, Madonna. Linked to the Stowe side at the summit by a short, somewhat downhill, trek across Sterling Pond, Madonna features north slope skiing with a 2,100-foot vertical drop, two double chairs, and a Poma lift.

The man most responsible for what Stowe is today is Sepp Ruschp, who arrived in December of 1936 to form a ski school. With the proprietor being the entire staff, business for that season was 1,100 lessons at one dollar each. Well-tanned, with dark eyes and a bright smile, Sepp is energetic and ambitious without being aggressive. Like most Austrians, he is very much of a gentleman, but more than his other compatriots he is a good businessman. Among all the Austrians who have come to this country he and Friedl Pfeifer have attained the greatest financial success. By 1940 he had expanded his ski school staff to ten instructors and had acquired part ownership in the Toll House. With some interest in the rope tow near the main lift, he also was the principal owner of the Mt. Mansfield T Bar, which was built immediately after World War II. Sepp's big break came through an association with Cornelius V. Starr, an insurance man with vast interests in the

Orient. In 1949, with Starr's backing, Sepp formed the Mt. Mansfield Company, which took over the single chair lift operation by buying out most of the original stockholders. Today the Mt. Mansfield Company, with Sepp as president and an important stockholder, operates all the lifts on Mansfield and the Stowe side of Sterling Peak, as well as the Lodge and the Toll House.

Sepp's influence has extended beyond Stowe. Interested in the organizational side of skiing, he has been president of both the Eastern and the National Skiing Associations. Also he has helped to keep teaching up to date in this country by bringing over a number of top Austrian instructors, some of whom skied for the Austrian national team. One was an Olympic Gold Medal winner, Othmar Schneider. Stowe has played a big role in racing, having been the site of the National Championships in 1938 and countless other races, including international races, which have been held since 1952 in alternate years to coincide with F.I.S. and Olympic races. For each of these races the Mt. Mansfield Company has brought over the best European skiers. Consequently, more of the world's best skiers have raced at Stowe than at any other Eastern ski area. Among them are Stein Eriksen, Toni Sailer, Josl Rieder, Jean Vuarnet, Ernie McCulloch, Christian Pravda, and Jean-Claude Killy.

There are many people living in Stowe who give it the character it has today, some of course, more than others. Two of my favorites, and two very different people are Bob Bourdon and Henry Simoneau.

Bob, who grew up in Woodstock, is about my age. In 1934 he was the first person to ride up the first rope tow in America, the "Ski Way," located on Gilbert's Hill. While working full-time as an instructor for Sig Buchmayr at Woodstock, he won the first official race ever held on the Nose Dive, the Vermont State Downhill Championship, on February 23, 1936, setting a record of 2 minutes, 35.8 seconds for the trail, at that time 1.4 miles long. Following Army service, Bob was on the staff of the Sun Valley ski school where he met his beautiful wife Mary. Married in 1948, they settled in Stowe, where Mary adjusted to small-town life in New England after leaving Philadelphia society behind. Mary is an excellent skier and instructor herself, and it is not surprising that she and Bob have two sons who are first-rate skiers.

Bob is a true Vermonter, like the early settlers of Stowe. A man of boundless energy, he has many talents. As a creative artist he gives great attention to detail without ever losing his overall sense of purpose. In his early years at Stowe he worked as a carpenter. On his 100-acre farm, he rebuilt the old house almost completely with his own hands. For many years he was the staff photographer at the ski school, and still does quite a bit of free-lance work, mostly ski movies. His book on skiing, *The New Way to Ski,* is available in paperback. He plays the best trumpet in the north country, sometimes organizing his own group to play at the Lodge, other times joining a big band to play at functions such as the Governor's Ball. His style is Dixie-Land and classic jazz. He has an interest in guns, particularly in old firearms. Forging new parts when necessary, he keeps his collection in good working order. He has learned to fire all of these guns, including flintlock pieces. Recently he has been spending most of his time doing original work with wrought iron, designing hardware and accessories for the home. These pieces are shown in a catalogue available for one dollar.

If Bob is an artist in the true sense of the word, he is also an artist on skis. Since his natural style is similar to the modern Austrian way of skiing, he has had to make fewer changes than any long-time skier that I know. Bob must have learned to ski without ever learning to stem, which logically is the way all skiers will someday be taught. Bob skis 100 percent parallel, in a graceful upright manner, not just on his skis but over them, reacting to the contour of the slope with unbelievable fluidity. There is such an absence of extremism in his skiing that sometimes he almost seems to lack a definite technique. He is a tall handsome man with a shy pleasant manner, but he is especially handsome when skiing down one of Mt. Mansfield's trails.

Bob's racing accomplishments are numerous. The winner of the European Army championships after the war, he has won many races at Stowe, even in his early forties beating some of the best college skiers and all but the top Austrian instructors. Today he teaches in Stowe, usually on a part-time basis, giving private lessons exclusively. He is a most respected, well-loved member of the community.

Henry Simoneau is a different sort entirely. To begin with, Henry is somewhat on the short side, and if he is not so handsome as Bob, he makes up for it by the twinkle in his eye and his own brand of humor, complete with authentic Vermont accent. If Bob Bourdon has spread his energy in various directions, Henry Simoneau, a real businessman, has channeled his energy, even to the extent of putting his skis aside.

Henry has risen to a high position in the management of the Mt. Mansfield Company. A vice-president and director, he runs the Spruce Peak operation, and in some ways is Sepp Ruschp's right-hand man. As a schoolboy, Henry was a bellboy at the Green Mountain Inn as well as the outstanding local racer. Henry loved to ski the Nose Dive nonstop and all out. In the days before the lift it was quite an experience to be walking up one of the schusses on sealskins and suddenly see Henry hurtling over the brow almost headed right for you. With an uncanny knack of knowing where the climbers would be, he whizzed right by them at fifty miles an hour. In 1940 and 1941, the Mt. Mansfield Ski Club paid his expenses to Sun Valley, where he always raced well, winning the Sun Valley Ski Club Championships in 1940. After winning the Sugar Slalom at Stowe in 1942, he went into the service like most of the rest of us.

As much as Henry loved to ski and to race, after the war he turned his attention to business. His skiing today is pretty much limited to early morning solo runs down the Smuggler's Trail, which he skis in a tuck as if racing against the clock, cutting all the turns, taking a high line against the boards on Hotshot Corner, and behaving in general as if his life depended on getting down the mountain in record time. Henry has a powerful pair of knees and skis in a fairly low crouch, somewhat in the old racing style. A rare treat for one of his friends is to catch Henry at midday and talk him into a run. Henry has special fun if the run takes place on the Mt. Mansfield side, which he doesn't get a chance to ski very often. Henry will always take the lead position. He likes individual sports—golf, hunting, fishing, and, on his terms, skiing. Follow-the-leader skiing with someone else in the lead is Henry's idea of turning skiing into a team sport. Serge Gagarin, one of the old Woodstock gang, is even shorter than Henry. An exceptionally good variable snow skier, Serge has the quickest reactions I have seen in skiing. He is therefore the hardest man to follow, and he takes special delight in shaming Henry into following him. Apart from this idiosyncrasy, Henry is a fine skier. He is also fun to ski with because of his great spirit and his appreciation for what little social skiing comes his way.

One day Henry was leading a group of Stowe kids down the Nose Dive Bypass. Following a traverse, a quick drop-off leads into a sharp, tricky right-hand turn. In the air after the drop-off, the skier gropes to get his skis back on the snow to make the right-hand turn and avoid soaring into the woods. Henry stopped at the top of the traverse, where the turn was in sight, and pointed out the problems involved: prejumping the knoll, stretching out to get back on the snow, not having the weight too far forward going over the knoll, and not sitting back during the turn. He got the young skiers fired up as if they were in their first race. Then with the confidence and arrogant manner of an Olympic racer, he said, "I want each of you to do it exactly the way I do."

After this announcement, he proceeded over the knoll, somehow missed his timing on the turn, and took a humiliating sit-down fall. He looked up to see one or two of the kids snickering. Then one by one they took off down the traverse, each in turn sitting down in the exact manner of the master. At the completion of the performance the whole gang laughed riotously while lying in the snow.

Another favorite story about Henry occurred about 1953, when he had his ankle in a cast. The inventor of the Cubco binding was demonstrating his new product on the concrete basement floor of the state hut at the foot of Mansfield. About fifteen or twenty of us watched with great interest as the inventor would slam the ski he was wearing against the floor, simulating one type of twisting fall after another, each time calling out, "Forward fall," "Fall to the right," etc., with the ski obediently snapping free in a most convincing manner. Henry hobbled in during the demonstration, and after watching one episode, he excitedly yelled out, "Why that's the damn binding I wore when I broke my ankle!" There was a stunned delay of a few seconds; then everyone, including the Cubco man, broke out in laughter.

The New York Times, reporting in October, 1965, on a light fall of snow, called it "nothing more than a nuisance," which interfered with last-minute maintenance work on the mountain. The article said, however, that Henry went up the Mt. Mansfield lift and skied down to a point where a trail crew was working. He announced, "It isn't really skiable yet, but I'm going to make sure. I'll be back. I'm going to test it again."

When the race time approaches, Henry's excitement runs high. Out on the trail to watch the international class racers feeling out the course, Henry gets a vicarious thrill out of the speed with which they ski. During a race he is always at the top of the course, functioning as the starter.

Henry lives in a large modern house on the Spruce Peak road. His wife, who breeds and shows dogs, is affectionately known as "Wogs." One of the owners and managers of The Foster Place, a former ski lodge, she is also the granddaughter of the tycoon who answered the question of how much it cost to run his yacht by saying, "Young man, if you ask such a question, you cannot afford the yacht."

So two native Vermonters, one creative and the other skilled in working with people, personalize Stowe for me. However, in a big area like Stowe the inn where one usually stays makes the town seem friendly and familiar. Stowe today has over seventy hotels, inns, and motels, plus countless farms and homes which put up skiers. For crowded weekends there are over 3,000 beds available in Stowe, as well as accommodations in neighboring towns. Twelve licensed bars, including several full-fledged night clubs, are also in operation.

My longest affiliation is with the Fountain, an inn two miles north of town on the road to Morrisville, where I always stayed during my Choate and Dartmouth years. A white clapboard farmhouse, it has an annex which is a converted barn with a large high-ceilinged living room. Here the walls have been left in the natural state of the barn interior, and are decorated with all sorts of interesting memorabilia and artifacts of Vermont life. The bedrooms are comfortably and tastefully furnished in the colonial tradition. The heating, which seemed unique to me, consists of a log-burning hot-air furnace. In addition the delicious and bountiful meals are representative of the best of New England cooking.

The name of the inn is derived from a small fountain in front of the house, centered in the curve of the driveway. Early in the winter it freezes into a still-life gusher, the state it remains in throughout the ski season. Driving back to the Fountain on clear cold nights, we could often see in the northern sky the spectacular pulsating shafts of light of the aurora borealis.

The Fountain was run by Mrs. W. C. Norcross, and in recent years has been run by her daughter Zelta. It is open all seasons of the year, and although completely democratic, has little change in clientele, since reservations are made well in advance by former guests. The style of living at the Fountain is relaxed and reserved, with the people staying there being friendly and yet showing respect for the privacy of the other guests. It was actually rather a conservative place for a student to stay, yet its warmth and hospitality made it seem like a second home to me. Perhaps young people need more security than they are willing to admit, either to themselves or to others.

In contrast, a ski lodge known as Top Notch attracted Barbara and me in the mid-1950's, before we were encumbered by family skiing. At that time Top Notch was operated by Dick Hood and Don Scholle. The magnificent contemporary structure, featuring elements such as varnished wood beams and trim, yellow clapboarding, stonework, and extravagant use of glass, breaks with tradition, both in order to exploit a hillside plot and to accommodate gracious living. The entry, with timber arches and a permanent canopy, suggests the proportions of a Shinto shrine. The bar and the dining room are well designed and arranged, but the living room is nothing short of spectacular. Jutting out from the main building, it has a high ceiling, and two walls of glass bisected at the end by a high wall of cemented round Vermont fieldstones. In the center of the living room a circular open fireplace topped by a black wrought-iron hood, is surrounded by low curved couches. The architecture, by Dick Hood's brother Ray, set the stage for a new mode of living in the north country.

In the mid-1950's there were fancy-looking girls as innkeepers and waiting on tables at Top Notch was a sought-after privilege almost as if screen contracts were up for grabs. Female guests and help both dressed in cocktail velvet pants and blouses, sometimes cotton with ruffles, sometimes silk printed in brilliant colors. For the first time, we were looking at a new fashion category, the après-ski costume.

Dick Hood and Don Scholle were a perfect business team. Dick was the efficient behind-the-scenes manager, aided by his sister Trientje, and redhead Don the gracious host, one minute playing the part of the clown to get a laugh, and the next minute introducing a prominent newcomer with a flourish. The inn, like a magnet, drew interesting people, well-known because of wealth, social position, or profession. There were show business celebrities, writers, artists, and a tight circle of Stowe skiers who hit the weekend circuit hard and were catered to more than any of the guests. If there was a race on, Top Notch was the place to find Brookie Dodge, Ralph Miller, or Chick Igaya. In the evening, even on a week night, the bar was a hub of activity, like the bar in a fraternity house after a home game.

In those days two other inns attracted skiers who in a way were part of the Top Notch crowd. In some respects, these places surpassed Top Notch, and in others fell short. One was Ten Acres, run by Darby and John Chambers. It would be an understatement to say that Darby had the best cooking in Vermont. It was and still is superb, and she either cooks or directly supervises all meals. A big woman, Darby has a beautiful face, and dresses with excellent taste. There is an unmistakable competence about her, which shows up whether she is involved in town politics, breeding dogs, or running Ten Acres farm along with her husband. The comfort of the rambling farmhouse and its cottages, the brilliant preparation of such meals as roast suckling pig, combined with the charm of Darby and John as hosts, make the Ten Acres group loyally partisan.

The Foster Place was owned and operated by a group of girls who started it the first winter of the single chair at Stowe. The main building had an undersized living room and a small kitchen, which was usually the center of activity, with Minie the cook at all times the most important person in the room. The walls of the paneled dining room were covered with a marvelous collection of eight-by-twelve black-and-white photographs of Stowe and Stowe skiers, mostly former habitués of The Foster Place, in various informal poses. The bedrooms, mostly bunk rooms chopped out of odd corners of the second floor, were reached by step-ups or head-ducks. The Foster Place was not lacking in authenticity, but it was short on comfort. If one was at ease in the living room, it was more because of a drink and good company than the furnishings. The innkeepers were perennially interesting crops of college girls who could ski circles around the innkeepers from Top Notch and Ten Acres. Sometimes these girls were as famous as attractive Sally Deaver, Olympic giant slalom star, who was killed in a tragic riding accident. The guests included college-age youngsters and people who were friends and contemporaries of the original owners. But dinner by candlelight Saturday night, with roast beef, mashed potatoes, broccoli hollandaise, and red wine, served at long sawbuck tables and benches by girls who were real personalities—followed by an after-dinner speech by Peter Wolfe, an ebullient geology professor—was the real treat of staying at The Foster Place.

The rivalry among Top Notch, Ten Acres, and The Foster Place usually consisted of good-natured ribbing both on and off the slopes wherever the guests from the three lodges convened. In the spring a three-way race called the Top Notch Trophy Race was held on Little Spruce. It was always a wide-open giant slalom with a fantastic assortment of skiers participating, from Olympic racers to snow bunnies.

One week when I was vacationing at Stowe the interlodge rivalry took the form of competition in après-ski games. All of a sudden it became fashionable to make a 360-degree jump-turn on the Bongo Board, a half-turn being nothing. Also, teams of three would try to keep two Bongo Boards going. At a given signal all three would jump—the man on the floor to the first board, the man on the first board to the second, and the man on the second to the floor. The trick was to keep both boards in play without fouling by a fall.

Then there were the beer-can races. At a signal, selected stars from each lodge would start from one end of the room balancing on beer cans. This was a little like crossing a stream by going from one rock to the next, except more complicated, because there were only two cans for each contender. After balancing on one can, the racer would reach back and pick up the other, putting it a foot or two ahead. He would then balance on that can, picking up the other, and so on. The minute a fall took place, the participant had to go back to the starting line and begin again. At times these games seemed a bit unfair, for the skiers who excelled on the slopes were also the ones with the necessary balance, thigh muscles, and confidence to star again indoors. One day it became apparent that we were taking the evening fun too seriously when Colin Stewart caught me taping my ankles to protect against injury in the Bongo Board jump-turn. This was like being surprised running a slalom course before a race.

Another parlor game known as "the feather game" was a form of strip poker. The players, holding a taut blanket between them, would blow at a white down feather. The person on whom the feather landed had to remove an article of clothing. To my knowledge the game was never carried to its conclusion, as the loser always "chickened out" at an early stage. At The Foster Place, there was often talk of the Japanese steam bath game. Supposedly on a subzero night, with the showers on full hot and the windows open, a mixed group seated on chairs would disrobe completely in steam so thick that someone just inches away would be invisible. This was actually no more than a good-humored threat, tried once a year by the old-time male guests on a group of new naïve innkeepers.

Today The Foster Place is no longer open as an inn, being used occasionally during winter vacations by the owners. Ten Acres is now run as an informal club. Top Notch, under new ownership, is a successful inn, but without the extravagant style of Don and Dick. Among the inns that I have visited personally, only the Fountain is completely unchanged—still living up to descriptions of it written before 1930, long before Stowe became known as a ski area.

Humor also personalizes Stowe, and Mt. Mansfield has often been the site of old-fashioned horseplay. Marilyn Shaw, a bright attractive blonde who is the daughter of the Stowe woodenware family, became a national downhill champion at Sun Valley in 1940 on her sixteenth birthday. She also won the national slalom championship in Aspen the following year. Like anyone that expert, Marilyn was full of confidence. One day two well-known racers arrived at Mt. Mansfield with a plot to play a trick on Marilyn. Edgar Bering, Harvard medical student, had decided to act the part of a mythical Polish woman champion, Paula Senkowsky, and outski his Yale friend, Peter Garrett, as well as all others on the mountain, skiing as no woman ever did before. Edgar had borrowed a gabardine ski skirt from Mary Bird Young, and with a well-filled out parka, a smear of lipstick on his mouth, and a few locks of curly hair protruding from the parka hood, he looked like a formidable, stockily built woman athlete.

Peter Garrett and Paula had made several Nose Dive runs before Marilyn got to the mountain, and the word had spread that a fantastic Polish woman skier was running the Nose Dive all out. On Marilyn's arrival, Peter broke away from his companion to ski with her, and Paula lurked behind. On the first run, Marilyn and Peter stopped for a few minutes in the Corridor, a broad open swath below the seven turns, hoping that Paula would run through. They were not disappointed, as Paula came screaming out of the seven turns, flying over bumps on an unprepared course, her skirt flapping like a luffing sail, running the Corridor absolutely straight. On another run farther down the trail, Marilyn and Peter again watched as Paula went racing through one of the lower schusses. Marilyn was stunned, and she turned to Peter and said, "I don't believe there is a woman in this world who can ski like that, and I won't believe this is a woman until I see her go in the Ladies Room."

Peter managed to get the word to Paula, and later on up at the Octagon, Paula came in, looked at the signs for the Men's Room and then the Ladies Room, and entered the latter. Marilyn, who had been watching, went right in after her, and scuffling could be heard. Finally a distraught Paula, with props askew and hood removed, emerged from the Ladies Room, chased by Marilyn.

My friend Willi Benedict, a fashion photographer who taught skiing at Stowe several years before the war, always brings his sense of humor to the mountain. One day as I was watching, Willi had a near miss with a tree, and politely turned around to address the tree in the middle of a deep-snow turn, saying, "So sorry, please." Another day he spotted me in the lift line, wearing a pair Kaestle skis which had been sold to me under the pretense that they were used by Toni Sailer. Willi said, "Ah, I see you are skiing on Mr. Sailer's skis. I suppose that means he is skiing on Mr. Tobin's." And then, looking at my bindings, bear-trap toe-irons with long thongs, he said, "I see you also have the latest safety binding, the one that releases at the knees." There are some who say that Willi Benedict jumps the lift line. My answer to this is that he never does it unless it is the sporting thing to do. In years when a gentleman knows where his place is in the lift line, Willi is well behaved. Nevertheless, for several years a "Benedict Trophy," a wooden wedge with silver plaque, was awarded to the person who distinguished himself by his agility in the Stowe lift line.

To the serious skier the mountain itself is the most important part of Stowe. I am sure that I could fill a book with the accounts of my memorable runs on Mt. Mansfield. There is no other mountain that I have skied which strikes me with such awe. I can get as worked up about a prelunch, fast run down the National Trail as I can about going in a big race. Perhaps the mountain itself excites me so that to race on it almost overwhelms me. Certainly I have never won any races on Mt. Mansfield's famous trails. I did win once on the Tear Drop, which runs from under the nose of the mountain down the western side toward Underhill, in the Intercollegiate Ski Union Downhill of 1941. But not being on the Stowe side, it was as if on a different mountain. Perhaps that is the reason I was able to master Mansfield that day.

I have never skied the mountain on days when I regarded conditions as poor, but for me it would probably be sufficient to have enough cover so that I could ski all the way down without taking off my skis. Fundamentally, there are such varieties of exposure and terrain that some part of the mountain always offers good skiing by any man's standards. I remember one weekend when Stowe's deep powder was to be found in granulated form on the Skimeister only, having been ground up by 2,000-pound harrows towed by Sno-Cats. Of course, it must be mentioned that I have at least one idiosyncrasy. I have considerably less fear of frozen surfaces than I have of deep snow. Some of my happiest days have been when I skied an icy, somewhat deserted mountain on wood slaloms with tuned-up offset edges. But no matter how critical one's taste, Stowe, weekend after weekend, can offer near-excellent skiing on most trails.

When I was at Dartmouth, my teammates Bob Meservy and Jake Nunnemacher used to spend Thanksgiving weekend at Stowe while I was cooped up in New Jersey with the family. Knowing how much I hated to miss skiing on Mt. Mansfield, they would send me a postcard, in which they made up stories about the trails all being open, the practice slalom they ran with Toni Matt, and the ten to twelve mountain runs they had a day. Actually skiing at Mt. Mansfield at that time of year was usually limited to thin-cover skiing on the Toll Road, or rare rope-tow slope skiing on the practice hill, with rocks and stumps projecting through on the big trails. However, during three of the last four years, Mansfield as well as other areas in the Green Mountains has had excellent skiing starting in mid-November. This seems extraordinary in the face of a long-term, 100-year-old warming trend.

Friends to ski with could always be found at Stowe. Sometimes it would be nonstop Charlie Stiassni, my long-term veteran rival, other times a group from The Foster Place, notably led by Bill Viall, a personality boy whose fame on skis was solely limited to his resemblance to Zeno Colo. Bill, like Zeno, is partly bald, but unlike Zeno, is not one of the great skiers of the world. Nevertheless in his deep crouch and with his downthrust hand action, steering as if he held the wheel of a bobsled, Bill seemed to be imitating the style of the great Colo. For years my favorite companion on Mansfield was ex-Olympian Dartmouth skier Colin Stewart, one of the most graceful skiers ever to ski at Stowe. Colin is a successful architect now practicing in Denver. His aesthetic touch was apparent in his every move on skis, and it was a real joy to tail him down the mountain. He was younger than I and a better skier in every way, and by mimicking him to some extent I sharpened up and became better too.

About ten years ago I was skiing down the National with Tom Watson, Wawa Lannon, and Mike Brooks, then a boy about twelve years old. The mountain was fairly icy, and Tom took a fall halfway down the steep upper section of the National, sliding rapidly over the moguls, his body relaxed, but looking as if it was taking quite a pounding. Tom skidded right down to the junction of the National and the Lift Line, for a distance of about three hundred yards. When he got back on his feet he was obviously bruised and shaken up, and there was some evidence that he had a slight concussion. I remember thinking International Business Machines stock would drop a few points if a news program were to show a film of his fall. One day on Madonna Mountain in 1964 I was skiing with Tom, his wife Olive, and Rod Stephens, navigator on that year's America's Cup defender *Constellation,* who at fifty-four was skiing for his third year. Everyone was skiing well, Tom and Olive with good speed, grace, and exemplary control, and Rod unbelievably well for someone who had taken it up at such a late point in life. But I was particularly impressed with how much Tom's skiing had improved, and what a contrast it was to his helplessness on the ice of the National years earlier.

On the Monday and Tuesday before Easter in 1961 a very bad thaw set in during which the trails lost much of their cover. Then a cold front brought six to eight inches of new light snow which blew off most of the runs, leaving an exceptionally slick surface. My family and I, skiing various areas in the snow corner of Vermont, found ourselves at Stowe on Good Friday. The Skimeister and the

Lord and Toll Road offered good skiing. Although the Nose Dive was closed, ironically the Lift Line was open. There was a considable amount of windblown snow in the troughs of the Lift Line moguls, with the tops of the mounds glistening wickedly in the sun. Few people took the trail, and those who did go down were foolish and soon regretted it. Unable to handle the abrupt change from ice to heavy wind-packed snow below the moguls, they were falling every few yards. Toward two o'clock in the afternoon I noted that just enough people had skied the Lift Line to break up the drifts of wind-packed powder. Also, after a full day of sun, the ice patches were softening just a bit. So I went down the trail, and after the first few turns I sensed that my judgment had been good and the slope was ready to be skied all out. The ice crust in places shattered under my edges, and in others held well. And the windblown snow was sufficiently broken out for easy handling. I skied two thirds of the Lift Line without stopping, and part of the fun was in knowing that some of the people riding up the lift would think I was Superman, after the difficult time earlier skiers had been having.

I went right back up, realizing that the sun was now behind the mountain and that this run would not be as good as the one before, because the crust would be firm again. While still on the narrow, extremely steep section near the third tower from the top, I came upon a skier who was obviously having trouble. "What am I doing here?" he asked.

"What are you doing here?" I replied.

"Those two b——s that I am skiing with said this was the best way to get down the mountain." I sensed he was talking about the two Kennedy brothers, Bobby and Ted, who were skiing Mansfield that day. Helping this forlorn fellow down the steep part beyond the Goat Trail, I spotted the two Kennedys. Bobby had his skis off, and was standing below a pine tree on blue ice, with a cut under one eye. Ted, with his skis on, was standing on drifted snow, and with outthrust pole, like a roped mountaineer, was helping Bobby step to safety. When Bobby got going again, I saw he was a strong, athletic skier with too much courage for his ability. Ted was somewhat the same sort, except that he was more polished and experienced. Bobby started too fast, found himself unable to turn, and shot across the slope in a rather helpless traverse. When he finally managed to stop, I skied up to him and suggested that he turn under each mogul into the soft snow. "If you miss one turn, make sure you don't miss the next, but always do your checking where the good snow is."

"Let's see you do it," he said. Fortunately I could. My advice seemed to work, and farther down the trail he thanked me graciously. "Well, as a partisan Democrat," I replied, "I'll do anything to help the new administration." Bobby and Ted chuckled, and we then skied down the mountain together.

One wintry January weekend I started off down the Lord Trail, making early morning warm-up turns. The granular surface was quite hard, and yet the sharpened edges on my beat-up year-old wood Kaestle slaloms seemed to hold. Feeling that the mountain was going to be easy for me that day, I swung over toward the Lift Line, taking a traverse which cuts across the top of the National. I was approaching the Lift Line at about twenty-five miles an hour, when suddenly I found myself on a stretch of glacier-blue ice. Immediately aware that my old skis were no match for this grade of ice, I instinctively shifted my weight slightly back. Suddenly I spun around on my skis, ending up in a reverse stem position and going backward at horrifying speed. This was clearly my most perilous moment on skis. Seeing the trees below, I was too scared to fall, and completely at a loss as to what to do. Fortunately, I left the ice patch as abruptly as I had come to it, and the wood skis took hold on the crust. The reverse stem position slowed me down, and putting my weight on the downhill ski steered me up the slope. Gradually I came to a stop, where I stayed for at least ten minutes, trying to collect my wits.

An extension of the same traverse goes through the woods past the Goat Trail and then into the woods again for a longer stretch, before culminating at the top of the Corridor section of the Nose Dive. This part of the catwalk evokes another mood, providing easy cross-countrylike downhill gliding through the quietness of the woods. The trail, not known to many, almost always has soft powder snow. So there is a true feeling of enjoying nature's midwinter tranquility. Even the noise of skiers on the other trails is muffled, and the sole sense of skiing is the softness of the powder snow under the skis. Yet surprisingly there is still the sensation of speed, since the trail is narrow and the trees go by only inches away.

In the late spring of 1962 I was as usual planning to ski in the Sugar Slalom at Stowe. During the week before the race there were several heavy rains, with warm days in between. As a precaution on Friday I called Alice Todd, then manager of The Foster Place, and she reported that it had been snowing all morning, with more predicted. I went on up, driving in the rain all the way until a few miles from the mountain. On Mansfield it snowed all night, all day Saturday, and was still snowing Sunday morning, the day of the Sugar Slalom. There was a total fall of about thirty inches of slightly moist powder.

After the race Al Sise and I, along with some young people, Ann McAlpin, Francis Woods, and Rosie Fortna, who became an Olympic Slalom skier, all went down the National. The sun was out, there was a whole new layer of snow flattening moguls carved out of the winter's base, and although the snow was partially packed out, there was as yet no new generation of moguls to take their place. Soft under the foot, the snow was fast as lightning for skis waxed for racing. And the smooth terrain was ideal for steep slope skiing. The youngsters were trying to prove that they could outski and outspeed Sise and me, but we all had a ball. When we got down, Sise turned to me and said, "That's the best run I have had in my life." And this was on the last weekend in April.

With the family coming along, and family skiing interest shifting to another area, Stowe has become more and more the place where I go on bachelor weekends. For I am happiest when skiing Mansfield. I now usually stay with my friends the Cookes. Nancy, who was a prewar national ski champion, and "Cookie," the head of Bayer Aspirin's Glenbrook Laboratories, have a handsome modern house high on the Spruce Peak road, looking over at Mt. Mansfield. A weekend with them adds many extras to the mountain's fun.

The most controversial ending to one of my bachelor weekends occurred a few years ago, when I still stayed at The Foster Place. On Sunday the mountain was going through one of the coldest days of the winter, with below-zero temperatures and a strong wind blowing through the Notch. It was one of those days when two or three runs suffice. I bummed a ride home with two college girls who were staying at The Foster Place, and we left about noon. Near Albany I called Barbara and asked her to meet me at the Suffern interchange on the New York Thruway. She said she was just about to leave for a cocktail party, but under pressure she consented to come and pick me up. At the scheduled hour we pulled up alongside Barbara. She took note of the spanking new white Chevrolet convertible and the two attractive girls who had driven me down, and when I got in our car she said, "Sometimes I'm not so sure it's the mountain that draws you to Stowe."

12

A Young Girl's Fancy

Many young girls learning to ski are carried along with the tide, joining skiing friends or possibly a ski club as a first step into the sport. There are some, however, who take it up completely on their own, so that the adventure of skiing starts with the purchase of an instruction book, a careful perusal of literature on ski resorts, and visits to ski shops, wondering how much to spend and what to buy. Even when a girl starts off with someone at her side who is knowledgeable about skiing, it is still a pretty uncertain procedure. We dedicate this chapter to a determined girl who has enough of the explorer's instinct to become a skier without having anyone to turn to for help.

This mythical girl is no ordinary creature. She may want to forget a boyfriend, without getting started with another just like him. Her hair is probably short, trimmed to a boyish style, more because it suits her than because it is fashionable. And she has to be quite a secure young lady to want to follow the single-life route to a sport like skiing. If her hair is short, the boy she is leaving behind probably has long hair and sideburns. He spends more time in front of the mirror with his comb than she does. Also, he seems to have more need for a continuing romantic attachment than she does. He is possibly much less secure than the girl leaving him.

There is a storybook life ahead of this young skier. For her skiing is a dream and the dream starts when she decides to ski. Best of all she knows that the dream will come true. It is almost unheard of for young people, once they have decided to make the effort to learn to ski, to turn their backs on the sport. Certainly she has sufficient spunk that this won't happen to her.

She sees skiing as a world where the sun always shines. In the literal sense this is untrue, but even on an overcast day, skiers radiate happiness. She knows that the double chair and the T bar are here to stay, and that a girl rarely has a lonely ride up the mountain. For wherever she skis there will be more men than girls. She has a pretty good idea, too, that these men will be a hardier breed than the type at home, and because they are skiers and skiing is so important to them, they will be a little less preoccupied with the comb and the mirror.

She knows that skiing offers its unique opportunity for her to find herself and lead a life on her own terms. Leaving her family behind to take up skiing probably gives her more of a feeling of independence than breaking away from the boy at home. For some people the mountains in themselves represent an escape, a chance to get away from society and to become closer to nature, where life's problems can be looked at more objectively.

Of course, the commitment to skiing sometimes poses problems, particularly for a girl. Any form of complete involvement provides tests of character, skiing as much as any. For some youngsters it is difficult to relate skiing to the other aspects of their lives.

Most ski bums do not have this difficulty. The ski bum may take one or two winters off to do nothing but ski. Sometimes he is a college student taking one semester off; sometimes he is taking a few months off before military service or graduate school, both of which would curb skiing over an extended period of time. For certain girls, who for one reason or another are not suited for college, ski-bumming can be a beneficial alternative. Skiing can even be a respected career or profession. Managing an inn, operating a ski shop, and teaching skiing are all legitimate ways to earn a living in the north country. A career of skiing can be balanced with farming, summer resort operation, and small-time industry of a seasonal nature.

There are some real bums in the ski world, like the handful of "surfers" who did their best to give Aspen a bad name during recent winters. These bums, wherever they may be found, are hangers-on, perennial loafers, parasites one and all, whose main stock-in-trade is a phony, slippery brand of charm. They seem to have forsaken a gainful life, and the vacant state of their minds is apparent in their vacant expressions. Skiing for them has become a disease the way alcohol or drugs may be for others. Their only hope is somehow to regain their self-respect by withdrawing temporarily from skiing or by putting the sport in a realistic proportion to their other activities.

Fortunately for our friend, there are few real bums on the ski scene. Also, since the girl we are addressing ourselves to has left a boy behind because she did not fully respect him, she is not very likely to become enchanted with the lowest order of man in the ski world. The kind of a bum we are talking about just barely gets by, economically as well as socially, in a ski community. He is a fairly rare bird, who never at any time is cast in a hero's role.

So much, then, for the good life and for the pitfalls lying ahead of our young lady who yearns to ski. The question is now, how does she get started?

First, the beginner buys a good book on skiing, such as *Expert Skiing*, by Dave Bradley, Ralph Miller, and Al Merrill. As the title implies, the text is fairly sophisticated, but it is both well written and well illustrated. Any how-to-ski book will have its limitations, because no one can learn to ski parallel from a book. Familiarization with the sport is useful, however, and there is obviously no limit to the background knowledge that can be absorbed. Some of the simple maneuvers, like walking on the level, doing kick turns, sidestepping up the hill, and herringboning, might actually be learned from a ski book. Also it is possible to learn the basics of downhill skiing, such as the snowplow position and the sideslip.

Nevertheless, since timing and not body position is the essence of the turn, the rhythm of skiing cannot ever be fully understood through reading. To show what little regard I have for text in a ski book, I once mailed to a friend, Jack White, a newcomer to skiing, the original German version of *Wedeln,* by Miki Hutter, Friedl Wolfgang, and Kruckenhauser—the latter being the dogmatist of modern Austrian technique. This book contains sequential illustrations which come quite close to approximating the feeling of skiing. Jack called me when he received the book and said, "What's the big idea? You know I can't read a word of German."

He did not go along at all with the point that the photographs were more important than the text and the subtitles. For the benefit of those who agree with him, *Wedeln* is now available in an English translation.

Second, after reading a ski book, the beginner must purchase equipment. Since our imaginary young lady has a burning desire to ski, we will not suggest the rental route. In most cities there are several ski shops, and her first move is to visit more than one, with an eye toward personal appeal, depth of stock, and fashionable styles.

Once a shop has been selected, our girl should become a trusting soul. It is important that she follow the advice of the shopkeepers. Women often have undue suspicions about the merchants they do business with. "Short weight" is virtually unheard of. In a competitive business, whether large or small, the retailer constantly strives for customer satisfaction, bending over backward to give fair treatment. The advice of people behind the counter is too often unsought or unheeded when given.

For the ski purchase it is particularly important to place trust in the retailer, who almost always is a long-time skier and fully experienced in advising a newcomer to the sport. Also, the equipment available being almost uniformly good, there is practically no chance of getting "hooked."

When women enter a ski shop they always gravitate toward the clothing section. When men enter, they head for the ski rack. When couples go into a shop, they split up. Our friend knows that she is going to be at home with ski fashions, and that she is going to look pretty nifty in stretch pants. This is another one of the many reasons she is attracted to skiing. Actually, because the selection of ski attire is always largely personal, I have little advice to put forward. Our friend does not need to be told that in stretch pants the skintight look is the fashion. Length should not be skimped on and pants should sit comfortably high enough on the hips. She should be able to sit down even if with discomfort, and also, since she must be able to get into her own binding, she should be able to bend down and touch an imaginary point a few inches ahead of the foot. For a first pair of ski pants, a conservative color like black is not a bad idea, because she will have more freedom to choose bright shades and gay patterns in jackets and sweaters. Also, good stretch pants have a long, useful life, and are worth the expense. Pants made of lightweight cloth at low prices should be avoided.

As for the rest of our friend's ski attire, ski magazines should be scanned for ideas. Feature articles in fashion magazines can be generally ignored as they are inclined to show flamboyant styles as an attention-getting device. For warmth, some sort of quilted parka is essential. Red long johns need no comment. Today's curon-lined slalom gloves are recommended for their surprising warmth, as well as for their quality of letting the skier feel the pole in her hand. Too, mittens are often the mark of a neophyte, and ski snobbery is part of the fun. There is great room for an imaginative approach in selecting headgear. Some inexpensive accessories can offer many color variations in the costume. I am thinking of nylon shells (lightweight-zippered windbreaker shirts), turtleneck jerseys, and knitted hats. Scarves at this moment are in, but not for skiing.

Choosing ski fashions should come easy. However, the essentials of boots and skis take our friend into uncharted waters. If I ran into her in the ski shop while she was mystified by the multiplicity of high-priced choices, I might say, "You look like a girl in a dilemma." I would then tell her that I'd like to help, and perhaps give a long spiel about boots and skis. In the end I would emphasize the importance of taking the storekeeper's advice, which she would probably be inclined to do anyhow after hearing about the marvels of present-day equipment. Here is what I would like her to consider.

Boots should be purchased for fit rather than for style, and again for fit rather than brand. There is no point in following a buy-American rule, since almost all ski boots except the new epoxys are made in Europe. There are many excellent brands, and faulty boots are almost a thing of the past. Boots fall into two categories—lace-up boots with inner boots, and the more modern buckle boots. The essential combination of good fit and strong support is possible through either type. Synthetic boots, such as the epoxys, are gradually but inexorably replacing leather boots.

The buckle boot, interestingly enough, is the first piece of equipment to be proved by the average skier and passed along to the expert. The quick relief of pressure, when pains develop in the bony projections of the feet and ankles, has definite appeal to both types of skiers. The main reason the expert prefers the buckle boots is that they enable him to endure an even stiffer, tougher boot than he would normally. The bonus for the average skier is that he tends to lace up conventional boots once during the day, and since boots invariably loosen, his feet are floating around by midday. Because the skier can flip in and out of the buckle boots, he always seems to be tinkering with them. A fringe benefit for our young skier is the speed at which she can get into a pair of buckle boots, eliminating part of the discomfort from bending down for protracted periods in tight stretch pants.

If the skier's budget cannot permit the buckle boots, a perfectly satisfactory performance may be obtained from laced-double boots. There is little necessity for people with normal feet to order custom-made boots. Through a careful process of selection, the average skier can get a perfect fit from boots purchased off the rack.

Some comment on fit is most important. The boot is the link between the skier and the ski, and for the ski to be truly responsive, the foot and ankle must be both securely supported and held tight. It is necessary for the sake of comparison to try on more than one pair of boots, usually several. A recent ski annual went to an extreme, stating that it takes three hours to get fitted for boots. And the ski shops were plagued by a few customers who actually went for the full time limit.

The big mistake most skiers make is to have the boots fitted over more than one pair of heavy socks, out of concern for the cold. One medium-weight pair of wool socks is recommended. There will be room for an inner pair of silk socks if this is necessary to keep the feet warm. Also, the boots tend to stretch, enabling the skier eventually to go to a heavier pair of wool socks. Anyway, toe wiggling keeps the feet warmer than a number of layers of socks. For this reason the boot should be long enough so that the toes can work, just missing but almost touching the front of the boot when it is laced up. The fit for width, especially through the instep and ankle is most important. There should also be the feeling that the front part of the foot is gripped snugly, with no play at the sides of the boot.

Some of the more expensive boots are built with an arch to match the curvature of the foot. The fit below the ankle bones and around the heel is also quite critical. The back of the boot fits snugly around the base of the heel, and a pad about an inch above the heel comes in under the ankle bones. Most good boots provide padded cups for the ankle bones, easing the pressure on a sensitive part of the foot. The laced boot should be left loose enough at the top for the ankle to bend all the way forward. The foot can barely be lifted away from the sole of the boot, and the heel can lift up no more than a quarter of an inch. The wearer can measure the support of the boot by firmly pressing either side of the sole against the floor. When doing this she should feel the pressure all along the sides of the feet. The modern boot is actually so stiff that wearing one is comparable to putting the foot into armor-plating. It must not collapse at all at the sides, and flex only enough to permit the knee to drive forward. For on the hill edging is accomplished by pushing the knees into the slope, not by bending the ankles. These stiff boots require a tough break-in period for tender feet, but through a good fit, extreme discomfort at the bony parts of the feet can be lessened if not avoided.

Beginning skiers often approach the purchase of skis with more trepidation than the purchase of boots. After all, in choosing boots our young friend can at least be comforted by the knowledge that since her feet are the ones being fitted, she is the expert on whether or not the boots fit. Skis, on the other hand, may seem more of an enigma, entailing the choice of many brands and lengths as well as the fundamental decision for wood or metal. Actually skis are no more mysterious than boots. The technology involved in the manufacture of both metal and wood skis, but especially metal, has assured such exacting standards that there is hardly any likelihood of getting a faulty pair.

The advent of Head metal skis in 1950 proved a tremendous boon to recreational skiing. These skis, nicknamed "cheaters," were thought of as wonder skis that automatically upgraded one's level of skiing. Through their design metal skis did offer certain advantages over wood skis. However, the main reason the average skier considered them "cheaters" is that he compared them with an imperfect pair of wood skis. The Head ski's real breakthrough was that for the first time skis were standardized, and manufactured by a process of skillfully putting together laminations of wood into a metal sandwich hermetically sealed with plastic. As a result there were no more warped skis, variations in camber, or deviations from a standard of flexibility.

Selecting a good pair of wood skis once required great skill. Before World War II most skis were solid hickory. One had to check the end of the ski for grain. A flat or horizontally grained ski tended to be fairly flexible and hard to break, whereas an upright grained ski was stiffer and harder to turn. Also the skis had to be inspected for warpage, for often there was a twist in the running surface or an added curve—sometimes even a bad S curve—along the side of the ski. It was equally important to determine that the skis were exact mates by first bending the tails and then the shovels, etc. The advent of the modern multilaminated wood ski has simplified the selection of a good pair of woods. It is unlikely that a matched set of wood skis made by one of the leading ski manufacturers would be mismates. However, between one pair and the next there are differences in flexibility. Here again the newcomer to the sport should follow the advice of the salesperson in the ski shop, who would undoubtedly recommend fairly flexible skis. An experienced skier would probably want stiffer skis, more like the slalom model favored by racers.

The real disadvantage of wood skis is that they are not nearly as durable as metal skis, and despite being sealed with a plastic finish, they tend to lose moisture. As the dried-out wood becomes brittle, the skis lose their resiliency and react sluggishly to variations in terrain as well as to the skier's command. Also their shape changes from the original design. Sometimes wood skis lose their camber, becoming so flat that the skier's weight is carried by eighteen inches of ski under the foot. These flattened skis are easy to turn, but unsteady going straight at high speed, and not too exact in carving out a turn. Sometimes the skis end up with too much camber. Then much of the skier's weight rides on the shovel and the tail, which dig in and make the skis extremely difficult to turn.

We have seen that selecting wood skis requires more care than selecting metal ones. And between seasons wood skis need special handling. However, even in the early days of wood skis it was perfectly possible to find oneself with an exceptionally good pair.

Wendell Hastings, a friend from Boston, who is a member of the Schussverein Ski Club, once purchased such a pair of skis secondhand in the Alps. They originally belonged to a German doctor who had bought them in 1928 for fifteen dollars from Sporta Schuster in Munich. Manufactured by Marius Ericksen, father of world champion Stein Ericksen, these skis were in many ways quite advanced. In place of the telemark tip they had a modern pointed tip, much like that of the Head competition model today. Made of laminated hickory, they had steel edges throughout their length, extending into the shovel of the skis, unusual for skis of that era. The original binding was a Bildstein heel-spring which attached to a jumper's hitch on the ski, offering downpull action. When the skis were two years old the German doctor sold them to Wendell Hastings for twelve dollars. The first time Wendell skied on them he recognized that they were exceptional skis. They had life, they turned well in all kinds of snow, and right from the start they upgraded his skiing. He continued to ski on them year after year, occasionally replacing a metal edge. And always each summer he carefully stored them away after blocking them and dousing them with linseed oil, then the standard treatment for preventing loss of moisture. When the Kandahar binding became popular in the late 1930's, Wendell converted the skis from the old Bildstein spring.

The skis seemed to have a quality of immortality. In appearance the tops began to look somewhat chafed and worn, and several metal edges had to be secured with rivets, which went right through the skis because of worn-out screw holes. Finally, in 1960 Wendell Hastings walked into the Hofstetter Ski Shop in Geneva with his Marius Ericksen 1928 model skis. He asked for the owner of the shop and said, "I really think it's time I bought a new pair of skis, but I've become very attached to these, and I like the way they handle. I want you to look at them very carefully and try to select a new pair which will have the same characteristics."

The owner was quite impressed by the museum pieces, and called his entire personnel over to look at them. He then carefully examined them for dimensions, camber, and flexibility. Surprisingly enough, he then chose a pair of Head standards off the rack, saying, "I think these will handle very much like your old-timers."

After Wendell got back to his hotel he took one of the Ericksens and one of the Heads and put them side by side, comparing them in every conceivable manner. The two seemed to be identical in all respects except that one was a sleek black metal ski and the other an ancient, weatherbeaten wooden one. Later, skiing on the new Heads, Wendell was also pleased with the way they handled. True to prediction, they behaved just like his revered Ericksens, which occasionally still have an outing. They are kept in Europe for members of Wendell's family when they ski there. When not in use, the Ericksens are stored very carefully according to the owner's specifications.

Wendell Hastings was fortunate in ending up with such a remarkable pair of woods. Happily he had the presence of mind to realize they had a charmed life, and treated them with great respect. Unlike Wendell in 1930, our young friend looking at countless skis in the rack today does not have astronomical odds against her in trying to choose a good pair.

Her basic decision in buying her first pair of skis will be whether to select wood or metal, with price being the deciding factor. Modern fiber-glass skis are more suitable for experienced skiers. If her funds are limited for equipment, wood skis will be her choice. However, over long term there is a saving on metal skis, since wood skis rarely last more than two or three years. The shorter life of the wood skis might have some advantage for our friend, because with her unusual mental makeup she might be ready in two or three years for a racing model or a more expert type than she selected in the beginning.

Whether metal or wood, her first skis will be flexible, easy to turn, and easy to handle. The storekeeper will undoubtedly recommend a pair with such qualities. As to length, there may be some confusion. There has been much talk about the short ski as a safer, surer, quicker route to skiing. Cliff Taylor, whose ideas on short skis have been well publicized, deserves credit for encouraging people who otherwise might never have skied. The short ski is the answer for older people and for those who for one reason or another have well-founded fears about taking up the sport. These skis are also good for people who ski only once or twice a winter. But for the young in heart, skis ranging from two to four feet in length are really "for the birds." The length of ski for the racer has not changed through the years, and the full-length ski is here to stay. The steadiness at any speed, the thrill of carving a turn, the feeling of utilizing the entire body properly on the skis, are lost on skis that extend just a few inches beyond the boot in either direction.

Nevertheless, the first pair of skis should be on the short side. There is less awkwardness, more ease in learning, and no need whatsoever for the extra length during the early stages of skiing. A good rule for our young friend is to choose a pair just over her height, using upraised elbow as a yardstick. In stocking feet the end of the elbow should coincide with the tip of the ski. More advanced skiers may buy skis as long as their upraised wrist, but some people are better off never quite going to full-length skis. Competence, weight, build, and strength are all factors, which the salesperson should be in a position to evaluate.

With the bindings there is little chance that the storekeeper will make a controversial selection. A tested safety binding is a must. The key is to stay away from a new binding or one whose design is modified each year. Marker, Look Nevada, Salomon, Miller, and Cubco are among the best brands. Chic as a long-thong binding might seem to a spirited beginner, our friend will find it absolutely unnecessary for a couple of years since its small margin of extra control will be meaningless to her. Setting the binding is very important. The salesperson's advice should be followed as to how often it should be checked and whether this can be done by the skier or by the ski shop. A good binding improperly set is no safeguard. During the first few days of skiing the bindings should be set to release with little thrust or strain. Our young friend should muster every bit of mechanical know-how she possesses, and learn all she can about the operational principle of her binding.

The simplest equipment to buy is a set of ski poles. A first pair should be inexpensive aluminum poles. These are ordinary poles without taper, and there is nothing fancy about the handles. But being lightweight, tubular aluminum, in a bad fall they can be bent without danger to the skier or risk that they will be broken. The length, right from the beginning, should be such that, when the poles are properly grasped, the forearms are nearly horizontal. Again the skier should be in stocking feet.

The stage is now set for our young friend to set forth on skis. She is fully equipped and eager to get started. If there is snow in the backyard, one of the best ways to begin is to walk around and get used to having skis on the feet for an hour or so. There is awkwardness in suddenly having the foot extended to five or six times its natural length—the impression one has wearing skis for the first time. Taking this first plunge by herself, she will avoid some of the embarrassment naturally faced by the beginner the first time out on the practice slope. Also it should be remembered that the how-to-ski book is of more use the first day on skis than at any other time. Walking on the level, the climbing steps, and the kick turn are all simple movements easily performed by the beginner who has done his homework.

The next step might be to go to some nearby ski area for the day, possibly to a hill with man-made snow. A beginner's slope and a beginner's class are essential, and usually both will be available at this type of ski area. After two or three trips our friend is a fledgling snowplow skier. Ideally the next move should be a week of skiing with daily instruction at a large ski area. Generally speaking, the bigger the ski school, the more chance the beginner has to be grouped with her own kind. The large ski school, in any learn-to-ski week, is invaded by a good number of newcomers to the sport. Another advantage of the big area is the beginner's immediate exposure to the full drama of the sport. The steep slopes, the presence of expert skiers, and the overall atmosphere of the resort reinforce the desire to learn to ski well in the shortest possible time.

Our young friend, like all beginners, wants to learn to ski parallel. This is a basic urge which I fully encourage. In fact, the parallel turn is the only essential phase of technique the instructor has to teach her. Upon reaching the parallel skiing stage, the skier leaves everything else behind except the snowplow—which always remains part of a skier's bag of tricks as an emergency braking mechanism. The stem turn in all its stages has no value whatsoever, no matter what the sharpness of turn, the steepness of slope, the speed of the skier, or the type of snow conditions. So my advice to a beginner is to become a "Young Turk" and advance as quickly as possible.

The biggest mistake beginners make is to try to perfect each type of rudimentary turn mechanically, overlooking the importance of getting the feel of skiing. All of the early types of turns and maneuvers should be viewed as exercises to familiarize the skier with some of the motions and rhythms of skiing. It is far better to be relaxed and somewhat sloppy about form than to be tense, trying too hard to have each part of the body making exactly the right motion at the right time. The latter skier is reluctant to move along to the next maneuver until the present one has been accomplished to perfection. My answer is that it is ridiculous to perfect a stem turn or a stem christie which will be useless once parallel skiing is learned.

Unfortunately, with very few exceptions, the ski school today conforms to the curriculum laid down by Hannes Schneider shortly after World War I. Here is a rationale for the importance of learning each stage of the stem before moving on to the next. It was written by Friedl Pfeifer in 1941, when he was director of the Sun Valley Ski School:

> As your speed and ability increase, one turn will fade into the next. The stem turn develops almost automatically out of the slow snowplow at the instant that it is correctly executed on a steeper grade and with a little more speed, aided by the rhythmical body swing of properly mastered skiing.

Friedl Pfeifer could not have known that he was defining a principle to be followed for the next twenty-five years. Ski schools are so tradition-bound that they have been unable to break away from the methods used by Hannes Schneider, even though the result of what they teach has changed tremendously. There must be a way—and certain radical ski schools have found a way—of teaching the parallel turn early by starting with the sideslip, which evolves into parallel turns, first up the hill and then down into the fall line. The modern parallel Austrian turn becomes the ultimate accomplishment no matter which road is taken first. As taught under the so-called American system, any differences are of a minor nature.

So each of the preliminary turns should be used by the pupil as the means to an end, as a way of getting the feel of skiing. The parallel turn itself should be perfected but with more emphasis on correct rhythm than on correct form, for skiing without rhythm is not skiing at all. In this book the challenge considered is the rhythm of skiing, with a description of the body movements involved largely left to the ski manuals.

To get back to our young friend, she immediately made a name for herself as a professionally dressed and well-equipped beginner who fought hard at the end of each day to be sent on to a more advanced class. Knowing that the only way to break the stem habit was not to get into it, she became a parallel skier after one week of practice. She had even skied the big mountain, having negotiated all but the steepest trails. She had met some of the hotshot racers training in the area. She had not yet had a ski romance, but she had met several young men, including two she hoped to see again. She knew that she would take to the sport as a duck takes to water. In fact, skiing had become part of her life.

13

European Adventure

There are many reasons for skiing in Europe, not the least of which is that each day is an adventure. Perhaps the mixture of nationalities contributes to this more than anything else, but certainly the grandeur of the Alps as well as the endless variety of runs with their resulting challenges, have an essential role in the adventures for each day the skier returns with some exciting new tale.

On Washington's Birthday weekend of 1962, Barbara and I, thanks to some help from a winner in the stock market, found ourselves on the Silver Lake Skating Club charter flight, heading for our first ski vacation in the Alps. We were not to be disappointed in any respect, and certainly we were to have more than our share of adventures during a three-week stay. My good friend Bob Schwarzenbach, thoroughly versed in Alpine resorts, had selected three famous areas for us. He said that for a "hard-nosed" skier like me nothing less would do for my first trip than St. Anton, Davos-Klosters, and Zermatt.

On the plane I chatted extensively with Bill and Dottie Blanchard from Morristown, old hands at European skiing from whom I hoped to get some last-minute tips. I told Bill about my plans to go to ski school in St. Anton for ten straight days. Although having had the benefit of coaching at Dartmouth, and in recent years an occasional private lesson from a top-caliber instructor, I had never been to ski school. Essentially I was hoping to get rid of my bad habits and learn to ski the modern Austrian way. Stressing one point, Bill Blanchard told me that on my first morning in St. Anton I should get hold of Rudi Matt, successor to Hannes Schneider as head of the world's most renowned ski school, and insist that I was a good enough skier to be in the top class. Bill said that if I was at all modest about my level of skiing, I would end up in the wrong class.

Barbara and I had flown the Atlantic before, but in a propeller-driven plane. In a jet there is the feeling of conquering space. This was particularly noticeable as Ireland, the southern tip of England, and the French coast seemed to slip by in a few minutes. After crossing the foothills of the Alps, we headed up the Rhine Valley for Zurich. As we descended through some momentary layers of clouds, the sides of a snowy spruce-studded valley seemed entirely too close to the wings of the plane. Our Swissair pilot then made such a soft landing that we were on the ground for a couple of seconds before we realized it. For this performance the passengers offered a spontaneous burst of applause.

Fortunately, we had a ride to the Arlberg with two people from our flight who had engaged a car with an Austrian driver. Driving through Switzerland on a perfect sunny afternoon, we marveled at the beautiful natural terrain and well-groomed look of the midwinter countryside. The Swiss, who have the reputation of being shrewd and resourceful, take a pride in their land which is evident at every turn. And the neatness of the scene with the quaint chalet-style farms and barns presents a pleasant contrast to the American countryside, which is not always respected, and rarely cared for with abiding interest.

Nearing Austria we touched momentarily on the rugged soil of Liechtenstein, and our driver entertained us with some of the fabulous history of that little principality. In Austria our interest shifted to the mountains among which the driver identified certain peaks and ski areas. He also told us about the recent heavy snows and avalanches that had curtailed skiing and closed the mountain passes.

Our friends, who were headed for Zurs, left us at Langen to take the train through the Arlberg Tunnel to St. Anton. We knew that we had arrived in the ski country when we saw two well-tanned friends from New York, Helen and Willi Benedict, with skis on their shoulders, standing in the Langen station. They had just skied the Albona and were on their way back to St. Anton. After the 7-mile-long ride through the tunnel, we were in the middle of St. Anton, which by this time was in darkness. Somehow a nighttime arrival in a ski area creates mystery and heightens suspense. You feel the mountains tower over you, but you do not know where they are or what they look like.

Our first trip from the station to our hotel in an Austrian Volkswagen bus-taxi was the only time we were transported in St. Anton without peril. Our inn was the Alpenhof, located several hundred vertical feet above the village on the road through the Arlberg Pass. If we did not know it already, the Wiener schnitzel we had for dinner made us sure that we were in Austria. Certainly not many people go there for the cooking.

The next morning I woke up early and rushed around to see the view through the windows at each side of the Alpenhof. The mountains were still bathed in the reddish glow of dawn. By the time I had breakfasted and gotten organized for skiing it was fairly close to ski school time. After putting on my skis outside the inn I headed down for St. Anton across vast sloping meadows covered with several feet of soft snow. I felt a little like the hare in the famous Hannes Schneider ski chase film as I descended gentle snowfields dotted with Tyrolean huts and barns. There were obstacles such as roads and fences, but without really knowing where I was going, I was confident that I would end up in the village. After about three quarters of a mile I came to a snow-covered road that appeared to go straight down into St. Anton. There was a fair amount of traffic, including one or two horse-drawn sleighs, and quite a few skiers on foot. On the iced track of the road I traveled at a fairly good clip, but since cars were moving at about the same speed, I did not think I would be arrested for speeding.

However, as I approached the village, with the railroad crossing ahead, I wondered how to stop, because I was hemmed in between the snow bank on one side and St. Anton traffic on the other, with nothing but a straight narrow track ahead. Still, drivers and pedestrians seemed to take me for granted, so I figured there must be a solution somewhere up ahead. As it developed, I did not have to cross the tracks, and like a ski jumper, had a nice little outrun before coming to a stop.

My next move was to get some Austrian currency at the bank, which took more time than I expected, and then I headed over for the ski school. A little on the late side, I found most of the classes already organized, with a number of skiers standing alongside of each instructor at his signpost. I bought a ticket for one week of ski school, and then sought out Rudi Matt, who turned out to be a robust, pink-cheeked man of about fifty, looking somewhat like a brewmaster. Remembering what Bill Blanchard had told me, I started right off with a bold opening:

"My name is Jack Tobin. I used to ski for the Dartmouth ski team. I am in good shape and a fast skier, and I think I belong in the top class."

"Wait a minute. I want to hear more," he said, scowling. Meanwhile he turned to others waiting to be placed in various classes. Finally he turned back to me. "So you think you are good enough for the top class?"

"Yes," I replied. "I skied with your cousin Toni Matt over the Head Wall in 1939, and I still race."

Again he stopped me to hear out the others. I was amazed at his efficiency. Someone would say, "I want beginning parallel." If he said it with confidence Rudi would tell him what class to go to. If not, he would ask one or two more questions before handing out the class assignment. Then he turned to me for the third time. "I have had six Americans in the last week who talked me into putting them in the top class," he said. "Not one of them was able to keep up with that class. What makes you think you are any better?"

My boldness undaunted, I continued to talk of my prowess. The interview went on through about six such interruptions. It was obvious that Herr Matt enjoyed listening to my tale, without believing one word of it. After a while my big talk began to wear down and there was an unusually long interruption for other assignments. At last he looked at me and stated in a rather condescending way, "Oh yes, I can't forget you. You must be at least a fair skier. Go with Robert Gluck." From this attitude I thought I had probably been assigned to a stem christie class.

Robert Gluck was standing by his sign, and unlike the other instructors, he had no students with him. As I approached him, I instinctively decided that I was going to like this fellow, who not only looked like a skier, but also looked like my racing friend, Livermore.

However, when I told him that Rudi Matt had assigned me to his class, he became very excited, and like the White Rabbit, said, "You're late, you're late, you're much too late. Go to the top but we may not wait for you."

I tried to converse with him to calm him down, but he cut me off, giving me a ticket and sending me through the side door of the Galzig tramway building. My ticket turned out to be a priority slip for the tramway, and after a short wait I was on my way up the lift. Although crowded in the car and unable to see very much, I was aware that we were going up, gradually emerging above the tree line to limitless open skiing slopes. When I got out of the cable car, some 2,500 vertical feet above the village, on a tremendous shoulder of the mountain, I was uncertain for a moment as to whether to wait there for Robert Gluck or to go up the next tramway to the top of the Valluga. Since outside the Galzig summit building there was no sign of a class, I decided to go all the way up. Upon arrival at the long corridor where one queues up for the Valluga, I was horrified. People were lined up five or six abreast and it seemed as if there were five hundred jammed between a pipe railing and the wall. I figured that I had no chance of catching up with the others, that I would spend the rest of the morning waiting in line, and that I would miss ski school for the day. However, keeping my eagle eye on the narrow corridor through which an occasional instructor would walk, I finally saw Robert and hailed him. He turned on me with vehemence. "You are much too late. We can't wait for you," he said, and in an overbearing manner proceeded down the corridor. Suddenly he stopped and came back. Standing by the railing he commanded in a quiet but firm tone, "Give me your skis." Next he made a beckoning motion, seemingly with his chin, which was my signal to sneak under the rail.

I followed him down the corridor, and passing countless waiting skiers who, if they did observe us, made no comment. Once again I tried to engage Robert in conversation. "Quiet, don't talk," he said. Suddenly he stopped, and without looking around, made the same motion with his chin—my signal to duck back under the railing near the head of the line. He then skillfully passed me my skis and went on. The entire maneuver of putting me almost at the head of the line had been accomplished with the craftiness of a jewel thief. The woman in back of me started to stammer a protest, but she was so confounded that the words never quite came out.

The ride up the Valluga cable car was awesome. I was fortunate enough to be in the front part for an unimpeded forward view. The Galzig shoulder is separated from the Valluga by a steep-walled glaciated ravine. Immediately in front of the Valluga summit is its twin peak, the Walfagehrjoch. On leaving the Galzig summit the aerial tramway descends slightly as it follows the steep side of the ravine which is famous for the Kandahar run. As this slope falls away, the passengers are more and more suspended in midair. At the extreme slack point of the cable, the car is over the center of the ravine. The drop is then about seven hundred feet, enough for a skilled parachute jumper to make a free fall for a few seconds before pulling the rip cord. The cable car ascends from its nadir in a gradual manner, but the passenger feels that he is suddenly going straight up, with the dramatically steep open runs of the Schindlerkar close below. As the car gets nearer to the slope there is a sensation of speed, and finally when the car swings by the tower on the Walfagehrjoch peak, there is a roller-coaster-like thrill. Then following another short drop-off, with an open-sloped bowl below, the craggy mass of the Valluga appears.

After getting out of the lift, I went into the restaurant, where

I was pleased to find Robert and the class. I was also delighted to see the familiar face of Nan Hewitt, a young member of the Amateur Ski Club of New York. Not only had they waited for me, but I had time for a cup of coffee and a chance to enjoy the view from the glass-walled side of the restaurant, a building which seems poised in space since it juts out over the mountainous Tyrolean terrain. Talking with Nan, who had been skiing in Robert's class most of the winter, I found to my relief that this was not the stem christie class. It was Class 2A, which meant that it was immediately under the top class that I had been trying to get into. The one big difference between the two was that Class 1A skied hard and fast all day long, whereas 2A would spend a good part of the morning doing exercises—the basic school maneuvers on skis, each one of which emphasized some element of the modern Austrian parallel turn.

We left the mountain station and put on our skis at the top of the bowl we had seen on the last stretch of the Valluga lift. Just above us was the actual summit of the Valluga, serviced by a short two-passenger sightseers' cable car. We had the choice of skiing down the steep outrun of the small bowl or taking a catwalk around its side.

The catwalks are an important part of the thrill of skiing in the Alps. The grade and the course of these narrow, somewhat flat trails were determined in the early days of skiing, when there were only a few hardy souls lumbering along on ridgetop hickory skis with natural wood bottoms, often without wax. Under the crowded conditions of today's European resorts, with skiers on fast plastic-bottomed equipment, both the expert and the average skier experience panic on the catwalks. The expert, riding on at least a residue layer of wax on lightning-fast Kofix plastic, and, because he is an expert, poling, pumping, and skating, can easily attain a speed of over twenty-five miles an hour. The average skier, on slower skies, often old-style phenolic-bottomed Heads, is wary of traffic ahead and behind. Disliking the narrowness of the track and the trapped feeling of not being able to check, he moves along at about half the speed of the expert. The uncertainty of the expert, who must constantly deal with overtaking skiers, is so great that he is almost as nervous as the person being overtaken.

Since the catwalk is a fairly level route cut out on the side of a mountain, there are all sorts of blind spots as it follows the mountain's contour. When the expert is alone he creates enough havoc both for himself and for the less-experienced skier, but when the expert is traveling in a pack, pandemonium ensues. The leader sets the pace as well as the passing tactics, with each overtaken skier being passed on the same side in pretty much the same way. The trouble is that there is a changing situation, for as the fourth or fifth member of the pack starts to pass the slower skier, the victim, having swung to one side or the other, may have veered without reason into the path of the oncoming hotshots, or may have fallen in such a manner that he blocks the trail completely.

It was fitting that my first adventure in Europe should begin with a run down the Valluga catwalk, in class, following Robert Gluck. We covered about a quarter of a mile as we rounded the shoulder of the mountain and emerged out of the ravine which seemed to curve as it unwound in almost a spiraling manner. It curved away to the right, and as we skied along we had a constant blind spot ahead. In the length of the catwalk we passed about twenty or thirty skiers without overturning one of them. However, to judge from their peculiar skiing postures we probably struck fear into the hearts of most of them. Sometimes we ourselves had plenty to worry about as we were forced off the track and had to ski on the steep side wall of the ravine, fighting not to tumble down or skid away from the catwalk.

When we finally came to a stop we had a slope under us several hundred yards long which had not been skied upon, but which, since it faced the sun, was covered with a half-inch breakable crust. I soon found out that Robert not only looked like a skier, but was a skier. And he had the reputation for being the best variable-snow skier at St. Anton. He skied down this slope with such a deliberate, methodical rhythm that he looked like a figure shown in slow motion on a movie screen. Since I am such a poor deep snow skier, I was humiliated on the first turn, but I was not alone. In the entire class, only Nan and one other person got down the slope without falling. But Robert's outstanding example, plus his verbal emphasis of key points, was helpful to all of us. Near the end of our run we were all doing better. We knew then that we were going to learn much from Robert, and that we were going to enjoy immensely our week together.

Since it was Sunday there was no morning session of exercises, and there was not even any more troublesome breakable crust. We skied out of the ravine on the other side in a long traverse, which took us around the Walfagehrjoch, down the Schindlerkar. This steep slope commands considerable respect. Average skiers steer clear of it and experts ski it only with a guide and always with a nervous thrill, for it is a slope so long and so steep that it is easily possible to take a header and fall away for a somersaulting slide of half a mile. There is also the possibility of sliding onto a rock face. But on this day Robert picked a route and a pace that we could all enjoy. We had excellent Alpine skiing, generally on an unbroken surface that was soft under the foot and yet firm enough so that our skis did not sink through. I remember one turn in particular, where we were skiing down a ridge that ended in a slight up-slope. We turned at the transition, with the slope on the other side giving us a rounded banked turn, and then headed down a not too steep section of the Schindlerkar, where we made long linked turns follow-the-leader style, at a fast but relaxed speed. We were all pleased with the run that Robert had selected, discovering that Robert was not only a first-rate instructor, but also a man who knew his mountain well. We finished our run on the Zammermoos and the lower wooded part of the Galzig, and skied down to the village. Then we took two chair lifts up to another large shoulder of the mountain, known as Gampen, and then another chair lift to Kapall. Here we did most of our skiing on another famous St. Anton run—the Matun. In one sunny day we had enjoyed superb skiing and had seen most of the St. Anton terrain.

Our group was to stay very much intact for the entire week. Occasionally a person would promote himself into our class, only to leave after a day of not being able to keep up with us. I remember a well-equipped American named George who tried to find his confidence by talking big as we went up the mountain. His easy manner and grand conversational style disappeared when he saw some of the steep pitches that Robert took us down.

Perhaps the most outstanding skier in the group, certainly the most graceful, was a tall Canadian named Bob. One day while skiing on the steepest section of the Schindlerkar, we stopped at the top of an even steeper slope where we could see only as far as a brow about two hundred feet down. Robert went ahead, stopping just below the brow, so that we could only see his head and shoulders. He yelled for us to come down, and make slow turns, one at a time. Bob went first and fell on about his third turn. He slid away on his back, not going too fast, but unable to stop himself. We saw Robert watching him carefully, then moving toward his path. Bob fell out of sight and we saw Robert duck down. We did not know what had happened for a few seconds, but Robert stood up and yelled, "Next!" Then we saw Bob get up and smilingly look toward us. Had Robert not been able to brace himself and stop Bob, one or both of them would have skidded a half mile down the slope.

There was a somewhat spoiled blond American youngster in the class, who was going to school in Germany. When he had his confidence, he skied as well as any of us, but when he was moody, he seemed to hold back and ski awkwardly. One day we were on the Kandahar section of the Galzig area, in an almost unbelievably steep ravine that went straight down. There were occasional dwarf spruce trees, particularly on the sides. Once again we were skiing toward Robert, with one man on the hill at a time. The blond American boy fell on a turn, sliding away fast. He reached out for Robert as he neared him, tripping him up as if he were trying to tackle him. Robert went down and the two skiers, one moment cartwheeling away from each other, one moment entangled, slid together down toward the runout, which fortunately was only about fifty yards away, and there they stopped. Robert as he got up was both speechless and expressionless. A few seconds later, the youngster got up and said, "I guess I flubbed that one all right."

At this point Robert's fiery temper let go and he told the lad off in no uncertain terms. The moral, of course, was that if you fall away on a steep slope when skiing with Robert, you do not grab him. You wait for him to grab you.

Ernie, a slightly rotund American, had become an expert in rotation. Unfortunately there was no place for someone with counterswing shoulder movement in Robert's class. Invariably when Ernie skied down solo before the class, Robert would saw away with his ski pole on an imaginary violin, singing his own verses of "Around the World."

We had two Germans in the class, one a somewhat serious man whose face had been badly burned in the war, the other younger, with a light, easy manner. Both were exceptionally dedicated pupils, excellent skiers, and in every sense good company.

Sig, a young Swedish boy, was probably our most athletic skier. Although he fell a few times, his edging was precise and his turns skidless. And he had a quickness and sureness of movement that made him look like a candidate for his country's national team.

Of all the people in the class, my clubmate Nan seemed to receive the sharpest criticism from Robert, perhaps because she had been skiing with him all winter, perhaps because she was so unusually good in deep snow or rough going. Robert obviously set higher standards for her than for the rest of us. But because she was a girl, the only one who skied with us every day, it seemed odd for her to be so abused by Robert. The day she suffered a slight concussion from a bad fall Robert dismissed her for the afternoon but insisted that she show up for the next day's class. Although she was still subpar, Robert kept after her with more than the usual storm of criticism, perhaps following the rule that when you are thrown from a horse you get right back on again.

For some strange reason, once we got by the first day, Robert was very easy on me, probably because of my unbounded enthusiasm about being in St. Anton and skiing in Europe for the first time. Also, I was the oldest member of the class, but I do not like to think I was so much older that I had to be treated with deference. In some ways I was the best all-around skier in the group because of my racing experience, yet, as I already stated, I was often helpless in heavy snow, and had many deeply ingrained bad habits. I skied in the Durrance crouch; I had a constant slight stem; I skied with my feet much too far apart; I did not use my poles with movements as light and easy and anticipatory as they should have been. Also my shoulders and upper body were not properly reversed and were too much involved in the turn. In many ways being in Robert's class was like learning to ski all over again.

For most of the days of the week I had an additional private lesson with Robert early in the morning. It was a thrill to be able to ski alone with him. After all, the St. Anton ski school is considered to be the best in the world, and Robert Gluck was certainly one of the top men in the school. Under Robert's watchful eye I could sense the bad habits disappearing one by one.

Skiing during these lessons, Robert and I really developed a companionship. There were few skiers on the mountain for the first hour that the lifts were running, there was usually at least a dusting of new snow on the track, and the snow everywhere sparkled in the sharp sun of the early morning. Also the still clear mountain air seemed to give the slopes a special mood.

One morning while going up the Galzig T-bar together Robert said to me in a serious tone, "I understand that you were a very famous Dartmouth racer." We both chuckled at his reference to my first day's bout with Skimeister Rudi Matt.

There was quite a change of pace when the regular school session got going on the second day. Thank goodness we always had a cup of coffee at the top of the mountain. Robert turned into a frenzied person as the morning exercises began, insisting that we do these exercises with complete involvement. The theory was that mastering all the exercises, each of which was designed to perfect some aspect of the turn, would assure a turn with all the elements put together in a beautiful integrated movement. We practiced heel thrusts, sometimes making slow-motion turns on an almost level stretch without any motion other than twisting the heels. At other times we would practice these heel thrusts on a steep slope, where we were to bring ourselves around quickly with exaggerated twisting. We practiced turns with and without poles. Sometimes we would make about three or four sideslips, each preceded by touching the downhill pole into the snow, and then make a complete turn, with Robert always insisting on a light easy touch with the pole, done with perfect timing and without any movement of the shoulder or the upper part of the body. We would do hop turns with and without poles. Body angulation was taught by exaggerating the lowering of the reversed downhill shoulder. The exercise for this aspect of the turn consisted of putting the ski poles over the shoulders, draping the wrists over the poles in the manner of one crucified, and skiing down the hill with the poles parallel to the slope. This threw the outside shoulder down, thus putting the weight on the outside ski at the beginning of the turn. Robert insisted that we ski at all times with our feet together and our knees actually touching. The exercise for promoting this togetherness was to ski with the gloves locked between the knees. Robert never asked us to do this unless there was something unusual about the terrain, like at the top of the Kandahar steilhang, where a dropped glove might slide down a quarter of a mile to the Steissbachtal. He also asked us to ski with our gloves between our knees in the moisture-laden rotten deep snow on the back of the Kapall. Robert had a very special smile for the occasion when we all would fall, confounded by a test that was impossible for everyone but our instructor.

If the exercise sessions were conducted with a bit of Prussian discipline and cruelty, Robert proved that he could be a fun-loving romanticist when the session was over and it was time to ski follow-the-leader style down the mountain. The key position was to tail the master. Sometimes this position was awarded because one of us had done something exceptionally well, and sometimes simply because it was that person's turn. But each of us sought to emulate Robert's exaggerated style. We were conscious that we were an elite class, and that other classes and groups of skiers often stopped to watch us go by.

Sometimes spotting Class 1A, the top class, Robert would figure out a way to outflank them, passing them in evenly spaced formation with each of us in egg-shaped racing tuck. One time we stopped and waxed our skis before passing them in order to put on a better show. Several times we overtook them late in the day, when they were spread out and obviously exhausted by a full day of fast mountain runs, following their wild leader Bertl.

Often at the end of the class most of us were still so exhilarated that we would leave Robert and go back up the mountain. So great was our pride in what we had learned that we each wanted to ski again on our own.

When the skiing day was finally over almost everyone returned to the village. St. Anton is not by any means the most picturesque Austrian town. One problem is that being surrounded by such steep mountains, it is in their shadow most of the day. It is astride the main railway line between Austria and Germany, the route of the Arlberg Express. Also the key highway over the Arlberg Pass becomes the main street of the town. But there are many colorful stores, including tea and pastry shops, boutiques selling ski equipment and Austrian clothes, and bootmakers' establishments.

Every afternoon the custom was to promenade down the main street of St. Anton between four and five o'clock, when the village had sunshine. As if strolling the boardwalk at Atlantic City, skiers would walk from one end of the town to the other, making occasional stops for shopping or an after-ski snack. The mixture of nationalities provided fun and interest whenever skiers bumped into each other both on and off the slopes. When someone you had misled on the mountain, pulled ahead of in the lift line, or cut off on a ski trail, accosted you, it was great fun to relive the experience in broken tongues caused by the language barrier. I remember telling one German couple on the Galzig slopes in the fog that the sun was breaking through on the Matun, providing good lighting and soft snow. By the time they got there, the lighting was flat and the terrain icy. The pretty German wife stopped me later on the main street, and shaking her finger at me, she said in a thick accent, "Shame for taking advantage of an innocent people!"

Invariably we would run into a Belgian dentist also staying at the Alpenhof, who always had interesting comments on the activities of the guests on and off the slopes. He was particularly well informed on two fun-loving, thrill-seeking American secretaries who skied even harder than I, and each night enjoyed themselves with a different group. We also would run into friends from the Silver Lake charter flight, notably a Mutt-and-Jeff-like pair from Philadelphia named Henry Reath and Chick Bolling.

There are several excellent tailors in St. Anton, and since the price of custom-made stretch pants is less than the cost of buying a pair at home off the rack, it is quite the thing to order a pair while staying in the village. I selected a tailor named Franz Zauner, and while in the shop, I ran into Barty Barstow, whom I had met skiing in Vermont. Having his final fitting for a pair of brilliant crimson pants, he saw me going through the swatch book, where I hesitated every time I came to a basic color like gray, tan, or navy blue. "You already own a pair of gray pants," he said. "Don't tell me you came in here to buy another conservative color. Why don't you follow my example and select something exciting?"

Acknowledging his point, I went through the swatch book with a new approach, finally picking out a lemon-yellow shade. Later in the week when I went to pick up my new pants, I left behind my 6-year-old gray Bogners to be taken in and retailored, and put on the yellow ones. As I had been skiing that day in a yellow sweater and yellow hat, I suddenly found myself in an all-yellow outfit during the St. Anton promenade hour. Because of all the catcalls, I seriously wondered if I would ever ski in my new pants. However, the yellow pants have turned out to be a lot of fun, being reserved for big-ego days when the sun is out. But never again have they been worn with a yellow sweater and yellow hat.

Perhaps the high point of the after-skiing promenade in St. Anton was watching the stop-and-go movement of traffic on the narrow main street. Much has been written of Paris traffic, where the Mercedes takes it out on the Renault, the Renault on the Vespa scooter, and the scooter on the bicycle. And in France sometimes a driver will drive on the wrong side of the road to avail himself of the sun. In St. Anton, too, there is an unbelievable assortment of vehicular traffic. Massive-tired heavy-duty German diesel trucks, European cars large and small, and a heavy sprinkling of brilliantly colored microbuses fight their way through streams of people. There is much tooting of horns and ineffectual voicing of authority by Austrian policemen dressed like members of Rommel's African corps, and active participation by heckling skiers turned pedestrians.

Austria has the highest per capita automobile accident rate of any country in the world. It is true that many young Austrian lads aspire to be another Toni Sailer. However, most of them have even more interest in becoming the daring young man behind the wheel of the microbus. The microbus driver often has a nonpaying passenger in the form of a shapely apple-cheeked blond Austrian girl sitting alongside of him. Before starting the motor he engages the passenger in bright witty dialogue that continues without pause during assorted near accidents, speed runs, and the grinding of gears. It only ceases as the bus stops to discharge a passenger. Making a K turn in the middle of St. Anton, the driver begins a run by backing into traffic without looking around. He uses only peripheral vision, side mirrors, and instinct. Pedestrians, knowing the peculiar noise of the Volkswagen power plant, which sounds a little like a rotary mower, start to move out of the way as the noise approaches.

One day we were in a bus speeding toward the Alpenhof on the narrow back road I had used to ski down into town the first morning. Near the top, where it was not plowed wide enough for two cars, we came upon three pedestrians—on the right a mother and child and on the left her farmer husband. Our driver, more absorbed with the fräulein seated at his side than with the pedestrian traffic ahead, gave woman and child good buoy room but left little or no margin of safety for the farmer. The latter seemed unconcerned about the impending disaster, until suddenly, twenty feet from the bus, he exercised the privilege of bailing out by diving head first over the snow bank at the side of the road and disappearing.

Some days, because of a scarcity of microbus taxis at the rush hour, I had to walk up the hill to the Alpenhof. This was not by any means a routine stroll, since my new pair of tightly fitted stiff Haderer boots made me painfully aware of each bony protuberance on my feet at every step. One day as I walked up the hill my consciousness of pain was interrupted for a few seconds when lovely Elly Newman smiled and waved as she went by in a microbus. Elly was the chief character in the great ski romance of the year.

On about our fourth day in St. Anton, we had joined our friends from New Jersey, Idoline and Bill Scheerer, for cocktails at the Hotel Post, the most fashionably continental place in St. Anton, and the center of après-ski life. Also there were Elly Newman and George Caulkins whose European adventure shortly involved us all. Elly was the 24-year-old daughter of family friends from home. George, a 40-year-old Yale man who had become a successful Texas entrepreneur, was one of the founders and promoters of the Vail ski area. George and Elly had met on Sandy McIlvaine's Chalet Plane, which had left New York a week before our flight. Right from the start it was apparent that a romance was under way. On Tuesday of the first week George proposed to her. On Wednesday she accepted. On Thursday they called Elly's mother to tell her that they planned to be married in Zermatt a week from Saturday, and that they wanted her to fly over for the wedding. Among the many problems that Elly's mother faced was the necessity of flying, which she hated. There had been several other conversations between George and Elly and Mrs. Newman, and needless to say, the latter was not giving her wholehearted support. Barbara and I had not been with George and Elly for more than a few minutes before we became strong partisan supporters of their whirlwind romance. And when as a friend of the family I agreed to send a telegram to Elly's mother telling her that we were a party to this madness, Elly threw her arms around my neck with gratitude.

Elly and George stayed for about half an hour and then left us with the Scheerers. Coming somewhat to my senses, I turned to Idoline. "You know, there are a lot of hurdles in any marriage, and it takes courage and staying power to overcome them. How does either one of these two know that the other has whatever it takes to stay with it and make the marriage work?" I asked.

Idoline, quick as a flash, made a classic comment, "Don't be an ass. No one ever knows that until years later."

The wedding, a colorful ceremony in the Alpine tradition, took place at Zermatt as scheduled, and although Mrs. Newman's first words to George as she got off the plane were "You rat!" she was soon won over by what turned out to be a happy marriage.

As for night life, Kitzbühel to the east has it all over St. Anton. The reason is perhaps that the town of Hannes Schneider is so completely devoted to skiing, or perhaps that the few nightclubs and cafés which do exist are always much too crowded. In any event, despite the international atmosphere and the abundance of good skiers who are also interesting people, St. Anton has never become a fashionable haven for the jet set. There is a certain snobbery about the area, but it is ski snobbery and not social snobbery. When members of European royalty or Hollywood actresses ski in St. Anton, they tend to become submerged in the ski community, having little opportunity to associate with their own kind.

Hannes Schneider exercised good judgment in choosing St. Anton as the location for his ski school. At an elevation of 4,200 feet, it is one of the higher resorts in Europe, but the assortment of steep slopes, fantastic terrain, and good snow conditions make it a skiers' ski area. Also St. Anton serves as an excellent hub for skiing in nearby areas.

There is the Albona at Stuben, where challenging powder snow skiing is available on north-facing runs. The vertical drop of 3,100 feet offers expert skiers one of the longest unbroken drop-offs anywhere.

Zurs, to the north, is a ski town located well above the timberline at an elevation of 5,600 feet in a dream-world valley of open slope ski country. There is a quaint Tyrolean look to the small cluster of inns and pensions that make up the town. Fashionable and quite expensive, Zurs is one of the most desirable places to ski in Europe. There are excellent runs on each side of the valley, all serviced by lifts. One of the most famous is on the west side, where after taking a lift one skis down a gentle slope to the Zursersee, a small lake in a natural mountain bowl. A short hike across the frozen lake brings one to another lift which goes to the top of the Madloch Run. This run, considered by some the finest in the Arlberg, starts in another bowl, between craggy peaks, and descends into a vast northern exposed traversing slope. Here a series of hollowed-out steep sections and interesting runouts provide a skiing place uniquely agreeable to both expert and intermediate skiers. Near the end of the run there are scattered fir trees, gentle traverses, and a magnificent view of the nearby village of Lech.

This town, larger than Zurs by some margin, is just as picturesque. Lunch at the Gasthof Post, in a paneled tavern decorated by Ludwig Bemelmans, proved to be one of the most luxuriously relaxing moments of the trip. Lech, too, offers a wide range of slopes and runs, particularly suited to less skilled skiers. Both Lech and Zurs have more sun than St. Anton. Lech, like Zurs, has a link to the other town by means of a cable car. From Lech, there is a gentle run back to Zurs on the opposite side of the valley from the Madloch.

St. Christoph, a small colony close to the summit of the Arlberg Pass, is really an appendage to St. Anton. It offers a gay, simple uncrowded life plus all the ski runs and facilities that go with St. Anton. One of the ski area's two main lift systems consists of a cable car up the back side of the Galzig, giving access from its upper station to all of the St. Anton ski terrain.

During the last few days of our class Robert continued to find interesting runs for us to ski. One of the most picturesque took us down the back side of Kapall, on an extremely steep avalanche slope which, gradually narrowing into a gully formed by two huge rock walls, became no wider than a two-lane highway. Then it opened up into a series of snowfields in lightly timbered country, bringing us down to the west end of St. Anton.

Another run took us toward St. Jakob on snow which had a breakable crust. Since this was near the end of our week with Robert, we were all skiing with strength and confidence, and the breakable crust became no obstacle. The farther down we went, the heavier the crust, and we took delight in demonstrating the reserve of power that Robert had built into our turns. We were able to produce a shearing action with our skis, breaking the crust into thousands of jagged fragments which skidded down over the slick surface and sometimes overtook us. We turned with extra heel thrust and exaggerated hop to release the skis, but essentially we used the same turn we had used on other parts of the mountain. Of course, our experience gained in skiing other types of variable snow had helped us to meet this challenge. When we got to the bottom of the run in St. Jakob, our boots bore scars from skiing through the crust.

On one of the last days at St. Anton, we planned to ski the Schindlerkar from the very top, which involved long traverses and some climbing to reach a point near the lift tower on the top of the Walfagehrjoch. There we ran into Class 1A, poised under a huge rock tower called the Gendarme, waiting to follow Bertl's lead. I stopped, fascinated, and let my group go on along the ridge. Down below, the rock tower cast a large shadow over the slope, making it perilously icy. Bertl sideslipped slowly, very much on his edges, across the ice, and then stopped after he had completed his traverse onto a surface softened by the sun. He was obviously putting his class through the supreme test. A mistake could not be permitted, as a loss of control could send a skier falling down the icy slope at such an extreme speed that he would be unable to stop before more than half a mile. Singly the skiers in the class followed Bertl's skilled example, meeting the test both with good form and a reserve of braking power. Only one skier, one of the two girls in the class, seemed really tense and uncertain—perhaps because she was conscious of being a girl. Originally situated to be the fourth skier to go down, she stepped back so that she was last in line. When her turn came, she hesitated, appearing unwilling to proceed. Then finally she went ahead to ski beautifully, accomplishing the difficult maneuver as well as any of her classmates. The tension still showed, however, and being a girl, she seemed to hate every minute of it.

On my last day I broke away from the class for the afternoon session and joined forces with Charlie Cole, a member of the famed Boston Schussverein. Charlie, who is something of a madman, had been skiing with Bertl's top class all week. We proceeded to chase one another down the Galzig T-bar area, having ourselves a ball. The faster we skied, the more we seemed to forget the technique we had been taught in the St. Anton ski school. Charlie's wife Fifi joined us for one run, and although she had been in Class 1A most of the week, she decided our skiing was a bit too crazy for her.

On one of our last runs I pointed out an appealing narrow glade alongside the T bar, a route through the trees which opened and closed several successive times, and which offered a fast, nearly straight run through untracked snow. When we got down to this part of the terrain, I was the lead man, and was soon going much faster than I cared to go. Making an impromptu quick turn, I ducked behind a large snow-laden spruce to come to a quick stop. Then I spun around to watch Charlie ride it out. With no skier and no tracks to follow, he hurtled down the spruce-studded corridor to apparent hell. I skied on down, and when I found Charlie he good-naturedly gave me the business for bailing out and abandoning him. Since at this point we realized that we were a bad influence on each other, Charlie left to go down the mountain and I went up the T bar for my last trip at St. Anton. I skied down at a slower pace, returning to the Austrian technique required under Robert's tutelage. I went down the last schuss, not knowing that Robert and the class had spotted me as they were about to disassemble. When I came to a stop I was surprised to see them, and relieved that they had seen me ski the way Robert had taught me, and not the crazy way I was skiing with Charlie.

We left St. Anton as we had arrived, with a meal of Wiener schnitzel, but this time it was at the railroad station. Like all Americans, we marveled at the European trains, with the private yet friendly wood-paneled compartments where you sit opposite other passengers. Riding in these trains is as relaxing as travel can ever be. They move along at great speed, and yet you have such a smooth quiet ride that you feel as though supported by a layer of air in some entirely new mode of ground transportation. To top it off, there is the interest of the European scenery, mountains, lakes, fertile valleys, and historic towns. In Switzerland the engineering aspect of railroading provides drama; sometimes you go through a mountain tunnel to find an entirely different sort of terrain on the other side.

Klosters, in Switzerland, our second port of call, was for us as different from St. Anton as anything could be. We were there only five days, about half as long as our Arlberg stay, yet in some ways it seemed longer. This was partly because being somewhat snowed in we lost a sense of time, and partly because the pace was more leisurely, with emphasis to some extent shifting from serious skiing to social skiing, with talk of snails, good wines, and fancy restaurants.

One of the most interesting aspects of Klosters was the almost complete absence of Americans, and predominance of the British, who, as I mentioned before, had been coming to Klosters since the 1920's. Their headquarters has always been the Grand Hotel Vereina, where we spent a couple of evenings socializing with them. And both times a charming Englishman, different in each case, completely captivated Barbara.

We also spent two enjoyable evenings with Reese Harris, his wife Sis, my old Woodstock friend, and her sister Susan Duval. The first evening we went to Chesa Grischuna, probably the best, and certainly the most famous restaurant in the European ski country. With Reese, suave sophisticated person that he is, selecting the wines and food courses, we felt that we were dining in grand style. The second evening Sis and Reese took us to one of their favorite places in nearby Davos, an intimate little restaurant known only to a rather select group of skiers, which specialized in *fondue bourguigonne.* Small chunks of beef are speared on forks and cooked at the table by the individual to his taste. There is a chafing dish of hot oil in the center of the table, heated by an alcohol burner, into which everyone dips his piece of beef. The cooking takes less than a minute, and when the beef is ready, it can be dipped into one of several sauces—béarnaise, rémoulade, sour cream and chives, horseradish, or ketchup for the conventional palate.

There are two other events that stand out in my mind about that evening. Reese, in ordering the wine whispered in the ear of the lovely Swiss waitress, and the wine, to my surprise turned out to be champagne. Reese then made a clever toast, which emphasized that we were celebrating an important occasion, and yet skillfully avoided revealing what the occasion was. We all touched glasses and drank the toast, and then everyone turned toward me, smiling in a knowing way. Baffled by my lack of awareness of what was going on, I hoped someone would help me out. Finally I had to humiliate myself by asking, "Will someone please tell me what this is all about?" As stern looks were cast at me from around the table, I suddenly realized that it was our fifteenth wedding anniversary!

The other incident of the evening concerned our waitress, who turned out to be rather naïve. For some reason she mistook me for Gregory Peck, and the bartender, whom she questioned about my identity, purposely misled her. The word got around fast that for the evening I was playing the role of Gregory Peck. I quite enjoyed making a fuss over the waitress who mistook me for the noted actor, but it was even more fun when I approached gracious Deborah Kerr at the bar and she kept up the deception by greeting me as a friend from the world of filmdom.

We also skied in Klosters; in fact, we skied every day, even through the first three foggy days. Going up the two-stage aerial tramway through the clouds to the top of the Gotschnagrat, a total rise of 3,500 feet, we could usually see the slope immediately below us, but we had no real idea of the mountain and its terrain. Fortunately, the trails were extremely well marked, with signs at all intersections and closely spaced red marker sticks. There was not much danger of getting lost because one could always see at least from one marker to the next. Of course, in above-timberline skiing, fog means flat light, where the absolute lack of any shadow or contrast hides bumps and drop-offs. One minute the skier feels a little as if he is falling through space, and the next as if his knees are being driven into his chest. Turning continuously helps to maintain control and to give better feel of the slope. In flat light the tendency is to tighten up and consciously try to direct the action of the knees, but it is better to let the knees relax and flex in a natural manner. The best trick of all, if you can manage it, is to find someone of about equal ability and ski as close as a ski length behind him, using him much like a blind person uses a Seeing Eye dog.

We enjoyed ourselves more on the lower parts of the trails in Klosters where the fog was less thick, the woods gave contrast to the snow, and the routes generally were easy grade, mostly traverses and catwalks. The farther down we got, the more crowded the catwalks, with several special narrow tunnels under railroad tracks adding to the confusion and excitement that always accompanies European catwalk skiing.

When the sun finally came out, the day was indescribably beautiful. Going up the lift, we emerged from a sea of clouds so flat that only the white softness of its surface made it look like a cloud layer rather than an inland sea among coastal peaks. But there were other monstrous cumulus clouds warring with the mountains for size, power, and occupancy of the sky. We saw for the first time the precipitously steep Gotschnagrat-Gotschnawang, a run unavailable at the time because of avalanche danger. This slope obviously requires precision skiing through the right slots in the rock faces, since there are too many points where a fall might be fatal. Skiing this slope marks a skier as being of top-expert caliber.

At the summit of the Gotschnagrat we heard the noise of cannon fire as the Swiss Army was breaking up dangerous cornice formations. Toward the open-slope Parsenn country there was a magenta glow in some of the clouds, and the entire Klosters-Davos ski terrain seemed to be at our command, covered with beautiful white powder snow marked by occasional tracks from other early mountain runners. Skiing that morning with Charlie Unternauer, a fellow veteran racer and the Eastern agent for Hart skis, I enjoyed the full luxury of perfect skiing conditions.

Barbara and I had two relaxing afternoons at Davos before leaving the area. We skied the expansive Jakobshorn and Bramabuel open slopes, which almost directly face the setting afternoon sun, and which are across the valley from the most famous mountain in the Davos area, the Weisfluhjoch.

Our last stop was Zermatt, in which, like prewar Bermuda, automobiles are *verboten*. Zermatt is reached by a railroad which goes from Visp up a long canyon into the mountains. The roadbed is so steep that sometimes the train must operate as a cog railway.

Since we arrived on a slightly hazy day, the town's famous trademark, the classic Matterhorn peak, was not in sight. Consequently the atmosphere, like our nighttime arrival at St. Anton, was one of suspense and mystery. But the authenticity of the mountain town of Zermatt was very much in evidence. Each train was greeted by porters wearing black caps marked in gold lettering with the names of such well-known inns as Zermatterhof, Mont Cervin, Christiania, as well as our hotel, the Perren—run by the famous mountaineering family. Each porter had a horsedrawn sleigh, and the trip through the quaint town was memorable.

The first afternoon I had time for one run up the Sunnegga lift, which is an interesting double-seater chair lift. It takes you up sitting sideways, in this case facing toward the ring of famous mountains at the headlands of the Mattervispa River. Only the base of the Matterhorn was visible this afternoon, but the lower part of its familiar profile revealed its identity.

Our first look at the majestic peak was by moonlight, through wisps of clouds, and its very sight made us stand still in wonderment. Thereafter the mountain in its many moods dominated Zermatt. We were always conscious of it poised over the town, seemingly ready to overpower us.

The next day was a beauty, and I was up early, well ahead of the lift lines, taking the cog railway to the fortresslike station at Gornergrat. From here two unusual cable cars go along an ascending sharp knife ridge, to Hohtalli first and then to Stockhorn. The higher up I went, the better on the right the view of Zermatt's ring of mountains separating Switzerland from Italy. The ring starts with Monte Rosa, the highest mountain in Switzerland, next Castor and Pollux, then the Breithorn, and finally the Matterhorn. Farther to the north I could see the perfect triangle of the Weisshorn, another famous peak.

Between Stockhorn and these mountains there is a sharp 1,000-foot drop to the Gorner glacier, whose flattened mass stretches out toward the valley. On the left side of Stockhorn the drop-off is steep too, but not so steep that it cannot hold snow. The snowfields below Stockhorn and Hohtalli offer superb open-slope skiing, partly on the Findeln glacier. Facing north, they stretch such a distance that there is powder snow skiing from almost any point on the knife ridge. Walking on a narrow footpath to the selected snowfield either from Stockhorn or Hohtalli is a bit like being on a tightrope. On the Monte Rosa side of the ridge the slope slants down at a 45-degree angle for twenty or thirty feet. Then the snow ends, marking the beginning of a rock-faced drop-off above the Gorner glacier. At one place, called the Bridge of Ice, the footpath on the ridge is especially narrow, and has steps carved out of blue glacier ice rather than snow. However, no one has ever faltered and fallen to his death 1,000 feet below.

My first day took me to all of Zermatt's famous ski areas. First I skied from Stockhorn down to the Findeln lift, for a short uphill ride to Sunnegga, where I skied the National Piste to Zermatt village, for a total drop of about 6,000 feet. I also got up to the top of Blauherd and then back over to the Schwarzee lift to try several of the runs at the base of the Matterhorn. I skied for a total of 24,000 vertical feet of downhill running, which is a lot for one day, especially on unfamiliar ground.

Barbara had an adventurous day near the end of our trip with Henry Reath and Chick Bolling, the "Mutt-and-Jeff twins" we had seen at St. Anton. These two interesting types are both ex-Princetonians from Philadelphia, the former a Main Line lawyer, the latter a drug industry marketing man, both traveling with their attractive wives. Each, despite victimization by this narrative, is a great fellow. The quiet humorous interplay between these two skiers—Henry the authority on form, and Chick the expert on skiing without form—involved a different plot each day, with each taking the same role. Henry, although a relative newcomer to the sport, had become a student of technique. As the self-appointed "lehrer" or leader, he always started the day with an easy run to demonstrate the importance of smooth rhythmic skiing. Chick, an ex-hockey player and always at ease on skis, skied with strength and confidence rather than style and rhythm. Obediently but reluctantly he went through the motions of being Henry's pupil. However, Chick fancied himself as a skilled organizer and did not at any time want to be a follower. Also, as an old-time skier he knew that he was more at home in the fall line than his Philadelphia friend.

The day's adventure began with a short confidence run on the Rotenboden slope. Then Nell Reath and Lea Bolling stayed behind as Barbara, Chick, and Henry decided to take the cable car up to the Stockhorn. Henry, skiing on a stiff, beaten-up pair of wooden skis, started off in the lead position. Heading down the steep slope leading to the Findeln glacier as though he were still on the confidence run, he soon took the first of several heavy somersaulting falls, which were somewhat unsettling to him since Barbara and Chick were able to negotiate the slope without a fall. Chick immediately pressed his advantage and took over as lehrer and organizer. On a narrow runout toward the bottom of the 3,000-foot drop-off at Stockhorn, Henry took a forward fall, vaulting over on one of his skis and snapping it near the tip. True to Quaker City thriftiness, Henry bemoaned the fate of his ancient ski, and angrily threw the broken tip into a gully at the side of the trail.

Chick, in his new role as lehrer, was then faced with getting Henry down the mountain on just one good ski. Pulling out his trail map, he spotted what looked like an easy traverse over to the lower station of the Gornergrat, known as Riffelalp. However, this turned out to involve an endless walk around the side of the mountain, with the left uphill ski always higher than the right one. During the trip, Henry kept reproaching himself for having thrown away his tip, saying, "I could have had it repaired and sold the skis." And along with Barbara, he became critical of Chick's route, particularly since they were confronted with two danger areas around which there was no alternative trail. One was the traverse of a steep, recently avalanched slope, bumpy and uneven, across which there were no tracks. The other was a narrow catwalk above a sheer drop of about 1,000 feet. The snow on the catwalk had built up so high that the guardrail was mostly buried. As a safeguard it was visible and available only at either end of the precipice, where it was not needed. Both of these pitfalls had to be met by simply looking straight ahead and plunging doggedly on, but they both required tension-breaking cigarette stops at the far side.

After about an hour of hard work and considerable complaining to Chick about his route, the three arrived at the Riffelalp station, where they waited for the train to come and transport Henry safely down to Zermatt. Barbara and Chick said good-bye to the unhappy Henry and then the two of them went on up the mountain for another trip down the Stockhorn.

Somewhere en route a cunning plan presented itself—what a feat it would be to retrieve Henry's ski tip among the many square miles of terrain below them! Fortunately Barbara remembered almost the exact spot of Henry's fall, marked by a peculiarly shaped rock near the gully where he had thrown the tip. Chick was able to find it with little trouble and the two congratulated themselves on their powers of observation. For the rest of the day they laughed as they thought of different ways of presenting the tip to Henry. Finally, securing a bottle of red nail polish in a Zermatt store, they painted "NOT FOR SALE," in large letters on the tip, and wrapped it up as a farewell-to-Zermatt gift to be presented to their lehrer at a party that evening.

The party had been organized for the Silver Lake charter flight members by "P. K." Smith, the director of the flight as well as a deep powder artist, whose skiing costume consisted of old-fashioned baggy knickers and a scotch plaid beret topped with an oversized pompom. It was an exceptionally gay evening, and to make it even more interesting, P. K. had brought some friends along. Among them was Robert Montgomery, who is as charming and distinguished off the stage as he is on. P. K.'s other friends were a marvelous international brigade of musicians who had negotiated the Théodule Pass with him on skis, from Cervinia in Italy. Among other activities that night, I ran a Calcutta pool on the Gornergrat Derby downhill event, which was to be held the following day, selling off the racers to the highest bidders in Swiss francs. But the real high point of the evening was the presentation of a special award to Herr Lehrer Reath. In all fairness to Henry, it must be recorded that he accepted his redeemed ski tip with grace and a few well-chosen words.

There were many other memorable aspects of skiing in Zermatt. One was skiing the Garten lift, a poma in the shadow of the Matterhorn, which as you ride up takes you toward Théodule Pass into Italy, and as you ski down offers easy dreamlike skiing on soft powder, with the mass of the Matterhorn right ahead.

Unfortunately, while we were in Zermatt, the lines for the

three lifts from the village to Stockhorn were long. In Europe people waiting for lifts can be rude—pushing and shoving, and showing no deference to women. The German nation, which on the whole has behaved itself so well in these postwar years, often shows its Teutonic aggressiveness in the lift lines. But the real villains are the boors of various nationalities who show no respect for others in this or any situation.

I especially enjoyed skiing at Zermatt because my thigh muscles had really become well conditioned after three weeks of continuous skiing. In fact, I was in the best condition I had been in since my racing days at Dartmouth. I even had a few reasonably successful deep snow runs with P. K. Smith and Vicky Shurtleff, a girl who caught on to powder snow skiing with ease, and Othmar Kronig, P. K.'s guide.

The last night in Zermatt we joined the Reaths and the Bollings at the Christiania, to listen to a Hungarian zither player—an exotic-looking girl with marvelous black eyes—who was our favorite entertainer in Zermatt. The next day, our last, we watched the slalom of the Gornergrat Derby. It had a top-rated field, fresh from the 1962 F.I.S. World Championship, including Perillat, Nenning, the flashy Willi Bogner, Egon Zimmerman, winner of the 1962 F.I.S. giant slalom, and Marianne Jahn, the graceful Austrian girl skier. The Americans were also on hand, and we had the thrill of watching Billy Kidd, young whiz from Stowe, score a second, in one of the best performances by an American in European competition. The race was surprisingly won by Minsch, a Swiss, and very much a local favorite. The slalom was a colorful sight, with the townspeople of Zermatt behind the ropes as well as seated on the rooftops of barns and chalets.

After the slalom and before our train left, P. K. Smith and I sneaked in one more run all the way from Hohtalli. Conscious of the newly acquired strength in my legs, I made fast giant slalom-like swings, skiing nonstop down the magnificent open slope with a 3,000-foot drop. P. K., who is a skier of the more ordinary variety when he is outside of his deep powder element, took his time. We were more than a little late when we finally got back to Zermatt. Since my hotel was on the way I could ski to the door, but P. K.

had about a 20-minute walk. He arrived to find that his wife Pat, faced with his nonappearance, had left for the train with all the gear, including his street clothes. The note she had written was rather succinct: "Get the hell over to the station."

At the station, Pat figuring he would not show up, was talking about spending the rest of her life without him. But the great P. K., as calm in a crisis as he is ebullient in a social situation, leisurely walked up in his knickers and scotch cap to board the train about a minute before it left. I walked away from the train for a few seconds to get a last look at the famous mountain where Whymper's tragic accident took place. I also looked at the slope toward the Gabelhorn, where snow fences, artificial terraces, and other embattlements play as important a role in defending present-day Zermatt against avalanche tragedy as the moats and fortifications did in safeguarding a medieval walled city from attackers.

The trip home provided a complete change from the flight over. On the way to Europe the clock is speeded up, a short night takes place, and the pace in general is hard on the nerves. On the way home the clock stands still, there is a long day, with the sun almost overhead throughout, and the pace is relaxed. A gay, champagne-drinking party atmosphere prevailed all the way home, and there was much talk of the many ski areas visited by the passengers. After all, Barbara and I had seen only three areas. And the European snowfields are so vast that the open-sloped Alpine ski areas are almost uncountable. *Ski Holidays in the Alps,* by James and Jeanette Riddell, discusses 250 European ski resorts jointly visited by the authors. Another man, W. Pause, has written as a personal observer about the one hundred top runs in the Alps, each of which is in a different area.

When Barbara and I return to Europe, there are many places we want to see, but I shall still hold out for St. Anton, and I would have a hard time talking Barbara out of Zermatt. However, because we both agree that three weeks of straight skiing is a lot of skiing, we plan to take time out for several days in Rome on the next trip.

14

Family Skiing

Picking an area for family skiing in America may not be as exciting as choosing between Zermatt, St. Anton, or Verbier, but it is an important decision which will involve many factors.

My family have become Mad River partisans. The reasons why we have settled there are numerous and well founded, and no longer does any one of us want to move to another ski area. For each family, as well as for each single person, certain areas have more appeal than others. No attempt will be made here to review all the places where one might ski. Nor will rules be laid down for selecting areas, since skiing is such a personal sport. However, in looking at Mad River and our reasons for liking it, others may discover what they are looking for in an area.

Ski resorts tend to develop their own personalities, and often the character of the area and the type of people who ski there have a greater influence on the decision than the more obvious features, such as terrain, uphill facilities, snow reliability, variety of slopes and trails, and distance from the home port. There is, of course, no ski area which is exclusively for single people or for married people. Family skiing takes place at every area, but even at Mad River it is only one part of the picture.

Single people need little advice in picking areas, tending to be influenced mainly by where their group goes. Sometimes it is not a group but a boy or girl friend who wields the influence. Some people might select a resort after taking a guided bus tour, which is the least discriminatory way of finding a ski area, since bus tours do not often go to the elite places to ski. Single people are probably too much inclined to become victims of habit, often returning to the area where the gang skis. As they have mobility in their lives they should take advantage of it. Usually they are not tied down either economically or socially to one ski area, any more than they are to one boy or one girl. The ski slope is one of the best places for meeting people. Single people should certainly be adventurous in trying new areas, and in meeting new friends.

On the other hand, family skiing means settling down, both in deciding on a ski area and in many other ways as well. Of course, until a couple start skiing with their children they can ski wherever whim leads them. But once the youngsters are in the picture, almost everything militates for skiing in one area. The high cost of skiing alone requires all but those who are independently wealthy to settle down to one area. Only in this way can financial shortcuts be taken. For a couple with four children, staying at an inn is almost prohibitively expensive. Some family budgets pretty much limit trips to one-day excursions.

Building your own house on land far enough away from the ski area so as not to be inflated in value is the best shortcut, but by building your own house, I mean literally building it with your own hands, with the countless weekends of work that go into such a project. By doing it in stages, completing one living space each summer, you can live in the house the following winters. Easier ways of doing it, such as erecting a shell house or one's own prefabricated house can be found, and are also long-term investments which will pay dividends in cheap skiing through the years. On tho other hand, your own house can mean a fifty-thousand-dollar modern ski lodge on highly desirable mountain land, accessible to and overlooking the ski area. No matter what type of house you build, when not being used by your family, it can be rented to offset most of the upkeep. And this income easily pays for taxes, heat, and power. Mortgage costs represent the largest expense of owning a house in the north country, but for a family who uses the house for a week of vacation plus about half the total number of available weekends in the ski season, the charges represent a considerable saving over the cost of staying at inns.

There are other ways of saving money on room and board. One excellent solution is to belong to a ski club which owns or rents a good-size house with plenty of bedrooms and bunk space. On a per night basis, this is the best arrangement short of an invitation to a private lodge. A ski club finds ways to use every bit of space and to make beds available to members at the lowest possible cost, usually subsidizing the lodge operation with income from membership dues. Another way of saving money is to rent a house either for specific weekends and vacation weeks or by the season. Often it is both economical and feasible in other ways to share the rental of a house with one or more families. By knowing a ski area intimately one can sometimes stay for very low rates with farmers or townspeople who are not in the lodge business per se, but who are glad to get the extra income from accommodating people they know and like. To get lodgings at reasonable prices, a family might find lodging a half-hour or more driving distance away from the ski area, often in the opposite direction from the main access road to the mountain.

The mobile home, usually known by the term "camper," might be thought of as a way to cut expenses in the ski country, but as yet it has not become popular. When used, it should serve only as transportation, and not as living quarters. These mobile homes are simply not designed for winter living, and the problems involved in sleeping and eating in one of them during the cold weather are almost insurmountable. My brother-in-law Chuck Scranton and Jim Heekin, an advertising agency president, rented an overgrown camper for a weekend, with the idea that it would put up seven boys while the fathers stayed at some plush inn. Among other problems, the defroster did not function, the heating was inadequate, the camper boiled over climbing hills, as well as clumsily got stuck in the snow. Furthermore, bottled gas for heating and cooking could not be found, and because of inadequate ventilation and an unwise menu the first night, the camper smelled of lobster for the entire weekend.

Another reason why a family settles down to one area is the lift ticket problem. Uphill transportation on a by-the-ride or even a by-the-day basis is inordinately expensive. For the determined skiing family season tickets are almost a must. There are some ski areas that offer little or no inducement to family skiing in setting up their rate structure. However, most areas offer a reduction in day tickets for children, and more and more areas sell specially priced season tickets for families. Okemo Mountain in Vermont has a flat rate for the season for a family no matter what its size. This bargain, plus the availability of wooded land alongside the lower slope, serviced by tiers of roads, has resulted in an influx of skiing settlers, all with children. At Mad River there are season ticket rates for adults, juniors, and children, and for the benefit of a large family there is a reduction in the season ticket rate for each additional member of the family.

I wish there were more information to pass along on savings for family skiing. As already stated, skiing is an expensive sport and the ways of reducing its cost are limited. However, by doing their own cooking a family can hold the cost of food down to what it would be at home, and by reducing the per bed expense, they can figure the expense of skiing vacations mostly on the basis of prices for lift tickets and equipment.

Some comment on equipment for children is very much in order. They do need good skis, bindings, and boots. Lightweight flexible wood skis with metal edges are not too expensive. Some of the Japanese skis are perfectly suitable, as well as low in price, and the Austrian Fischer skis are excellent. Although children can handle regulation length skis, they do not need them except for racing. Certainly youngsters can perform very well on skis that are on the short side. There are several good safety bindings for children, one of which is the Dovre. The double boot is essential, and although a good fit is rare, it is just as important for youngsters as for adults. There is always a lot of activity in the secondhand equipment market for youngsters. Boots in particular get passed around quite a bit, since they are outgrown so quickly.

Driving to the ski country is another expense, but an ingenious skiing family selects a car offering good gas mileage as well as good adaptability to winter. Also there are ways of taking the drudgery out of ski trips. One of the best is a sustained dinner hour en route, complete with many courses, including a single serving of martinis from a thermos, hors d'oeuvres, soup, sandwiches, dessert, etc. This entails some organization, but it results in economy of time as well as money, and makes the trip seem shorter. However, when we head north, the chore of the trip is lightened most of all by the glow of smiling young faces. It is enough for the children to know that they are on the way to Mad River skiing to make them enthusiastic and eager.

Skiing is a most welcome relief to the regimentation of school, but in family skiing the sport is often subordinated to the area. For instance, for a day of skiing in the Catskills, our children might have to be prodded to go with me. Obviously, Mad River comes first and skiing second with my ski team. There are many reasons for this, chief of which is the personal aspect. My youngsters know the manager, Ken Quackenbush, the lift personnel, Rudi Mair and his instructors, and many die-hard Mad River skiers of all ages. They are completely at home on the mountain, having skied even the most difficult slopes like the Fall Line and the Chute. And they take on adult responsibilities in skiing the mountain, making up their own groups and setting up their own rules of conduct. Their time is completely their own; they even have their own night life with other youngsters in the skiing community. For Barbara and me, skiing vacations at Mad River have helped us know our children better because we all enjoy the same sport, but each in his own way. Somehow, as skiers, adults and children seem to be on the same level in a natural, unforced way.

Mad River is located on General Stark Mountain, part of the Green Mountain Range immediately north of Mt. Lincoln (Sugarbush) and Mt. Ellen (Glen Ellen). General Stark, like the other Green Mountains, has hardwood forests on the lower slopes and mostly evergreens on the upper slopes, with no above-timberline areas.

The full name for Mad River is Mad River Glen. All the slopes and trails funnel into a fan-shaped hollow or glen, an arrangement recommended for family skiing since it tends to bring everybody together at least once in a while. Ironically, the bottom of the mountain, even though a meeting place for friends, is unfriendly-looking to the beginner, since the hollow is formed by a series of ledges which give each trail a rather steep ending. A nursery slope is nowhere to be seen. The only visible part of the so-called practice slope is the fairly steep slalom section. To create an easy way down the practice slope would require a vast amount of blasting, which not only would be prohibitively expensive, but which would destroy Mad River's long-held reputation as an area for expert skiers. However, in truth, Mad River, in addition to having four or five expert trails serviced by the original single-chair lift, also has a variety of intermediate slopes and trails, most of which are reached through a newer double chair. A novice area has even been developed. Although this area is well hidden, up the mountain out of sight, it can be reached by riding the double chair to the midstation. Known as "Bird-Land," the novice area has its own double chair.

One reason the Mad Riverite is so proud of his area is that the Mad River Corporation makes few mistakes. For instance, a badly laid-out trail does not exist and the newest trail—finally called the Antelope because Mad River founder Roland Palmedo successfully fought attempts to name it for him—is one of the most interesting runs in New England. Starting off as a narrow easy grade through the woods before coming into a series of S turns with drop-offs, the trail offers constant variety, sometimes opening up into fairly steep traverses with beautiful vistas of the Vermont countryside, always developing interesting different types of turns. On the whole it is an intermediate trail, but provides excitement for the intermediate and the expert alike.

Despite the informality of the area, Mad River has always been run on a businesslike basis. When Jack Murphy was the manager, he had the reputation of being the best area manager in the East. After he moved on to Sugarbush, Ken Quackenbush took over, acquiring the same reputation. A true woodsman, keenly attuned at all times to the mountain and its trails, he is completely at home with the Mad River skiers, all of whom like and respect him. Although he appears to be an easygoing person, he has the knack of getting things done.

The man behind Ken, Roland Palmedo, president of the Mad River Corporation, leaves the day-to-day operation of the area completely up to Ken. Aristocratic-looking and somewhat austere, Roland is a fundamentally warm person. As trim as he was during his college years, he looks at least ten years younger than his age, which is probably around seventy. His influence and interest is long term, looking toward new trails and lifts for the mountain and taking a strong hand in attracting new ski club lodges and private chalets to the glen. A pioneer skier at Williams, Roland maintained a continuous interest in the early stages of downhill skiing in this country. Besides being one of the leading founders at Stowe, he was also the originator of the certification system for ski instructors. In addition he has always been interested in the organizational side of skiing, including Olympic and F.I.S. competition. His indirect influence at Mad River is nothing short of stupendous.

Mad River was started immediately after the original Mt. Mansfield lift company sold out to the Starr and Ruschp interests, with most of the Mt. Mansfield stockholders participating in the new Mad River Corporation. The beginning was slow because the lift was not completed for the first winter, which was a heavy snow year. The first two years of operation, 1949 and 1950, had little snow. Also, since Mad River had only a single lift up until 1958 and was a full hour's driving time from any other major area, it was unable to attract middle-of-the-week vacation skiers. Ironically, its years of greatest growth resulted from the establishment of Sugarbush and later of Glen Ellen, both of which are major areas within 12-minutes' driving time of Mad River.

A great source of pride to Roland Palmedo is the type of races which are held at Mad River. A longtime proponent of amateurism in sports, he has always believed in races for recreational skiers. Mad River has an open-door policy toward ski club activity, taking on ski club races, interclub regional races and even interlodge races —such races being limited only by the number the area can physically handle. Mad River has instituted no-stop, no-fall races, which are held every Monday, and which are especially interesting to children. Each year during school vacations there are children's races. There is also a family race, in which points are scored by each member of the participating family on the basis of how each does in his class. This race is usually won by well-known old-time skiing families like the Bob Joneses, the Sises, the Everdells, and the Goodriches.

The big race held at Mad River every other year is the New England Kandahar, a giant slalom with a top-seeded field. The run covers almost the entire mountain, down the Chute and through either the Beaver or the Grand Canyon. The length and layout of the course as well as the nature of the terrain are comparable to an Olympic giant slalom. And the race, which is held late in the year, has usually been run on superb snow under a brilliant spring sun. There is an over-forty class in this race, enabling veteran skiers like me to ski at least part of a championship caliber course. This class has been won each year by a different skier—Bob Bourdon's record being perfect, since he won it the one year he showed up. My turn came in 1962, when I had the unfair advantage of having strengthened my legs during three weeks of skiing in Europe.

Mad River, not known for downhill racing, has seen few downhills held on the mountain. Yet in 1955, when Norwich University was host for the National Collegiate Championships, the downhill event took place on a course which combined the Catamount and Grand Canyon Trails. It was won by Dartmouth's Chick Igaya in 1 minute, 29.3 seconds, probably still the fastest trip ever made down the mountain. Walter Prager, who was the Dartmouth coach, called this racecourse the best downhill test in the East, chiefly because of variety of terrain.

Roland Palmedo's influence is well manifested in the grouping of club lodges and private chalets both in the glen at Mad River and on the mountainside. It is always a privilege to be able to wake up in the morning and ski right over to the lift. Perhaps at Mad River a higher percentage of the skiers have this advantage than at any other area in the East. On the other hand, there are no inns on the mountain property, the theory being that they might in some way commercialize Mad River.

My own ski club, the Amateur Ski Club of New York, put up a lodge just before the 1959 season. Since we are a large club made up of geographically scattered members who have varied interests, the lodge has helped us to become better acquainted and to be a more unified club. It has been a boon to family skiing on vacations and a great meeting place for the college-age members on weekends. Designed by one of our members, Sandy McIlvaine, the lodge has the peculiarity of utilizing half its space for a large glass-fronted living room under a peaked chalet-style roof. This room has been highly successful for cocktail parties and club outings, even though the space takes away from sleeping quarters.

The growing colony of people who have built private chalets on the mountainside call themselves the "Mountain Folk." They have their own trail, which they cut themselves. It is of the narrow, bush-whacking variety, but serves the purpose of linking all the chalets with the mountain and the lifts. It is appropriately known as the "Rat."

The ski school, which until recently was run by Bud Phillips, is informal, personal, and friendly—suiting the style of Mad River. The fear of taking lessons in a big school is the fear of being regimented and being treated impersonally. Bud Phillips had an uncanny knack of knowing each person and how well he could ski, and of seeding him in the right group. It means a lot for someone returning to Mad River to reenter the ski school and find that he can pick up where he left off.

There have always been a number of Austrian instructors in the ski school. One of them, Rudi Mair, blond, blue-eyed and handsome, now runs the school—in the same characteristically informal and effective style. Famed journalist, ski author, and top instructor—Austrian Miki Hutter—was with Bud for two years immediately before he was lost to the newspaper world. Two Mad River standbys were Austrians Otto Egger and Egon Bresnig, who added lots of color as well as style correctness to the ski school. To our children these two fellows were heroes. Both men were very much aware that children can sometimes learn more by indirection than they can by what they are told, placed no curb on laughter, pranks, and horseplay. And the children, who have the knack of being imitative, learned much from these two, even emulating the details of their personal styles.

During some years, Don Powers was a star of the ski school. Tall and slim, he was light on his feet as a prima ballerina, and capable of all sorts of feats on skis. He could make quick zack-zack linked turns on a glacierlike section of ice, his skis holding by touch and timing rather than because of extra sharp edges. A feature of each year's Easter Parade would be Don in costume, caroming down the Chute, doing somersaults, bouncing off his rear end, grabbing the tops of small spruces, disappearing into the woods, and occasionally fitting in a superb turn, with the whole Mad River flock on hand for the performance.

Bud Phillips is my only acknowledged double, although he is younger than I, and I always claim he looks older. During the war, when Bud was with the ski troops at Camp Hale, the Dartmouth boys called him Jack Tobin, and Bud often used my name when he took out local Colorado girls he never expected to see again. At Mad River he started the Dipsy Doodle, perhaps Vermont's first winter nightclub. It was a poorly heated, unadorned barn, with Bud and his staff performing the same old pantomime singing acts, with the same old records, for the same old gang each Saturday night. As repetitive as this sounds, the Dipsy Doodle was anything but dreary, with a great exchange of spontaneity between the audience and the performers.

Often on Sunday mornings people who had seen the show would approach me for a ski lesson, and get turned down, or would congratulate me on the previous night's performance, and receive the straightforward comment, "I thought we were pretty good too." I trusted that the victim would inevitably find out that there were two Bud Phillipses at Mad River.

One day in the spring of 1964 I had just got the word that François Bonlieu from France had won the Olympic Giant Slalom at Innsbruck. As I spotted the Austrian instructor Egon at a table in the Basebox, the restaurant at the foot of the mountain at Mad River, I told him that the Frenchman's victory was a national disgrace for Austria. Warming to my own humor, I added that Austrian ski instructors would soon become a drug on the market and that Bud Phillips would have two or three French instructors in his school the next year. I was almost completely carried away when I noticed out of the corner of my eye the attractive young girl seated near Egon, who seemed to be listening with interest. As my monologue ended, this girl left the table to go out on the slopes, and Egon informed me that she was Princess Christina of Sweden, then a student at Radcliffe. Naturally I felt foolish having become so absorbed in my joke that I did not take a good look at the group I was addressing, especially the handsome young princess.

The lift line at Mad River does not always contain princesses, but you can count on an attractive crowd. Adherents say the wait never exceeds twenty minutes. And the atmosphere is friendly, with much mixing up of the sexes and ages. There are always a few Harvard boys, who certainly are not drawn to the area because of family skiing. As a matter of fact, Mad River gets more than its share of college boys and girls. But in the lift line the children are the stars, being so full of fun they communicate their happiness to others. The youngsters get a lot of attention, and the college students as well as the adults act as if they are talking to a group of celebrities.

On the mountain the children, usually skiing follow-the-leader style with their own groups, always seem to be having a good time. Six seems to be the average number in a group, with rarely more than two being from a family and with all of about the same age and ability. The coveted spot is that of leader, attained by the simple maneuver of passing the head man when he isn't looking.

Another sport is to attempt a flight off moguls. Often looking pretty ineffectual, the group members try above all not to make silly sit-down falls on landing. According to some people on the hill, the moguls are carved out as skiers successively turn in the same places. The youngsters claim that this is not so, and that the moguls simply grow. Their proof is that if one gets shoveled away by a trail maintenance crew, it grows right back in the same spot. The kids have nicknamed a huge perennial mogul on the Beaver just below the midstation the "Jinx Mogul." By legend, if one member of the group falls on this mogul, a hex will spoil the run of the entire group.

Other challenges on the mountain include a near-vertical short pitch under the lift at the very bottom. It is quite a thrill to see small-fry skiers poised at the brink, trying to get their nerve up to plunge down. Great fun for a group is to overtake and intercept a less able group, splitting their formation and sending them off in different directions. If the victims are four or five years older than the overtakers, the game becomes especially sporty. Also, it would be an oversight not to mention an important characteristic of the young skier—the noise level, which consists of hoots, catcalls, rocket sounds, singing, and whistling. One of the funniest sights I have seen was my number-two daughter, then aged twelve, skiing down under the double chair with the number-three son of my friend Jack White. The two of them were doing the watusi and the monkey on skis, supplying their own music, and seemingly not encumbered at all by their ski poles.

The only thing that can curb the youngsters is extreme cold. No matter how well bundled up they may be, when the temperature is twelve degrees below zero and the wind is blowing, they probably will not make more than two halfway trips up the mountain. Generally children seem to be sensible about skiing in the cold, but because some have a greater tendency toward frostbite than others, they must be watched very closely.

Apart from cold, little deters children from skiing. Our friends from the European trip, Chick and Lea Bolling, pulled into Mad River from Philadelphia late one evening with their four young children. They had accommodations in an apartment known as a "hutch," consisting of a bed-living room, kitchenette, john, and sleeping loft separated from the main room by fiber-glass sliding panels. In the middle of the night Lea woke up to the noise of people entering the adjacent Garden City Ski Club apartment. She then noticed that the light was on in the loft, and that there was some activity up there. Since it was 2:30 A.M., she climbed up, slid back the panel, and lo and behold, found her two youngest boys getting dressed for skiing! One of them was completely dressed in parka and ski pants, and the other one even had his ski boots on and laced up. They had apparently mistaken the arrival noises of the Garden City group for waking-up noises, and weren't at all discouraged by the darkness outside.

Living on the mountain in Mad River, our children have a long day on the slopes even if they don't get started until daylight. Consequently, we are always amazed that the youngsters still have energy at the day's end. During our cocktail hour at the ski club lodge, the youngsters congregate in a corner of the huge living room on a low couch, consisting of full-sized upholstered foam rubber mattresses and pillows. Here they listen to records, play the guitar, play cards, sing, wrestle, bounce on the mattresses as if on a trampoline, have pillow fights, and even occasionally surprise us by having quite serious bull sessions. After dinner, while the grown-ups sit in front of the fire, their heads occasionally nodding after a full day of sun and skiing, the youngsters are out enjoying Mad River. Their night life might be compared to the kind of fun children have on a summer night in a small town or simple lakeside summer colony. We never know exactly what they are up to unless, right under our noses, they are jumping off the second-floor balcony of the ski club lodge into the snowbank eight feet below. Sometimes they are engaged in organized activity, such as Ping-Pong or discothèque dancing at the Basebox, known as the Catamount Club in the evening. Here the preposterous notion reigns that kids from ten to seventeen can have fun together. One treat for our kids is to join up with the Godfrey Rockefellers' grandchildren and ride the private aerial tramway running from the parking lot to the Rockefeller house, built on a Mad River ledge. Another favorite pastime is sliding down the practice hill on flattened cartons or trays from the Basebox. Sometimes someone produces a toboggan, and raccoon coats, for the lucky ones, provide a not-too-fast, cushiony backside trip down the hill.

One New Year's Eve there was a boy from Australia at Mad River who had never skied before. The kids thought it would be fitting for him to be the first person in the New Year to ski at Mad River. Surrounded by a whole flock of "ski instructors," none certified, none over eighteen, none on skis, he was submitted to a machine-gun barrage of conflicting advice. Apparently the idea was for him to learn to ski on the easy upper part of the unlit practice slope, and then to ski the last more difficult section of the hill by himself. As an athletic representative of a country of athletes, he surprised the youngsters by surviving his many falls and actually skiing down the last part of the hill.

On the same night, part of the group—the older ones who did not face an early curfew—climbed up to the Appalachian Gap on the McCullough Turnpike, where there is a one-hundred-foot steel microwave tower. They selected an assault team of four climbers to go to the top. Although they carefully balanced their team with one person on each side of the tower, about three quarters of the way up, the tower began to sway, and they reversed course rapidly.

On the night before April Fools' Day, my oldest daughter and a friend made a neatly lettered wooden sign which they carried up the mountain in the dark and nailed to a tree. The next morning skiers coming down the mountain were surprised to see a sign at the junction of the Porcupine and the Bunny, reading "Two Minute Stop—Elephant Crossing."

Youngsters in their late teens looking for more sophisticated night life will find many spots in the overall area, generally known as Sugarbush Valley. Among these are Gallagher's, the Blue Tooth, the Inside Edge, and the Fat Cat. The Dipsy Doodle, which ran a country-style discothèque with fiddler, drummer, and horn player, has been replaced by posher places featuring music with a modern beat.

Some comment should be made on the serious skiing done by expert youngsters at Mad River. The ski school will put together a slalom class if there are two or three prospects. In the winter of 1965 a new slalom slope was opened on a newly cut steep section of the mountain, completely independent of the trail system. It is serviced by a high-speed rope tow, and on any weekend day or vacation day the young long-thong set can be seen running gates hour after hour, working hard to become Olympic racers. But Mad River's best-known training ground is the Chute, the steep fairly narrow upper section of the lift line. Somehow the moguls are the young hotshots' meat. National racers Lee Hall, Rosie

Fortna, and Duncan Cullman really learned to ski by running the Chute fast and nonstop, putting in one turn after another at a fantastic clip, and never "chickening out." This is by no means an easy feat, and when one of these young racers is working on such a run, everyone riding above him on the lift is spellbound.

Although Mad River is a small area, in combination with Glen Ellen and Sugarbush there is immense variety, all within about fifteen minutes' driving time. Walt Elliott of Glen Ellen and Sara and Damon Gadd of Sugarbush deserve as much credit for making their areas click as Roland Palmedo does for Mad River. If this chapter on family skiing had been written by a Sugarbush adherent, the tale might have been very much the same, with only the names and numbers of the players changed.

But for this skier, one of Mad River's big assets is that Stowe is only fifty minutes away. Even though Mad River is our family skiing headquarters, one member of the gang sometimes sneaks off to Stowe. However, I can't get away with a thing, and the day after one of my Stowe expeditions, countless die-hard Mad River skiers tell me, "You missed a great day here. You shouldn't have gone to Stowe."

Racing Against Father Time

There are many differences between the veterans' circuit and big league racing. With no training camps, no coaches, and, to hear us talk, not even any practice sessions, veterans ski for fun. And this chapter will start by describing the greatest fun-skier of all—Alec Bright—someone who has never been seen practicing slalom, and someone we all want to be like.

Alec, one of the few racers born before the turn of the century, has been known affectionately by skiers as "Gramp" ever since the mid-thirties. Technically it has been premature all along to call Alec "Gramp" because he only recently became a father, having married prewar racer Clarita Heath when he was just over sixty. They now have two children under ten. According to reports, Alec, who as a bachelor had the services of a butler, delights in all the simple chores that befall a head-of-household, insisting on drying the dishes, shoveling the snow off the walks, etc. As a father he derived more than the usual pleasure out of his first baby. Those of us who knew Alec as skiing's most notable bachelor have enjoyed hearing about these domestic moments.

Alec graduated from Harvard in 1919, where he was a star on the hockey team. Continuing to play hockey for several years after he graduated, he was on a team that was runner-up for the National Amateur Championship. Among his other sports were white water canoeing, amateur auto racing, and fox hunting. Starting in 1927 he became a flyer, and he has great skill as a sailor, having won Class D in the 1964 Bermuda Race.

Alec was part of the vanguard that started modern skiing in this country. Along with Al Sise and Bob Livermore he remembers the race to the opening in the stone wall on Gilbert's Hill in Woodstock, long before the first rope tow was built on that site. With a geschmozzel start, all but the winner faced the prospect of a fearful pileup at the gap in the wall. As some measure of how things have changed, a promoter out in Aspen Highlands a few year ago held a somewhat similar race on a "bash for cash" basis. Following the geschmozzel start, skiers headed together for the nearest gate of an open fast giant slalom. Because of the many injuries, there was much criticism of using cash-hungry young racers as gladiators.

The first downhill race in this country took place in 1927 on Mt. Moosilauke on the Carriage Road, and since it was an all-Dartmouth event, Alec missed it. However, he entered the first national downhill in 1933 on the same Carriage Road. The *Boston Transcript* reported as follows:

> A former Harvard hockey star, Alexander H. Bright representing Hochgebirge Ski Club, made a remarkable performance in finishing third. He is reported to have fallen three times and yet his time of 8:17.6 was more than 10 seconds under the old amateur record for the course. He has concentrated on skiing only for the last two years, as relaxation from office work and so the feat of the 35-year-old broker is noteworthy.

Alec was one of ten charter members of the Ski Club Hochgebirge, a distinguished Boston club founded in 1931. From the beginning a purpose of the club was to hold a downhill race each year to make certain that the members had "the proper dash and abandon in their skiing." Known as the Hochgebirge Annual Invitation Team Race, it is the oldest of its kind in the United States. In 1933 the race was moved from the Carriage Road to the new Taft Trail on Cannon Mountain, and in 1934 Alec placed second to Dick Durrance. Today a ski-club team race, it is closed to college competition and dominated by the East's top veteran racers. The gathering continues to be friendly and spirited.

In 1936 Alec was chosen for the United States Olympic Team, and in the downhill he made the second-best showing for an American. His last outstanding victory was in 1939, when he won the Massachusetts State Downhill Championship on the Thunderbolt Trail, setting a new course record and prevailing over a strong field. In the same year he placed fourteenth in the famed Mt. Washington Inferno, which was commendable for a 41-year-old racer on such a long arduous course.

In his skiing style Alec comes from the "point-'em-straight-down" school, with speed rather than form being the objective. Consequently, Alec often skis with quite a bit of air space between his knees, but he is a joy to watch coming down a schuss in his steady characteristic style. An article in the February, 1950, issue of *Ski Magazine* said that Alec, as he crossed the finish line of a fast downhill, wore "the pleased grin of a small boy." Always a favorite with the crowd, he got a tremendous cheer as he appeared at the top of the steilhang in the 1947 Harriman Race.

He is a pleasantly good-looking man, with a ruddy complexion, a full head of sandy, now gray, curly hair. There is great evidence of character in his jaw, which head-on is somewhat square, and in profile quite prominent. If such a jaw indicates stubbornness, all Alec's stubbornness is reserved for his strong vociferous defense of the uncontrolled downhill race. He has written many articles and often debated his stand at Eastern Ski Association conventions.

Alec is actually a soft-spoken relaxed sort of person who is an attentive listener. And in dispensing his dry humor he always has a boyish twinkle in his blue eyes.

A fine extemporaneous speaker, he has the reputation of being skiing's greatest toastmaster. Above all, there is a warmth about the man that is difficult to describe. In New England his last name is rarely heard, since the terms "Alec" or "Gramp" can only refer to one person. His friends are almost uncountable. Many years ago he was flying over New Hampshire in his own plane when he had to make a forced landing, coming down into a farmer's pasture. Expecting an angry pitchfork greeting he was mildly surprised when the farmer recognized him and yelled, "Hi, Alec."

There are many legends about Alec's bouts with the law over speeding violations, and his numerous leg breaks from speeding on the trails. All sorts of stories recount Alec's putting his charm to the test of talking policemen out of tickets. His skiing accidents number about one for every ten years of his life, but since a few of them were closely spaced they seem more numerous. At one time he was president of the Broken Bones Club, the presidency being awarded to the club member who has had the greatest number of leg breaks.

When the veterans are racing, a good field is determined by the quality of entries from the old-timers rather than from the not-so-old veteran hotshots like Brookie Dodge, Tom Corcoran, George Macomber, and Tony Carleton. And what makes it a real race is to know that Alec will be coming down the hill.

Another leading veteran racer is Bob Livermore, who started serious skiing while at Harvard. And through the years, although ten years younger, he has been a close compatriot of Alec's as well as a fellow member of the Hochgebirge. He is a most attractive, engaging Bostonian, all his life looking young for his age. With Alec at Garmisch-Partenkirchen for the 1936 Olympics, Bob also has won many racing laurels. One of his big victories was the 1940 Eastern Downhill Championship on Mt. Greylock, but he has also won many medals in veteran races in recent years, like first place in the 1960 New England Kandahar over-forty class.

I remember best his downhill run on the Cannon Mountain Trail in a National Veterans' Championship in 1954. Only a narrow track was packed out for much of the length of the trail, which had two feet of moist powder. Most of us were waxed well, and the snow was exceedingly fast. The speed of the snow combined with the dearth of places where one could check made conditions quite dangerous. Also the finish was on a fairly steep slope and the runout was inadequately packed. We knew that someone would surely get hurt making a stop turn in 2-foot powder. Yet at the top of the course before the race Livermore, far from showing any hesitancy, had a keen excited look in his eyes. True downhiller that he was, Bob took second, right on the heels of Bob Bourdon. Unfortunately, one person, Curt Bricklemeyer, did break a leg after he had crossed the finish line, trying to stop in the heavy deep snow.

As for myself, I was racing under a slight mental handicap that day. The year before while practicing for the same race on the same trail, I had the one accident of my skiing career. I do not count ankle wrenches, the bruised thigh muscle at Alta, and a broken bone in the hand from forerunning a race at Stowe, since these minor injuries did not incapacitate me for any period of time. Trying to avoid Dave Bradley, who was skiing slowly but who suddenly came into my path, I turned toward the side of the trail, found myself in midair, and sailed off a snow bank into the woods. Instinctively I ducked a tree with my head, led with a leg as if it were expendable, and crashed into the base of another tree. I had excellent medical attention, since Dave is a doctor, and he was joined by Walter Crandall of the Hanover hospital staff. Just before they straightened out my leg I took my first look at the way it was wrapped around the contour of the tree. Despite its frightful appearance the leg had a simple fracture that healed in routine time. However, since there was nothing routine about the dislocation to my business life, the following year I skied not just to avoid an accident but to avoid all possibility of a fall. Placing sixth in the downhill, I was applauded at the banquet that night for returning to the scene of my downfall. In the slalom, with no excuses whatsoever, I did a little better, placing third.

Al Sise, another seemingly ageless person, is perhaps skiing's most colorful veteran. In one of the earliest Mt. Moosilauke Carriage Road races Al went off the road on one of the sharp switchback turns. He found himself skis up, in a ditch alongside of Llewellyn White, another racer who had encountered the same difficulty. As Al tried to get back on his feet, Llewellyn said, "I have a flask in my hip pocket. Why don't we each have a nip before we go on?" Al was agreeable to the idea, and the two enjoyed a moment of relaxed conviviality while the stop watches ticked on.

In races before the war Al Sise was no Livermore or Bright,

skiing not at all as if his life depended on it. He was thought of more as the friendly outgoing personification of the Schussverein, the Boston ski club which has always bristled with interesting people.

Now, however, Al Sise, without any organized program for self-improvement, skis better, acts younger, and enjoys it all more each year. Al is so loaded with personality and enthusiasm for the sport that his presence in a race is felt by everyone there—racers, officials, and spectators. It is hard to believe that Al is now sixty-three. Up until the last two seasons, when he has usually been tagged by Rod Aller, a young bull of an entry in the over-fifty class, Al has very much dominated this age group. In 1968 at the Crotched Mountain Race, the name of the area apparently dictating the need for a veterans' event, Al placed high in the overall field, having fun beating all the skiers in the youngest age group, as well as those over fifty.

Just as Madame Tussaud's wax figures illustrate history, so do veterans in a race provide examples of earlier ski technique. Since you can't teach an old dog new tricks, most of us ski very much as we did when we raced as youngsters. But Al Sise, pushed by hot-shot daughters who made the national team, has made a few concessions to modern technique. For instance, he skis with both hands forward. To a modern-day racer, however, Al almost looks as though he is waltzing with a beautiful lady as he gracefully skis his way down a slalom course.

Joe McNealus of Pawlet, Vermont, who races for Killington, is a short, somewhat slight skier with one lung that collapses unpredictably. He has a bright friendly personality, though he often looks as though he has missed a night's sleep. Nevertheless, his alert eyes reveal a mind that is constantly at work. An entrepreneur, he has been successful in several different types of business. His accent is all New England—some Vermont but part of Maine too.

Joe in his younger days had some inspired slalom runs. He has a great sense of skiing a line, and as he comes down a course you can see how intent he is on skiing his exact planned route. There is a classic story about Joe, which could only have happened to someone very concerned with skiing a line.

Aspen's first International Race was scheduled shortly after the 1948 Winter Olympic Games at St. Moritz. Joe McNealus and Norm Richardson, neither of whom was on the Olympic team, had skied at Aspen all winter. They wanted to make a good showing against Jack Reddish and the other members of the American team, but knew that the Olympians had many advantages, like faster plastic-bottomed skis, better training and conditioning, plus racing experience against the Europeans. Knowing that it would take extraordinary efforts to beat them, Joe concocted a wild scheme.

The day before the race, late in the afternoon, Joe and Norm were at the top of the downhill course. Both carrying knapsacks, they persuaded the patrol to go on down, because they planned to take some pictures. After the patrol got out of sight Joe and Norm opened their knapsacks and pulled out blowtorches and two gallon cans of gas. Then, using the searing flames to ice the course, they created a set of icy tracks across all the traverses and flat sections. Since the course covered most of Ajax Mountain, starting high up in Tourtellotte Park before descending into what was to become the F.I.S. course through Spar Gulch, they had many hours of work forming the ice slicks on which they planned to ride to victory. They did not leave the mountain until about ten in the evening.

Unfortunately, the next day the hot sun spoiled their plan. The snow under the slick melted, and when they came down their private route, the tracks collapsed to make the going heavy and slower than on the conventionally packed sections of the course.

Consequently, both Joe and Norm placed fairly far down the list, way behind the American team. And thinking that everyone would be amused at their efforts, they told the story of the blowtorches. This was not the case. Some of the racers and all of the officials were so irate that for a couple of hours Joe and Norm were threatened with disqualification. The rule book said that skiers were not allowed to work on the course with anything other than their own skis. Joe and Norm defended themselves by pointing out that for a number of years many of the top racers worked on their lines for the Roch Cup by using shovels to build small platforms to help them in their jumps over the road crisscrossing the lower part of the course. Finally after a long heated discussion, Joe and Norm succeeded in blocking their disqualification, but somehow the two of them felt that the humor of the situation had been overlooked.

In mid-March of 1965 before a long giant slalom at Glen Ellen, Joe McNealus once again studied the icy course with great care. This time a blowtorch was unnecessary. His line all the way down would keep him on a hard fast icy surface. There was one especially perilous section of the course which caused many falls among the top runners. But not Joe, who stepped his sharp nonskidding turns, edge-checked with great skill, and held his line every inch of the way. Joe didn't just win in the over-forty age group. He won over the entire field, taking the Eastern Veterans' Giant Slalom Championship.

One of my great rivals is Tony Hyde, former owner of Madbush Chalet, between Sugarbush and Mad River. Before Tony settled in the north country he had never raced, and had not even skied very much. However, after much practice, he has become one of the best veteran skiers. When Tony and I vie with each other, his tuned-up technique is pitted against my experience. We know much about each other's weaknesses, and when the course and the snow are to one's advantage, the other pushes his gamesmanship and makes a great show of confidence. If the course is smooth and requires getting maximum speed out of every turn, Tony is a difficult man to beat. He is apt to be as polished on skis as he was as host at Madbush. A tall, handsome fellow with grayish-blond hair, Tony is competitive in several fields besides skiing. He was one of the best go-cart men on the Vermont circuit, as well as a demon on the tennis courts, having won several championhips at Sugarbush. Soaring, which has become very popular up there, is another of his interests. Today, Tony is a Boston businessman, preoccupied with a new career and a new wife, and he has slowed up ever so slightly.

Bob Skinner is another veteran skiing star. Bob lives in Sunapee, New Hampshire, where he has a ski shop and runs a ski equipment distribution business, handling several well-known lines for the East Coast. Graduated from Dartmouth in 1940, Bob was an exceptionally bright mathematics major. Now he is a big man, perhaps a little heavier than he should be. At the beginning of each season we always hope to see him fatter than the year before. Sadly enough for the rest of us, he doesn't seem to put on any more weight.

His personality, well understood by the competitors, is a puzzle to some of the officials. When Bob arrives for a race he goes up to the desk where the numbers are handed out and immediately starts "beefing" about the course, his number, or the behavior of certain people—almost as if this were expected of him. Certainly it is an oral exercise carried out with no malice toward anyone, and most decidedly with no threat of withdrawing from the race.

But he is sometimes misunderstood. For instance, during the mid-1950's Bob had earned the reputation as the number one veteran runner in the East. One day he pulled into Top Notch at Stowe and asked for lodgings. The management somehow got the impression that he was posing as Bob Skinner to gain entry. It seems hard to believe that Bob could get in trouble for using his own name, but it could only happen to him.

On March 7, 1965, a Senior Veterans' Giant Slalom was scheduled at Stratton Mountain for skiers over forty. As I pulled into the parking lot with several other Amateur Ski Club cohorts, in the rear mirror I saw Bob Skinner's big blue Ford station wagon. He maneuvered alongside, parking in the slot to my right. After getting out of the car I immediately noticed that two beautifully waxed Head Competition skis were lying flat on the floor of his station wagon, the rear seats having been folded down. I leaned on the edge of the car and stared at the skis with wonderment. Bob, without saying a word—our usual way of greeting each other—got out, walked around, and stood next to me. "That's a beautiful wax job," I said at the appropriate moment.

"Yes," Bob replied, "I painted it on very carefully. And the skis haven't been skied on more than half a dozen times. Not one nick in the bottoms, and the edges are perfect."

Later, outside Stratton's tremendous base lodge, we had just gotten our numbers and were putting on our skis. Bob swore a few times as he struggled with his bindings. "Who in the hell borrowed these skis?" he asked.

Finally he picked them up, held them alongside each other, and found to his consternation that they were mismates. One ski was a 210 Giant Slalom Model and the other a 205 Slalom ski. What followed is unprintable.

Finally he borrowed a pair of 210 mated Giant Slalom Competition skis from Gene Gillis, but was so unnerved by the mix-up that he did not race well that day. In fact, a good many of us even managed to beat him, since he finished eighth. Tony Hyde won the race and I came in second.

But Bob Skinner doesn't stay down very long. At Killington one week later, Bob got off to a beautiful start in a controlled downhill, running skillfully through some fast gates on a steep slope. His performance through the section we could see was flawless, and we knew he would do just as well on the flatter stretches below where he would keep his weight low, back slightly over the tails of his skis to make them plane. Here, also, he would benefit from his smooth style on the fast gradual turns. Several young Class A skiers racing as veterans for the first time—among whom was Charlie Gibson, an excellent competitive skier who had been Harvard's ski team coach for several years—thought a veterans' race would be a sure-fire way to win a trophy. But these fellows, who had just turned twenty-seven, were all beaten by Bob Skinner, then forty-six. He also defeated Joe Jones, Tony Carleton, Bill Prime—Amateur Ski Club star, Dick Weber, Joe McNealus, Tony Hyde, Al Sise, and myself, among a strong field of over fifty competitors.

The next day in the slalom the young Class A hopefuls got a good look at another over-forty skier, Joe Jones from Rutland. The snow for the slalom was good old Eastern boiler-plate, quite representative of 1965's lean crop of snow. But Joe, one of our greatest stylists and finest skiers, skied with such a delicate sure touch that it seemed as though the officials had moved a blanket of soft-packed powder on the course for his runs. Joe won the slalom as well as the combined event.

Rutland has a long tradition of turning out good skiers. The late Karl Acker, head of the ski school at Pico, took great interest in youngsters, and should get some credit for Andy Mead Lawrence's success as America's greatest woman racer. As a more recent part of this tradition, Joe Jones, who started the mid-Vermont Junior Skiing Council, has worked with talented young skiers from the Killington-Pico area, helping develop racers like Rick Chaffee, Rip McManus, Rebel Ryan, and Crandy Grant.

Joe's wife, Ann, a brilliant skier, came within 2 seconds of beating Andy Mead Lawrence in a downhill race on the Nose Dive. Joe and Ann, one as blond as the other, are as compatible on skis as any expert skiing couple I know. She can go anywhere he goes and do it just about as well and as fast.

No discussion of Eastern veteran skiing would be complete without mentioning Brookie Dodge and George Macomber. These two do not show up for all our races, since they still enter top Eastern competition. Needless to say, they are both so excellent that they are two of our best skiers. Brookie is in his late thirties and George is just a few years older. Their accomplishments are too vast and too numerous to cover. Brookie, the son of Pinkham Notch's Joe Dodge, grew up with Mt. Washington in his backyard. Lean in build and light on his feet, he is one of the most graceful skiers I have ever seen. In Europe, in F.I.S. and Olympic competition, he had America's best alpine record up until 1964, having twice been fourth in world championship slalom. When Brookie is on the hill we have a chance to compare our speed with that of a real skier.

George, who had some bad luck with bone breaks, never saw as much European competition as Brookie. In 1950, a few weeks after the Aspen F.I.S., George outskied many international stars, including the top Austrians, to win the Eastern Downhill Championship. A sturdy strong skier who is not as pretty to watch as Brookie, George is usually just as fast, and sometimes beats him.

When veterans are skiing together but not racing, there is always lots of fun. One very exciting day about a dozen of us were skiing down the Lift Line at Stowe. Joe and Ann Jones were both there, as were Livermore and Bright. There was sort of a mad spirit to the group. We were all skiing fast and getting just a bit competitive about our recklessness. Sensing that something was about to happen, we feared that someone would get hurt. Alec Bright, who must have had this feeling to a pronounced degree, decided not to let us down. Skiing the schuss below the midstation, Alec took the lead in a spurt of speed, overshot the turn to the left at the bottom, went head over heels into light timber, and completely disappeared down the uncleared drop-off below. As we skied down to look for him, suddenly Alec's smiling face appeared over the knoll. He had obliged us by going off the trail, but we were delighted that he had not hurt himself.

Another skiing-for-fun story concerns Brookie, George, Joe and Ann Jones, and an unidentified Austrian ski patrolman. The foursome, dubbed by George's wife "The Grim Group," was in Europe skiing at St. Anton. One morning they were looking for unbroken powder on the Hutte Run, a trail that was officially closed. On a catwalk in a narrow gully which opened up to the valley below, they suddenly heard a ski patrolman yelling at them in German. Although they didn't understand what he was saying, the message was unmistakable. Nevertheless they kept going and the ski patrolman, carrying a shovel, skied down the steep side of the gully toward their group. On the catwalk Brookie was leading, then George, and Joe and Ann were trailing. Like a *Focke-Wulf* fighter plane diving in on a formation of B-17's, the patrolman bore down on the group as if to split their ranks, while all four looked up with interest as they continued on down the catwalk. The patrolman, shovel and all, came in between George and Joe. Then he proceeded to pass George, possibly intent on going after the lead man, Brookie. Passing George more on the lower side of the gully than on the catwalk, he touched his shovel to the snow almost as if it were a ski pole. However, this maneuver caught him off balance, throwing him into a spin. He did some somersaults and ended up in the gully fifty feet below, still holding the shovel and shaking his fist. The four American skiers continued on down the catwalk, looking to the rear rather than at the trail ahead, having seen the gyrations of the spectacular fall. Perhaps the patrolman at this point realized that these skiers who were so perfectly poised while looking backward and going down the catwalk at twenty-five miles an hour, were no ordinary skiers.

Since deep powder skiing on world-renowned mountains is not often available, most veteran skiers will pass up a day of pleasure skiing for a day of racing. Not much is required from course and snow conditions to hold a race for our gang, and the race inevitably offers so much fun that we do not miss social skiing.

Veterans' racing defies the laws of time and logic, particularly in the East, where distances are short and schedules are heavy. Many ski areas regard any kind of racing as something of an organizational pain in the neck, requiring time, personnel, and slope space. From a purely commercial viewpoint, nobody has much interest in watching a bunch of more or less over-the-hill skiers trying to recapture their youth. Even members of a veteran racer's family often pass up the opportunity to watch the old man. Newspaper sports pages also reflect this lack of interest, rarely reporting on a veterans' event.

Nevertheless, the tempo of veteran racing has stepped up considerably in the past several years. The 1967–1968 competition schedule listed an Eastern event for veterans for nearly every weekend in the season. Every event drew a flood of entries, several over 100, three over 150. The Eastern veterans' list has 423 names. The situation has become somewhat like junior racing, with fields so numerous that there is now a system of eligibility classification.

In their headlong fight to prove that seniority doesn't necessarily mean decline, these veterans have, in a measure, discovered a kind of Fountain of Youth. They are, as a group, so healthy it is almost overpowering. Among the active veterans in the East, there has not been one single heart attack or death from any natural cause, even including what is known as old age, since the first National Veterans' Pace at Cannon Mountain in 1953. Most of the oldsters carefully preserve a state of total dishonesty about subjects like conditioning, the object being to convince their competitors that they never run slalom gates, never indulge in anything but casual fun skiing, and never have occasion to undergo such off-season miseries as calisthenics, jogging, or vigorous sports. As lean and muscular a group of adults as you'll find anywhere, they obviously employ propaganda more than a little suspect. To find out how a veteran keeps in shape, you have to ask his wife, who will usually be quick to make fun of her husband's strenuous surreptitious efforts to maintain his youth.

In veterans' racing, the goal is not so much to win one's class—although the competition for silverware is heated—as it is to see how many younger competitors one can outski. A racer becomes eligible for veteran competition at twenty-seven. If this seems young, it works out well in practice. Actually, once a Class A racer leaves the big-time circuit for military service or business, or for the early years of marriage and family, his competitive edge drops fast. There are four age classes, twenty-seven to thirty-one, thirty-two to thirty-nine, forty to forty-nine, and fifty and over. The so-called Class II, between thirty-two and thirty-nine, dominates veteran racing, mainly because these skiers have become settled in business and have the time and money to take weekend skiing seriously. Another reason for their dominance, particularly in the East, is that Class II contains many of the great Dartmouth skiers of the 1950's who were prominent in international racing.

As a measure of the big-time aspect of veterans' racing today, it is interesting to cite the 1968 National Veterans' Race at Waterville Valley. In the first event, the downhill, the most notable victory was that of 48-year-old Vermont dentist, Bob Middleton, who beat 40-year-old George Macomber and other strong contenders in that age class. George, undaunted, went on to win the other two events plus the combined.

Another double winner in this race was the bright and genial Tom Corcoran, the president and general manager of the host area. Tom, who placed fourth in the Olympic Giant Slalom at Squaw in 1960, competed for three or four subsequent years as a part-timer, holding his own against America's best in his giant slalom specialty. His first race as a veteran was three years ago in the Hochgebirge. He won that and every other veterans' event he entered, right up until the 1968 National Slalom at Waterville. Shortly after his first run of the slalom, he was astounded to see his time bettered by Bill Beck. Immediately skating up to Bill, Tom slapped him on the back and exclaimed, "Becker, that's the very first time you ever beat me in the slalom!" When all the years are considered that Bill and Tom have raced against each other, during which Beck made his reputation as a downhiller (fifth in the 1952 Olympics, fourth in the 1954 F.I.S. for the best showing of any American male ever in world championship downhill), it was a remarkable occasion.

Neither man, as it happened, won the event. After the second run of the slalom, the final class winner was Franz Schemmel, and overall winner was a Class I entry, Al Hobart, who untypically won a veterans' trophy while still racing on the big-time circuit.

There were two triple winners at Waterville, one of them a girl, Cricket Mackinley, from California. The ladies' events in veterans' racing have not been as overwhelmingly successful as the men's, being limited to sectional and national championships with comparatively small fields composed mainly of veterans' wives. Nothing, however, should detract from Cricket's accomplishment. Her leading competitor was Tom's wife, Birdie Corcoran, who is an excellent skier. Both girls are well under forty and look well under thirty. One has five children and the other four. Both are extremely attractive, Cricket being the outdoor type and Birdie looking more like a European model. Cricket captivated everyone by innocently waltzing off with downhill, slalom, and giant slalom titles; Birdie won us over with her style as a skier and her sportsmanlike attitude about being beaten.

The other triple winner was 51-year-old Rod Aller, a lawyer from Lakeville, Connecticut. Rod won the downhill by 5½ seconds, the giant slalom by 3 seconds, and both heats of the slalom, making him a kind of graying Toni Sailer. After the slalom on Saturday, I took a recreational run with Rod down one of Waterville's broad trails. We were skiing alongside each other, doing opposing S turns, playing a kind of "chicken" as we skied toward each other, turning away at the last possible second. After about half a dozen such maneuvers, I decided it was the wrong day to play chicken with Rod Aller. As I stopped, I noticed that Rod had given approximately the same treatment to four college girls who had stopped at the side of the trail. I went over to explain that my friend was a good skier, and that there had been no threat to their safety. I went on to say that he was still a little elated after winning some national championships in the last few days. Rod had whizzed by in a light nylon jacket, with no hat and a good head of hair, showing speed as well as control, and the girls were quite impressed. I couldn't resist divulging that he had won his victories in the over-fifty age group, but that didn't seem to make any difference. For, as I was about to ski down, one girl said, "Tell your friend that since it's Leap Year, I'd like to have the next dance."

And we all have our big days. One of mine came in the 1964 Hochgebirge Invitational Team Race. Three of us from the Amateur Ski Club wisely drove up to Franconia on Thursday, two nights before the race. Franconia, principally a haven for Boston skiers, is not the easiest place to get to from New York City. We had a good day of skiing on Friday, and took a casual look at the giant slalom course after it had been set up late in the day. Sometimes this is an excellent way to implant a course in the memory, letting the mind subconsciously absorb its basic flow.

The next morning the sun was out strong, which meant that I would wear my yellow pants. That day my feeling was one of general well-being. I was not exuberantly happy, but rather calmly, inwardly sure about myself and my prospects for a good run. Although the snow was hard, my Giant Slalom Head Competitions were almost new, and there is nothing like new skis on icy snow. Also, having done the Royal Canadian Air Force exercises for a year and a half, I sensed that I had an advantage in conditioning over my cohorts.

As I was making my last-minute preparations—taking a trip into the bushes, lacing up, and then slithering my skis on the snow —I recognized this as one of those rare moments in racing when fear is completely under control. The race was on the Zoomer Trail, a broad swath cut through the trees. The start was over on one side, almost in the trees, and the first gate was across the hill on the opposite side of the trail. To gain a couple of seconds, I decided to head almost down the fall line toward the second gate, and then step up to my line for the first gate, skating for speed as I worked my way up the hill. My plan worked beautifully as I got to the gate, and back on the line with plenty of speed. In my mind I could see the entire course. There were no uncertainties about where I should be or how fast I should go through any of the combinations. I had no special feeling of skiing well or rhythmically, yet I knew I was holding my turns and getting speed out of the course. As I went into my tuck after the last gate, heading for the finish line, I had the satisfaction of knowing that no matter how I had done in relation to the others, I had skied the course without a single mistake.

After stopping and looking around I could sense from the expressions on the faces of the timers and spectators that I had had a good run. There were many skiers on hand who had been associated with the sport since its early years. Most of the people mentioned in this chapter were there, plus others like Ted Hunter, Sel Hannah, with his lovely wife Paulie, and Roger Peabody, managing director of the United States Eastern Amateur Ski Association. Most important of all, Alec Bright was on the hill, and turned in a stellar performance.

There was considerable suspense about the team race for the forty-and-over class. However, it looked more and more as if I had won that age group by a good margin. For top individual honors, there was no doubt about the contest's being between Brookie Dodge and George Macomber. Before entering a three-gate flush, Brookie performed an impressive instantaneous edge-check, which was certainly effective, but which slowed him down too much. His club mate and arch rival George was able to defeat him that day. In the overall field only four skiers beat me, all better skiers and in younger classes—Macomber, Dodge, Carleton, and Jones. I came within 5 seconds of George, which particularly pleased me, and I won in my age class by 6 seconds. Also the underdog Amateur Ski Club team, consisting of Charlie Stiassni, Haig Costikyan, absentee Tom Clement, and I, won the team event, in which only three were needed to score. Tom Clement, who stayed behind at his farm in Maryland, must have been clairvoyant, knowing that he could pick up a team pin without making an appearance.

Later, at the Hochgebirge clubhouse everyone made quite a fuss over my yellow pants—even commenting that my ego got such a boost from wearing them that I had had an unfair advantage over my competitors. But it was a great day, and one which I shall never forget.

I should mention that in the same race a year later rival Tony Hyde won the over-forty class without the benefit of yellow stretch pants, but otherwise in very much the same manner, within 5 seconds of the overall winner, Rato Schmid of Switzerland, who edged out Brookie Dodge. And, coincidentally, Tony placed fifth in the overall results, but I was unable to get quite the same thrill out of Tony's victory as I did out of my own the year before.

16

The Male Ego

I hope that many aspects of this chapter, despite the masculine title, will have a message for women. Essentially there is much basic information to be passed along to all intermediate skiers, little of which is new, but all of which, as far as I am concerned, has never been put in the proper perspective.

The confidence factor, very important in all sports, is critical in skiing. When the skier is "up," keenly attuned to the snow and the feel of the snow, he skis in a relaxed way with reflex action rather than deliberate movements. There is a natural rhythm to his skiing. His ego is in its most healthy state and he literally knows that he can ski to his best capability. It is much easier to talk about the skiing ego than it is to find it, yet there are ways of helping a skier find his ego.

If this chapter is oriented toward a male skier, perhaps it is because a man's ego is more easily understood than a woman's. A man's ego may take many forms, getting its satisfaction from duck-shooting off the eastern shore of Maryland, from a shrewd well-timed business deal, or from cracking a golf ball 250 yards down a famed fairway. Even building his own house can be a source of masculine pride, either through the role played by his architect in designing a home that reflects the owner's personality, or through that part of the house which he has actually built with his own hands. Of course, the classic way for his ego to be satisfied is through the conquest of a woman, sometimes on the dance floor when he dances so well with his partner that the two dance as one, or sometimes in life when he has through his charm, sincerity, or even his masculine directness, completely won over a woman, who perhaps becomes his wife.

A woman's ego seems to be entirely related to how she feels as a woman—a feeling which often changes according to her relationship with a male partner. If the woman's ego appears simple in its form, within this form it is infinitely complex and hidden deep below the surface. At my age I have learned a lot about women, partly because I have three daughters, yet how ridiculous it would be for me to think I understand them. In a rare moment when I do and say just the right thing, I can make a woman feel as if she is on the stage, and accordingly her ego becomes unveiled for a fleeting second. However, to write about a woman's skiing ego would involve an entire book.

Actually the mystery of women is as elusive on the slopes as off. Women usually have more trouble finding their confidence on skis than men do. Physically they are suited to skiing, because of their grace and adaptability to skiing's rhythmical movements. Since they are not as aggressive as men and have less compulsion to ski fast, they should have fewer fears and be more relaxed about the sport. Sadly enough, this is not the case, for women have definite problems with the mental challenges of skiing.

To take a look at a typical male intermediate grade skier, let's assume that he has been skiing for over ten years and that he has the undeserved reputation of being a hardy skier. He looks, talks, and acts like an expert. Burdened with only a small share of life's problems, he might be a 32-year-old bachelor, a success in business, and a ladies' man.

We find this well-attired young man in one of his most impressive moments, standing with drink in hand at the Club 10 bar at Sugarbush, talking to a group of six or seven other skiers. A New York model he knows slightly comes over to congratulate him on his run down the Organ Grinder which she saw while riding up in the Gondola. This fellow's turns had looked very impressive to her, possibly because of the combination of his distance from her, his smart colorful costume, and his reputation as a good skier. Also, because the hour was high noon, the sun bright, and the snow a soft-packed excellent surface, he had skied especially well on that run. So, when the model told him how good he looked, he remembered the moment quite well, and was inclined to agree with her.

In fact, later on over at Orsini's, he thought about what the model had said to him. He reflected on his level of skiing, suddenly realizing that he had been on a plateau for much too long. It seemed to him that the main reason he hadn't made any progress was that he did not feel ambitious, already having a slight edge on the group that he skied with. Originally skiing had come fairly easy to him, and he could now ski all the trails with few falls. Musing over his demitasse after dinner and watching some fancy twisting on the dance floor of the discothèque, he decided it was time for him to go on to greater heights. He resolved that it would start with his first run down the mountain the next day. And with a new exhilaration he sensed he would become a new skier.

So the next morning he could hardly wait to get back on skis. For his early morning run he chose the steep lift-line slope under the Valley House Chair, known as the Mall. Unfortunately, the mountain was in a new mood. With the sun obscured by clouds and the slope scraped clean of powder, there was a hard mogulled surface. Nevertheless, feeling full of confidence at the top of the slope, he shoved off a couple of times with his poles and built up to an unaccustomed speed. His first turn was an old-time jerked christie which he had gone into with too much speed. As he unweighted, in his anxiety to slow down, he rushed his turn, producing an edge-chattering skid rather than a carved turn. His next few linked turns were more controlled, but still stiff and awkward. Spurred on by the desire to ski better, he was accomplishing little other than skiing faster and more aggressively. About halfway down he stopped, very much out of breath, weak in the legs, and emotionally let down. Having resolved to ski to the full measure of his ability, he was worse than ever. The experiment was a failure, and he longed for his regular skiing group.

The frustrating thing for this skier is that he knows he has ability, balance, coordination, and judgment. However, like many recreational skiers, he has no focus in his approach to the sport. He is a skier without a plan, enjoying it in some ways because he really likes the sport and wants to get better at it. Among the solutions to his problem, some would take time, some would take effort, and others money. And before appraising whether or not improvement is worth the trouble he must know what has to be done. Most skiers in this category have little idea what steps must be taken to upgrade them from intermediate skiers to experts.

Let's take a look at the list of requirements for this skier to earn his promotion. Ultimately he will have a healthy male ego working for him. But the skiing ego must be built step by step; it cannot come into being by having an attractive female say the magic words about one's skiing. For the skiing ego depends upon the right equipment and confidence in that equipment, as well as upon knowledge of the simple elements of the parallel turn and confidence in the ability to make rhythmical turns under varied conditions. But above all the skiing ego is the confidence to rise above the physical challenges of the sport—to think one's way down the mountain—and it is in this final category that the recreational skier is so abysmally weak. Stated more prosaically, there are actually only three elements that go to make up the skiing ego: equipment, mastery of the parallel turn, and "trailsmanship." Naturally all three interrelate and are important, and strength in two categories does not compensate for weakness in a third.

Taking these three elements in the most logical order, we shall first consider equipment. Here equipment means the complete skier, his physical being as well as his clothing and ski equipment. We have seen how the racer has such a personal feeling about his clothing, his muscular power, and his boots and skis, realizing that all this is part of an entity which he pits against the course. The average skier in a less intense and less preoccupied way can have the same sort of awareness of himself as a total skier.

Conditioning gets too little attention from the average skier.

Just doing a few deep knee bends several days before going out on the slopes is not enough. The rewards of conditioning are high, both in terms of safety and of ability to enjoy the sport. Yet because of human inertia the majority of skiers resist and overlook this aspect of the sport. A desire to be in shape has to come from within the skier and will not be too successfully promoted by me or anyone else. However, I have been skiing long enough to have a good idea how much conditioning is required for a successful ski season.

Every year of my skiing life I have done something about preparing my muscles for the sport. Up until a few years ago it was spasmodic road work, an assortment of calisthenics, with frequent deep knee bends. The road work nearly killed me and too many deep knee bends resulted in sore thigh muscles and creaking knee joints. I accomplished something, but was never really in shape until after the first month or so on skis.

I now use the popular Royal Canadian Air Force 5 BX system of exercises, along with some special skiing exercises, including a number of muscle-stretching maneuvers. I try to stay in shape all year round simply because it makes me feel so fit and energetic, giving me much more reserve for tackling daily chores.

There is undoubtedly much to be learned about physical conditioning. In recent years study of the heart and circulatory system has indicated the tremendous importance of exercise as a way of increasing the efficiency of the human body, expanding the capacity of the heart and lungs, and therefore reducing the incidence of degenerative heart disease. Even more certain is the role which exercise plays in controlling weight, reducing nervous tension, and contributing to a general sense of well-being.

The routes to good physical conditioning are not by any means clearly mapped. I like the Royal Canadian Air Force procedure mainly because it is simple and easy to do in the home, takes little time, and most important of all, builds one up, according to age groups, to two levels of physical fitness—either so-called flight fitness or a somewhat lower level for the average person. Furthermore, there is a prescribed rate of advancement. There is, however, some necessity for caution here, less for skiers perhaps than for others, since skiers are generally fairly lean, hardy, and fit, even without special exercises. Among the four million people who have followed these exercises there have been quite a few victims of back problems and even of heart attacks. One of the R.C.A.F. exercises should be eliminated completely—the one in which a person lies on his stomach and arches his back—since it is notorious for causing back trouble. Three years ago on a plane I sat next to Captain Benson, U.S.N., who is a doctor in charge of the flight surgeon team responsible for our astronauts. He told me that the Navy gave up the Royal Canadian exercises because there were a few heart failures among men who were unable for one reason or another to keep up the prescribed pace. I felt much more comfortable when he told me that there are no risks once the proper level has been attained; the risks occur during the buildup period. Obviously, people who are overweight, or who have a record of back problems or previous circulatory trouble, should consult a doctor before taking up any program for conditioning. Also, anyone over forty who has been exceptionally inactive should either see a doctor or proceed on a most cautious basis.

My friend Dr. Hans Kraus, one of the finest muscle rehabilitation men in the world, who served on the Physical Fitness for Youth Committee under two presidents, also has some reservations about the R.C.A.F. exercises. He points out, as does Captain Benson, that not everyone is capable of the recommended pace and that the exercises do not properly stretch or relax the muscles. Hans is a great advocate of running, walking, hiking, and climbing. He would rather see us attain physical fitness in more natural ways. I am sure Hans is right, but few of us have the time or the will to discipline ourselves to this degree.

Considering that the R.C.A.F. workout only takes 11 minutes a day, the results are good. And once you have reached your level the exercises do not have to be done every day. Just doing them two or three times a week will keep you there without any strain. Also, it is not by any means necessary to attain the flight level of physical fitness. I try to stay at my age level in the nonskiing months and to upgrade to the flight level for my age as the ski season approaches, in order to be in shape for racing. Any skier who takes up this program will be aware of a tremendous new reserve of muscular power and endurance when he is on the slopes.

As winter draws near, one or two special exercises for skiing can be added. For the bobbing jumps I usually substitute an exercise in which I use the first three steps of a staircase. Placing one foot on the third step from the bottom, I then bring the other foot up, and then step back down, alternating feet each time. For me this seems to approximate the way the thigh muscles are used in skiing. I still do a few knee bends, although I don't go all the way down, because football trainers have determined that deep knee bends can actually weaken the knee joint. Stein Eriksen has a great little exercise, in which you put a shoe box on the floor and jump quickly over it on both feet from one side to the other. The body centers over the shoe box, and the feet go back and forth somewhat in the manner of wedeln. This exercise develops timing and coordination as well as muscle tone.

To help stretch and relax muscles I do several other exercises. One from the Swedish rhythm series is a high kick with upraised, stretched arms. In the position of the drop-kicker on the football field, one kicks the toe to shoulder height. Another is a yoga exercise in which one lunges like the fencer, with the weight on the bent leg, the other leg stretched out behind. The knee of the trailing leg as well as the hands touch the floor. For both exercises a good count is to build up to fifteen with each leg.

In deference to Hans Kraus, a bit of hill climbing, or the recently popular jogging, would be the best way of all for a skier to get in top shape.

What seems extraordinary about any exercise program is that so many people continue to follow it once they get started. Naturally, a skier is more motivated to stay with such a program than a nonskier. What is really needed is a scientific, efficient way of getting into shape for skiing. And a good ski-oriented regimen would probably include much of the modified yoga used so successfully by the French racers.

Obviously, equipment in the more literal sense is very important, and some of the engineering that goes into the modern ski has already been discussed. For the intermediate skier there is much to be gained in going from skis like the Head or Hart standard to high performance skis, either metal or epoxy fiber glass, often labeled "Competition Model." Among the three "Competition Models," the Giant Slalom best serves the intermediate-expert recreational skiers' needs for mountain skiing. Today's racing model is engineered to provide a skidless, precision turn without an inordinate amount of stiffness. Consequently, one of the shortcuts for the intermediate skier aspiring to an expert, is to put himself on the expert's skis. There will be no problems in going from the soft standard model to the somewhat stiffer racers' skis. After only three or four runs, the intermediate skier will be used to his new high performance skis, and feeling more like an expert, wonder how he got along without them. The great Killy says that any good skier could handle with ease the fiber glass skis he used in winning the giant slalom in the 1968 Olympics.

The racers' skis have these properties: they track well, they absorb bumps in a steady manner, and they flex in a uniform way, helping to carve a smooth, well-rounded turn. One of the most outstanding characteristics of the metal skis is the absence of torque or lateral twist, a quality almost lost in a soft slithering metal ski. In the more skillfully stressed racers' model, this advantage results in a quick, hard bite when the skier is edge-checking. Of course the perfectly squared hidden edges play their role in giving the skier more skill in turning and checking. Finally, the fast high-density polyethylene-type bottoms (more and more available on all types of skis) almost give the skis the speed of a waxed surface, and despite conventional belief, a waxed ski is easier to ski on than an unwaxed one. There is more feeling of lightness, of turning properly and rhythmically, on waxed skis.

These expert skis will even help the average skier to fight falls. After all, the racer is constantly scrambling to get over his skis or back on his line. The fact that these skis will track better when tracking and turn better when turning will enable a skier to recover from an unsteady position and therefore to some extent avoid falls. However, since they are fast skis, they do not eliminate the useless sit-down fall which occurs when a skier lets his skis run away from him, and a moment of timidity seems to coincide with a moment when his weight is back on his heels. If it is just a little harder to start a turn on racers' skis, the handicap is small. The actual beginning of the turn should be a simple maneuver with the real finesse being required to finish the turn, as we shall shortly attempt to prove.

But these hotshot skis have one definite liability. As highly tuned, somewhat fragile instruments, they must be treated with care. They should not be used for the first snow of the season, since the soft plastic bottoms gouge out quite easily and the edges may be badly damaged when nicked by rocks. The solution is for every above-average skier to own two pairs of skis, one of which could be old Head standards, serving for deep snow as well as for poor snow conditions. It is my contention that the ski manufacturer has not received his full share of the skiing dollars, since some of the original Head skis are still in use. In fact, there is a cult among people still skiing on standards with less than four serial numbers. Ann Murphy Garrity could afford to spend recent winters skiing at Aspen but still does all her skiing on pair number 247 made in 1950. Even though physically intact because of many reconditionings, these skis are so floppy that they almost flutter in a slight breeze. I seriously think she is ready for a new pair. She may even need two new pairs, since the old Heads are ready to be mounted on the wall, complete with engraved plaque.

With two pairs of skis, there is an incentive to keep the "Competition Grade" pair in top-notch working order. The average skier never works on his skis from the beginning of the season until the day the snow melts. The skis, if they are lucky, may get one trip to the ski shop, for a grindstone edge-sharpening job. Once the skier owns such classy skis, he should be introduced to the file—in fact, to a special Austrian-made file called a Vixen. It has sharp raised teeth appearing on its broad working surface in the form of short parallel arcs. No more than ten minutes a day with this file can keep edges almost as sharp as they were when the skis left the factory. The file is used mainly on the sides of the edges, being held perpendicular to the running surface and worked lightly down the length of the ski. Occasionally it should be used on the bottoms of the skis, where its teeth file the plastic surface as well as the metal edges, shaving off equal amounts of both to keep the soft bottoms flush with the edges. This eliminates a channel which grooves out on the bottom near the edges, causing a bothersome condition known as "railing." *

The whole point of taking care of these skis is that most of the tremendous advantage they offer is lost unless they are maintained in superior condition.

As fast as the soft plastic bottoms are, they should be waxed, both to lengthen the life of the skis and to give them greater potential for speed. Even waxing once a week is better than not at all, for each of the many little fibers on the bottoms has the property of retaining minuscule amounts of wax for long periods of time. And waxing can be so simple. Some waxes can be rubbed in by hand, but an inexpensive travel iron is ideal. With an iron the process takes just a few minutes. First the wax is held against the hot iron and allowed to drip on the running surface of the ski, then the drops are ironed flat. Also the types of wax that can be bought in tubes, such as Toko, provide a fast smooth running surface with a minimum of fuss. For racing, special care must be taken, and hot waxes are normally painted on, a process which takes nearly an hour. But the average skier needs only five minutes of waxing to enhance the day's sport, especially appreciated when he passes everyone on a runout.

Boots for experts, like boots for novices, must fit well. And boots outlive their usefulness not by looking worn or beat-up, but by losing their stiffness and support. In modern ski technique, the knee drives forward to provide the dynamism of the turn, and drives into the hill for an edge-check or an edge-set for the beginning of a new turn. When the knee drives into the hill, the ski must respond with sureness and power, but this is not possible if the boot is stretched too much or the leather is too soft. There comes a point when boots are as comfortable as a pair of slippers, but are almost worthless for their main purpose—to transmit the action of the knee to the ski. One piece of good advice is to buy

* The 10 Mil Bastard file is easy to obtain and very effective for edges alone, but not as good as the Vixen for bottoms.

new boots in the spring of the year. When the snow is soft and moist, not much edging is required, and the boots are pliable because they absorb moisture. These two factors ease the break-in period for new boots. (One of the more extreme, and not to my knowledge approved, ways of breaking in leather boots is to wear them in a bathtub full of water so that when thoroughly moistened they are molded to the contour of the foot.) Additional reasons for buying boots in the spring are that the feet have been toughened by a winter of skiing, and there is the good possibility of a spring discount.

The relatively new epoxy boots are certainly here to stay. The Rosemont and especially the Lange boots are an important American contribution to ski equipment, nearly rating with Head metal skis and Scott lightweight poles. The advantage of the synthetic material is that it retains its stiffness better than leather, providing strong support and a positive link to the ski. Perhaps some day epoxy boots will be lined with leather to give perfect feel as well.

For the expert skier, in fact for any skier, the less sock material between the boot and the foot, the better the communication to the ski. At a recent Louise Orvis Race on Bromley, one of the young hotshots was seen to pull a bare foot out of a Lange competition model boot before the start, on a day ten degrees below zero. For five years I wore an exceptionally snug pair of Austrian Haderer boots over only one thin pair of Italian silk socks. I never had any frostbite, although there were times when I had to keep my toes going. One of the great skiers, Ernie McCulloch, always broke in his boots with bare feet.

The new expensive lightweight poles are in greater evidence than the high performance skis. Contributing to balance and ease of movement, they make it simpler to anticipate the turn properly with a pole plant. As costly as they are, these poles turn out to be a bargain since they last so long, providing they are not "lifted."

I have always discouraged pole thieves by tying skis and poles to the wooden ski racks with my long thongs, a system that has worked perfectly. Once, however, at the top of Mansfield late on a gloomy day when there were few people skiing, I decided not to bother, merely slipping my skis and poles into the slot on the rack, before heading into the Octagon for a hot chocolate. Ten minutes later I came out to find my Scott poles missing. I let loose my wrath, announcing to the others who were there that I had been the victim of a pole thief. Someone said, "There was a girl here who lost hers too." I then proceeded to look around, hoping that my poles had only been misplaced and that I would find them in another rack. Having no success, I returned to my rack and again cursed and bemoaned my fate. This time a man said, "There was a girl here who had her own poles stolen, and then took someone else's. She must have taken yours."

"What did she look like and where did she go?" I asked. He had noticed nothing about her except that she was on Head standards, and was skiing with a boyfriend, with whom she had gone down the Toll Road. I jumped into my skis, not even bothering to fasten my thongs properly, raced up the knoll to the start of the Toll Road, and took off, minus poles, down the trail. I skated along on my fast skis, having no trouble passing Toll Road-grade skiers. Each time I passed a group they must have thought there was something strange about me, since I looked them over so carefully as I went by. After passing about a dozen groups of skiers, almost half a mile down I saw a couple stopped at the side of the trail. As I pulled up close I recognized the scars on the gold aluminum finish of my Scott poles. Before I had even come to a complete stop I grabbed them from the girl, saying, "These are my poles. What are you doing with them?"

"Someone took mine, leaving me with a pair much too short for me," she replied.

"Two wrongs don't make a right," I declared. It was my generation against hers as I proceeded to dress down this young mascara-eyed beauty. When I got through with her she was most apologetic and near tears, but at least I had retrieved my poles, being luckier by far than most victims of pole-snatching.

The new lightweight poles are of little use if the skier is burdened with a heavy jacket and too many layers of clothing. The quilted parkas are recommended for cold days, but when the sun is out and the temperature is over twenty degrees, they can be cumbersome. No racer would ever be caught wearing heavy gear in competition. I find that a light sweater under a nylon shell and one heavy sweater on the outside allow me to feel free and easy and yet stay warm in temperatures down to fifteen degrees. A sweater on the outside has become my trademark. One of its advantages is that if I fall on a steep hard-surfaced slope, it grabs the snow, whereas a nylon parka slides like greased lightning.

The second feature that goes to make up the skiing ego, after my broad interpretation of equipment, is mastery over the parallel turn. And as stated before, the parallel turn cannot be learned by the book-knowledge route. The rhythm of the turn and the infinite subtleties that go into it must be learned on the hill with a certified ski instructor. Each year I go back to have my turn reworked. In fact, almost every good skier I know makes a point of getting some instruction every winter.

Without attempting to teach the parallel turn, I at least want to break the turn down into its elements.

Colin Stewart, claiming that the motions of the parallel turn could be duplicated by a nonskier in his own living room, once said, "You simply have someone push a corner of a rug a few inches toward its center so that there is a raised fold. Then you have the person stand on the corner of the rug, bend his knees, and on the command 'Twist the rug,' the person reproduces the unweighting and heel-thrust of the ski turn."

Such unweighting as takes place is quick and almost unnoticed, as with the expert skier, but the heel thrust is definitely there. The body position, even if not fully angulated, is correct for skiing, the shoulders having moved in the opposite direction from the feet, to conform in this respect to the simple law of physics that every action has an opposite and equal reaction. In a jet plane this is the reason why the plane goes in one direction and the jet exhaust in the other. Die-hard Arlbergers can perform Colin Stewart's stunt (and make it prove the importance of rotation) by using a slower windup. Their feet hold their position during the counterrotation and then move with the shoulder near the end of the rotation, conforming to the law of inertia, which says that a body remains at rest or in uniform motion unless acted upon by some external force. Therefore rotation works too, but my dear Arlberg friends, only at the end of the turn, when it often results in "over-turning," especially on ice. This is one of the worst disadvantages of the old style of skiing.

On the mountain the skier's turn is incredibly simple in its mechanics. But the more difficult part of putting the motion together can only be done if the skier thoroughly understands these mechanics. First, we should forget the steered turns, which are stem turns in their various stages. The parallel turn on skis is accomplished by unweighting, edge change, and heel thrust. Of these three, edge change needs no comment, because somehow the skier, with his unweighting and subsequent sliding out of the tails of the skis by means of heel thrust, accomplishes a really quite complicated shift from one set of edges to the other without even thinking about it. So let's not create a problem by studying edge change.

The turn itself is so simple that a good one can very neatly evolve from a correct sideslip, but the sideslip starts from good body position in the traverse. The skier moving across the hill in the traverse position has the upper part of his body facing more down the hill than square to his skis. His knees are bent, and as close together as his skis, so that his legs can work as a unit, with the uphill ski leading slightly. To sideslip, the skier releases his edges, which is a form of unweighting, and applies heel thrust. If this sideslip is accompanied by a quick motion of rolling the knee into the hill, the result is an edge-set. Sometimes this can be a hard speed-reducing check, but always it is an excellent maneuver for setting up a turn. When neatly timed with the planting of the downhill or outside pole, it establishes the rhythm of the turn.

When the skier is making linked turns, either wedeln or longer radius open-slope turns, the end of one turn becomes the edge-set for the next. The real skill of skiing is in the feel of the edge, or, as it is more properly known, edge control.

Oddly enough, the beginner-to-expert skier, if he worries about his turn at all, worries more about its beginning than about its end. This is partly because the beginning of the turn obviously takes the skier down the hill, creating worries about speed and loss of control in the fall line. But the beginning of the turn is the easy part. There is the relaxing rhythmical motion of unweighting, and the fun of going down the hill. The only sure way to botch up the beginning of a turn is to start it late, which unfortunately may happen if one worries about beginning the turn. And a late turn is a misplaced turn, often rushed and skidded. The skill is used in applying pressure to the ski to make it hold toward the end of the turn, or if substantial checking is necessary, in digging the knees hard into the hill.

The average skier's absorption with the beginning of his turn is reflected in the fact that as he starts his turn he is looking at the place where his skis will be pointed down the hill. Sometimes this grade of skier looks no farther ahead than the tips of his skis. The racer is usually always looking ahead down the hill. If he does look at any part of the terrain where he is about to turn, he is scrutinizing the place where he will finish the turn. The racer knows how much finesse is required to end the turn smoothly. First off, he has the objective of staying on his line. If he skids, he not only goes off his line but he loses speed. Second, he can be perfectly on his line but lose speed by "over-turning." Sometimes at the end of an easy turn in a slalom, a crisp motion can be noticed, where the skier momentarily edges his skis to be assured that they have stopped turning and are tracking toward the next gate.

The average skier who wants to turn like the experts not only must understand the mechanics of the turn, he must also know something about the rhythm necessary to shift gradually from the unweighted position, in which the skis start their slithering motion, to the weighted position, in which the skis must be made to hold without sliding. Even if the unweighting is easy, it can be done improperly. For instance, on ice there is little unweighting required. Lifting the skis off the snow is unwise, because the skier needs to communicate by feeling the hard surface throughout the turn. Also the skier can unweight improperly, without taking his skis off the snow, by combining too much and too quick up-down motion with too much heel thrust. This sets up a skidding action, guaranteeing the jerk christie, which is disastrous on ice.

The errors in judgment in the beginning of a turn should be easy to correct. On the other hand, constant effort is required to gain skill in ending the turn. Billy Kidd, silver medal winner in the 1964 Olympic slalom and one of the top ranked skiers in the world, has a reputation for the smoothest turn in skiing. This skier, of course, has great natural ability, but he has also practiced continually to perfect that turn.

There is much talk about the racer's ability to carve a turn. To my knowledge this has never been properly explained to the nonracer. When carving a turn the racer rhythmically applies pressure to incline the ski sideways so that its edge carves into the snow surface rather than skids over it. This can't possibly be understood in the abstract, but should be tried on ice or hard-packed snow. A skier with good edges and good skis experiences a revelation when he properly applies power to the outside ski. The trick is to go to the outside ski as soon as possible with an even, rhythmical application of power. As the skier begins to weight his outside ski, he twists his foot to steer the ski slightly and immediately pushes his knee into the turn. He thus gains a swooping edging, timed so that the knee movement is beautifully integrated into the turn. While performing this carved turn, the skier becomes aware that the skill and effort is not in starting the turn but in making the skis carve and hold. This more than anything else is the essence of a good turn, especially on hard-packed snow.

Round turns are here to stay. Even among racers, the ability to make them is what separates the Brookie Dodge from the run-of-the-mill Class A skier. One way to make a round turn on ice is to make a long-radius turn, but under glazed ice conditions even Brookie could not go down the National making long-radius skidless turns. The tug-of-war between speed and control would be more than even this fabulous skier could handle.

Skidded square turns, as the average skier knows, are not the answer for ice, since they result in uncontrollable sliding all over the hill. The way to ski on ice is to make round turns, which are not so difficult. The edge-check setting up the turn is a hard, quick motion, with the skis sometimes pointed up the hill slightly, the weight hard on both uphill edges, and the feeling that for one second the skier has stopped completely. The unweighting takes place with very little up-down motion, as the skier wants to get on with the important business of weighting the downhill ski, making its inside edge hold with a strong though quick application of power. On the hardest ice, a quick rhythmical turn actually holds better than a long-radius turn.

In soft-packed snow the skier probably thinks he needs little help. Yet the same turn he uses for hard-packed will be an additional asset when conditions are excellent.

The basic turn also works in deep snow, although certain changes have to be made. In deep snow the skier is never riding on the edge of one ski. If he is on one ski he is riding on the entire bottom surface of that ski, but if he is skiing correctly the bottom surfaces of both skis are equally weighted. An unweighted ski in deep snow is going to drift, taking a direction of its own and giving the skier trouble. If the up-down motion on ice is unpronounced, in deep snow it should be exaggerated. The deep snow skier bounces from one turn to another, for if he does not bounce up at the end of one turn he does not start his next one soon enough and with sufficient release from the snow. In movies of skilled deep snow skiers, two points are apparent: One, a tremendous updrive with the upper body in addition to the knee is used to unweight, sometimes resulting in the skis even emerging from the snow. Two, the skis are kept working together. You can see them drawn together when the tips start to separate, and the skier's knees are often touching. It is generally understood that the weight is not forward in deep snow skiing, but not too far back either. Momentarily in a neutral position when unweighting, it then goes slightly back.

Deep snow skiing can be simple, especially if you follow this inelegant tip, which might be the best piece of advice in this book. The good Eastern skier can attain immediate success in Alta powder by working the tails of both skis. Skidding both tails out from under him, he turns as if the only part of the ski was from the boot back. This is a simple little reminder which, after unweighting, keeps the weight back and on both skis.

When not in deep snow, the skier should be over his skis. This means at almost all times being slightly forward. Balance and dynamism come when the skier is forward, whether he is going over bumps or making turns. In a race on a tough turn the skier drives forward. On a steep slope it is just not possible to get down the hill without having the weight forward.

Most of the basic motions of the turn discussed so far have been used by better skiers for some thirty years. Only in describing Colin Stewart's parlor turn and the edge-check have we dealt with aspects of the modern Austrian parallel turn.

A skier who thoroughly understands the importance of round turns and of the carving action to make the skis hold will have no problem with the modern techniques. The two simple keys are readiness and below-the-waist skiing, which work together. With the modern turn there is no windup in going from one turn to the next. Even the edge-set is the crisp ending of one turn. And when there is no need for checking or making an unusually short turn, the skier does not make an edge-check, the alignment of his skis going smoothly from one turn to the next. The upper body, facing in the same direction throughout linked turns, seems almost inactive. It also, through the so-called comma position, leans down the hill and away from the turn. In this manner the upper body serves as a giant counterweight. Its neutral position makes it always available to provide thrust to the turn. When Stein Eriksen skis, the action is below the waist, but the position of the upper body balances the effect of centrifugal force as well as gives thrust for the turn. The skier feels the action below the waist, almost as if he were on the dance floor doing one of the Latin dances. Some expert skiers, when they really have things working for them, feel as if they are skiing with their toes.

Certainly the feet and the knees work like a unit, and the skis are always parallel, usually just a few inches apart. The boots should not touch each other. The trick is to let the knees occasionally touch, but only when the skis are about an inch apart. The downhill knee can fit into the hollow behind the uphill knee, which automatically gives the uphill ski the correct amount of lead.

One of the worst errors in skiing is to slam the boots together by bringing the uphill ski against the weighted ski. This action sometimes trips up the downhill ski, causing a quick fall. But by having the skis together without touching, the skier can work toward a smoother turn. If the skis are separated it is slower and more jerky to go from one turn to the next. Also, most people are surprised to learn that a wide stance is not the steadiest platform. Keeping the feet together in a correct manner reduces the number of falls.

The most unpardonable error in technique is to bring the hips around on quick turns on rugged icy terrain. The key objective in these conditions is to make the skis hold, and to get off the edges onto the next turn. By bringing the hips around, the skier overturns and skids. Furthermore, he is not ready for the next turn. So when on an icy steep slope, if he thinks of one thing only, he should keep his hips facing down the hill.

Readiness for the next turn is essentially achieved by having the pole ready to be planted. If a turn to the right is coming up, the right arm is almost cocked, prepared for the pole plant, which through a light touch to the snow, automatically sets up the entire sequence of the turn for the good skier.

Of course, rhythm is the element tying this sequence together. And rhythm cannot be learned from this or any other book. The skier develops rhythm on the hill, working with a certified instructor. Words alone cannot communicate it; the skier must emulate the instructor's motions after observing the rhythmical way the turn is put together.

Actually, there are two rhythms to skiing. There is the rhythm of the turn and the rhythm between the skier and the mountain. The result of the first rhythm is one good turn; the result of the second is pleasurable, controlled skiing. Strangely enough, mastering this second rhythm has little to do with the skier's latent ability. It is a know-how to which the skier can easily be introduced, and at which he can become extremely proficient with some thought and considerable experience. The rhythm between the skier and the mountain is what I call "trailsmanship."

In discussing trailsmanship we must study the skier's mind and the way he bolsters his confidence. In other words, we are finally coming to grips with the male ego.

Paradoxically, becoming confident on skis may start long before the first snowfall. A publisher friend, Eric Swenson, says that his ego may hit its peak when he skis with zest in the Corridor of the Nose Dive, but he gets better between seasons by just thinking about skiing. Ni Orsi, top United States Olympic downhiller, must have the same approach, since he broke a leg going downstairs during the summer, probably while going through the motions of a hairpin slalom turn around a stairway landing. But thinking about skiing when off the slopes does help one to visualize the turn in its simplicity; it also helps to put some of the challenges of skiing in the proper perspective.

Going up the lift in the morning, the skier can use a certain amount of bravado to work up his confidence for the day's skiing. But if there is a pace to the skier's day, mind and body can gradually work up to a peak-performance-before-lunch ski run. The racer may spend several days preparing his mental attitude for a race, but the average skier has at least one advantage over him since the nonracer has probably had a good night's sleep before approaching the mountain.

The average skier can have a simple plan to get the mind and the muscles going for the day's skiing. The muscles can be warmed up in several ways: by bending over and trying to touch his knees with his head, by sidestepping for at least two minutes up the mountain, or making slow deliberate turns down an easy section, almost as if he were a beginner. Incidentally, deliberate turns are important because they can set up the use of good technique throughout the day. Good heel thrust and body angulation are never so well ingrained that they come naturally to us. Making a good turn where it really counts comes from having thought about the idea of the turn, from having practiced it on an easy slope, and from having developed the rhythm to do the turn at the critical moment.

The skier should also get the feel of the snow under the ski. Some skiers start off early in the morning by heading straight down the first drop in a frozen position. Just slithering the skis back and forth on the snow can be helpful as the skier gets under way. Putting the poles into the snow, first merely touching the snow, then pushing with them energetically and rhythmically, the way a racer would at the start of a course, helps both to warm up the muscles and to give the skier the feel of the snow. The skier may take a few gliding steps, exuberantly skating from one ski to the other, as an aid in starting.

The feel of the snow is just an awareness of the type of snow on the track. To ski well the skier must have something more—he must have the "feel of the edge." He gets this from making an instantaneous edge-check, from finishing a turn well, from using the finish of a turn as an edge-set to start the next turn. Suddenly he has confidence in his sense of timing, his ability to make the skis hold. He is ready to make rhythmical turns.

The first couple of runs down the mountain should be part of a skier's warm-up. Just getting the muscles working takes some doing, but this is only the first step. Even when the skier has his turns under control he is still not at peak form.

His next step is to get his mind working, for the intermediate skier who wants to become expert must have some of the mental makeup of the racer. He should work up to one run, preferably the one before lunch, when he pushes himself to ski just a bit faster and a bit better than he ever has before. This may mean leaving his group for one run, or better yet, breaking away with one skiing partner whose ability nearly matches his.

This run should take place on familiar ground. On an earlier trip down the same trail the skier should have looked the terrain over carefully, even planned the placement of some of his turns. The difficult sections should have been carefully scrutinized.

Before starting down the skier should be somewhat exalted. This feeling can come in various ways, sometimes from permitting himself the luxury of a philosophical thought, sometimes from an aesthetic appreciation of the winter day on the mountain. More usually the exaltation is the result of a fervent desire to ski the mountain well and of confidence from having tried the mountain out on earlier runs.

The skier does not have to take dangerous chances or to pour on unaccustomed speed. This kind of recklessness is always folly. But on the other hand he is not at this moment going to be merely content with stylish skiing, with making rhythmical turns. He is ready now to establish a relationship with the fall line. He wants to be able to ski on the steep pitches in and out of the fall line in relaxed high-speed style. To do this he has to be able to look steepness right in the eye. He has to comfort himself with the knowledge that the extreme pitch of the slope makes it easier for him to turn, and that if he does fall, he is less apt to be hurt than if he falls on a flat runout. He is suddenly aware that steepness is his friend, not his enemy, and that going into the fall line can be the most relaxed, satisfying moment in skiing. He knows that he can ski steep pitches without getting out of control, that he has the means at hand always to check his speed. On a difficult slope he knows that he can maintain a constant speed by putting in a sufficient edge-check at the end of each turn. He relaxes at the beginning of each turn because he knows he can check his speed at the end of the turn. He knows that the rhythm of his turns becomes a key to establishing a rhythm with the mountain, and this means mastering the mountain.

He knows how important it is to use his eyes, so that by looking ahead his mind will be thinking ahead. Just looking at the tips of his skis is in his past. His eyes are now trained even to look beyond the turn he is making and toward the next one ahead. Constantly moving, his eyes see the entire width of the trail as part of a big picture. Automatically his eyes keep track of other skiers as well as the main obstacles on the slope, even finding an out in case of trouble.

He must be prepared to ski as if the mind is released from the body, making turns as a function of reflex action rather than as the result of conscious mental processes. By skiing on reflex action he can be almost completely relaxed. Always starting a turn down the hill with a light easy unweighting, he momentarily applies muscle power as he turns back into the hill to control his speed and make his edge-check.

With muscles, mind, and even eyes in such a state of readiness the skier has a memorable run ahead. He is assured of success. He is completely prepared for the challenge of the mountain, even if the conditions are adverse. For the skier is part mountaineer, and merely to take the mountain in its easy moods is not to know the mountain.

James Ramsey Ullman has said:

> Challenge is the core and mainspring of all human activity. If there's an ocean, we cross it; if there's a disease, we cure it; if there's a wrong, we right it; if there's a record, we break it; and finally, if there's a mountain, we climb it.

For us the only difference is that if there's a mountain, we ski it.

17

The Best Years Are Yet to Come

The first weekend of April in 1965 found me at Aspen to take part in the National Veterans Alpine Championship. A sales meeting I had attended in Kansas City the week before made it possible for me to enter this race, but the same sales meeting kept me from reaching Aspen before Friday afternoon on the day of the downhill. Most of the competitors had been there all week practicing. That afternoon I had time for a couple of hours of skiing on Ajax Mountain. The weather had been exceptionally warm and sunny, but by three o'clock began to threaten rain. Almost miraculously the air cooled slightly and instead of a downpour we were treated to a fairly heavy though brief snowstorm, with giant snowflakes.

As I skied from the top of the mountain down to the upper terminal of the main single chair lift, I saw an unusual sight—a fairly long line of skiers waiting to ride *down* the lift. True, the lighting was flat, but to an Eastern skier who had survived the East's most snowless winter, the mountain was in superb condition, having over a hundred inches of snow, a soft-packed powder surface, and only moderate-sized moguls. I skied a couple of extra runs on the Zogg Park lift, finding myself almost alone on the hill.

In the slalom on Saturday, I skied conservatively—partly because I was worried about not having adjusted to the altitude—and failed to qualify for a second run. Actually I was surprised at the strength of my legs after the long course, but as a nonsmoker in excellent condition, I probably needed very little acclimatization. Knowing I did not have to worry about my legs in the giant slalom on Sunday I placed eighth in the over-forty class. This would have been equivalent to third place in an amateur division, and Joe McNealus' fine third place would have given him the national amateur championship for the over-forty group. The Aspen race, unlike the Eastern veterans' events which are for amateurs only, was an open competition in which the bulk of the field consisted of full-time ski instructors.

However, our Eastern contingent of five skiers was tremendously impressed with the high level of competition and with the extraordinarily good physical condition of all the competitors. Never have I seen a leaner, more fit group of men. Of course, it is not surprising that some of these men looked fit since a skier can enter veterans' races at twenty-seven. But speed and crispness of style were the qualities separating the younger men from the older ones. Skiers in the over-forty and over-fifty classes looked just as fresh at the bottom of the course as Class A skiers. The winner of the over-fifty class was the hero of the race. Toni Woerndle, of Red River, New Mexico, beaten by only a handful of younger skiers, won the over-forty class as well as his own. He is certainly the best skier of his age in both style and performance in the entire country.

On Monday after the races Joe McNealus, Dick Weber, and I had some marvelous skiing on Ajax and Bell Mountain, with cigar-smoking one-lung Joe usually the leader. I am sure that my two companions reflected on the wonders of Aspen's mountains as much as I did. Although I haven't seen Squaw, Vail, or Jackson Hole, I think that Aspen offers the finest combination of snow and terrain in America. And from almost any skier's point of view, the West has a tremendous advantage over the East. If I have seemed particularly attached to Mt. Washington, Mt. Mansfield, and some other Eastern ski areas, this is because I know them best. Also in recent years the Eastern skiing resort has been underappreciated. But the East is still turning out outstanding skiers, partly because they have to be tough to measure up to the East's conditions. Most of the Americans who have done well in international races have been Easterners, and it is quite likely that in the future, at least half of our Olympic and F.I.S. skiers will come from the East. Even if these skiers do all their training in the West, if they learned to ski in the East they are Easterners in my opinion.

But whether they are from the East or the West, the boys and girls who have made up the United States Ski Teams have always been a dedicated group. During the past few years international racing has moved toward outright professionalism, still the United States Ski Team has held fast to the highest ideals of amateur sportsmanship. Credit for this goes to our racers as well as to the former Alpine director, Bob Beattie. I hope that someday United States skiing will catch up with European competition. But above all I hope that this can be done without government or ski industry subsidy.

In late March of 1969 I went out to Boise, Idaho, to ski in yet another National Veterans' race which took place at Bogus Basin, a relatively new but fast developing area. Unlike my last minute arrival for the Aspen races, this was serious business, almost as if we veterans were in junior racing camp for a week. Of fourteen Easterners, three girls were medal winners—Mary Beck, who won two firsts, Joan Skiff, and Birdie Corcoran. Woodie Woodall, our unofficial though highly knowledgeable coach, was first in the Alpine Combined for his age group, and I won a second and a third.

When I missed two winters of skiing while in the submarine service, I seriously wondered if my skiing would ever again be as good as it was at Dartmouth. I regretted having given a girl at Woodstock some pictures taken of me racing, for I wanted some documentation of my form at its peak.

Actually the main incentive for veteran racers is the feeling of getting better each year. And we all ski better than we did as youngsters. The sport has moved along rapidly, and to some extent its momentum has carried us along with it. The tremendous developments in equipment and technique are more exciting for us than for youngsters because these improvements enable us to offset the disadvantages of age. Consequently, we probably get a bigger kick out of skiing on the current "hot" ski, the Rossignol Strato, than the racers do. In fact, now we can accomplish things on skis that we were never able to do before. We can ski faster on long-radius turns, we can carve sharp hairpin turns on ice, and we race with so much control that we hardly ever fall. Above all skiing is more fun than ever because our turns are faster, smoother, and almost skidless. Only the fast uncontrolled downhill is part of our past, but not by choice. Downhill veterans' races are held on easy runs like the old prewar Class C trails, only wider. The test is not to see who can hold speed, but who can cut corners, hold a tuck, and ski with the least amount of edging.

Now I know that I can plan on skiing well at least twenty more years. Three friends, all sixty-five or over—Alec Bright, Ragnar Naess, and Carl Gray—inspire people who watch them ski. Anywhere they go, few skiers on the hill are better. Recently when I ran into Carl Gray, now president of the Sun Valley Ski Club, I asked him about his health, remembering that he had had a leg operation a few years before. He replied he was in good shape, still playing a fair game of tennis. Then he went on to say, "I'm sorry I haven't skied with you lately. During the last three or four years I have really worked at my skiing, and I am better than I ever was."

So my fears when I was out in the Pacific were groundless. I now feel that as long as I can walk around a golf course I'll be able to ski. And since skiing is so important to me, I am delighted the future looks so good.

Sometimes I marvel at how I can be such a complete skiing enthusiast without letting it dominate my life. Most of us fight convention in our lives. This book has not related much about my nonskiing life, yet I have few complaints concerning this life. Certainly skiing alone is not what has kept it from being dull. As a skier I may seem to have the heroic role in this book, but I am not one of the great skiers. If I had been one of them I doubt if my keen interest in the sport would have continued to grow. And I would never have waited until my mid-forties to write a book.

Last winter early in the season a local New Jersey snowstorm took me out to a recreational ski slope in South Orange known as the Deer Paddock. While skiing there, I noticed a small boy about four years old going at the sport with great vigor. His equipment was inexpensive—galoshes for boots, short poles without straps and with solid wooden wheels for baskets, fairly short solid maple skis, and a marvelous binding with heavy rubber toe straps and lighter heel straps of inner-tube rubber. This young skier was falling all the time: he fell when climbing and he fell when skiing down. Each time he would jump up eagerly. If a ski was twisted in the wrong direction, he would lift his foot and the binding would quickly snap the ski back in place. Never have I seen such spirit, such determination. He seemed like a rubber-legged boy on his rubber bindings. Falling just seemed to be part of the fun. Others on the slope were watching him, but I was the most interested of all his audience. Going up to chat with him, I found that he was Terence Ringwood of Summit, New Jersey. And I told him that one day he would be a fine skier.

What I was watching was myself, had I started skiing at that age and with that equipment. That's the reason I was spellbound by the boy's energetic efforts. But he's even luckier than I. Think of the many more years he has to enjoy the sport.

Index